ART BOOKS

FROM CRESCENT MOON PUBLISHING

Leonardo da Vinci
by James Pearson

Early Netherlandish Painting
by Rosalind Mutter

Piero della Francesca
by Naomi Haskell

Giovanni Bellini
by Julia Davis

Eric Gill: Nuptials of God
by Anthony Hoyland

Minimal Art and Artists In the 1960s and After
by Laura Garrard

Postwar Art
by George Knighton

Vincent van Gogh: Visionary Landscapes
by Stuart Morris

Max Beckmann
by Stuart Morris

Egon Schiele: Sex and Death in Purple Stockings
by D. Simon Eade

Mark Rothko: The Art of Transcendence
by Julia Davis

Jasper Johns
by L.M. Poole

Brice Marden
by Laura Garrard

Frank Stella: American Abstract Artist
by James Pearson

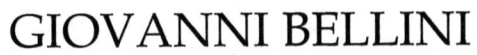

GIOVANNI BELLINI

GIOVANNI BELLINI

GEORGE HAY

CRESCENT MOON

First published 1908. This edition © 2018.

Printed and bound in the U.S.A.
Set in Book Antiqua 10 on 14pt.
Designed by Radiance Graphics.

Thanks to the authors and publishers quoted.

British Library Cataloguing in Publication data

ISBN-13 9781861716064 (Hbk)
ISBN-13 9781861716910 (Pbk)

CRESCENT MOON PUBLISHING
P.O. Box 1312, Maidstone, Kent, ME14 5XU
Great Britain, www.crmoon.com

CONTENTS

NOTE ON THE TEXT

The text is from *Giovanni Bellini* by George Hay, published by T.C. & E.C. Jack, London and Frederick A. Stokes, New York, 1908, as part of the Masterpieces In Colour series, edited by T. Leman Hare.

The illustrations discussed in the book are included in the illustrations section, along with many other works.

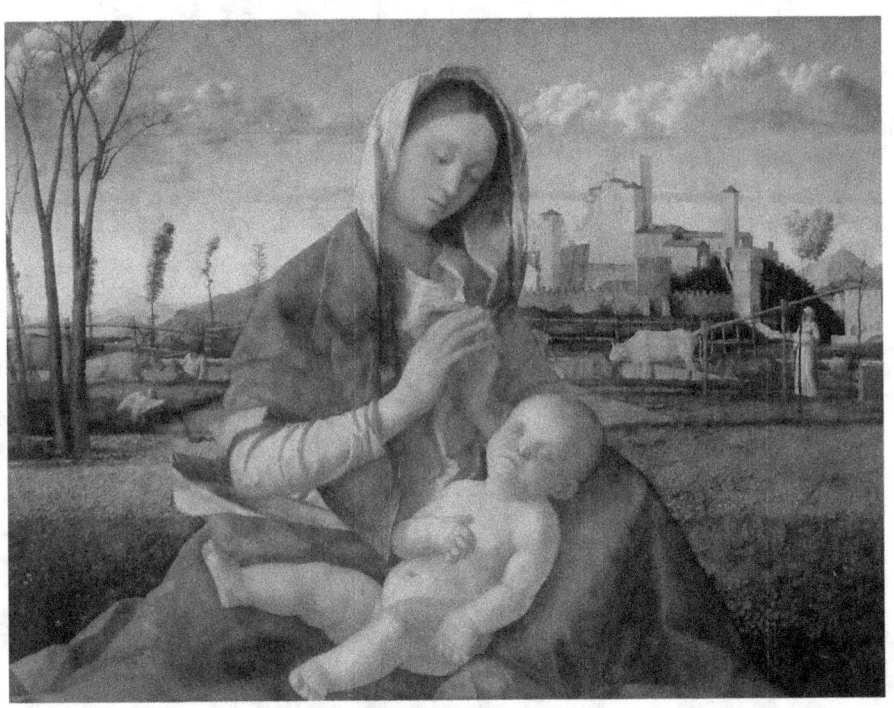

Giovanni Bellini, Madonna of the Meadow,
National Gallery, London

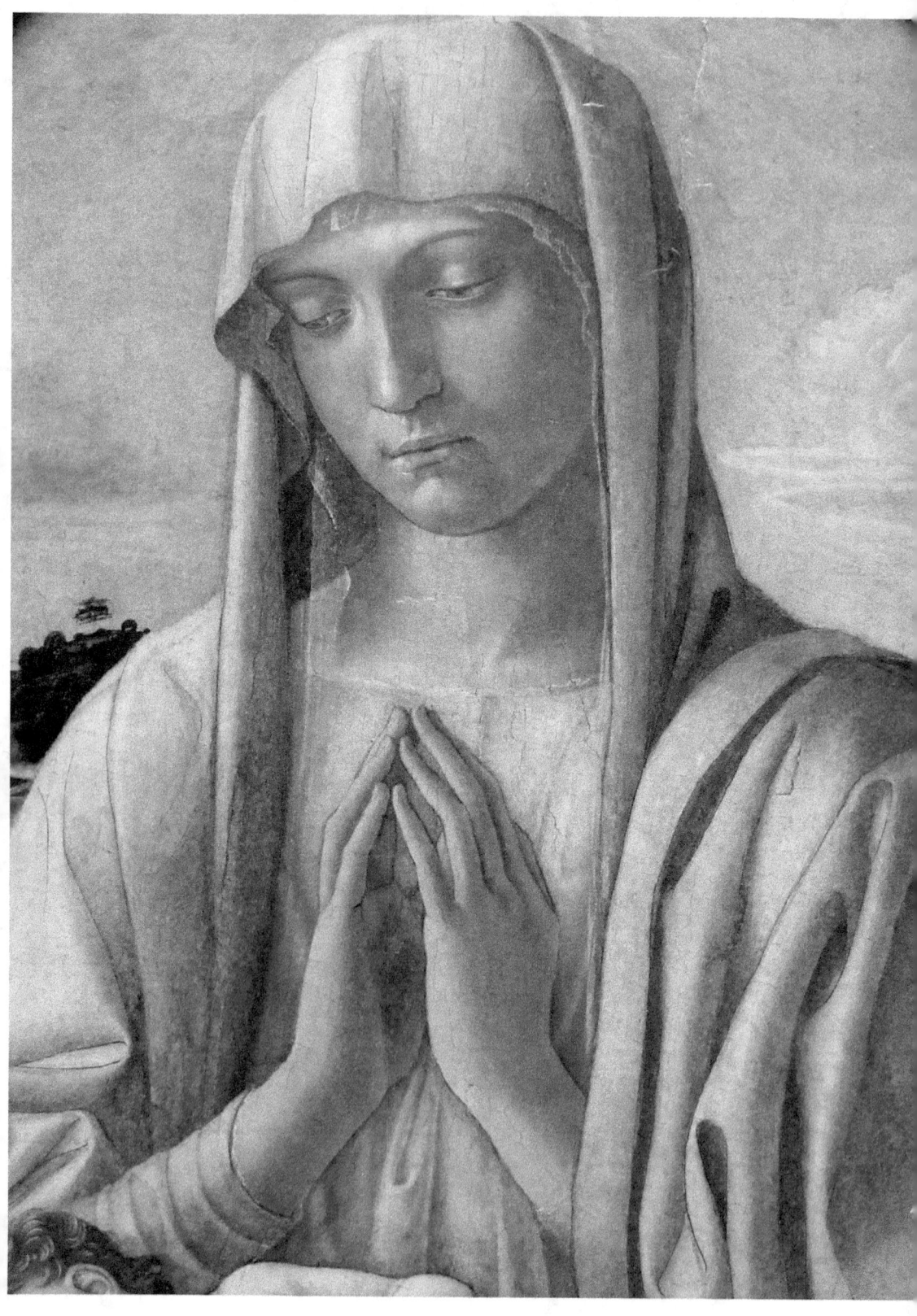

Giovanni Bellini, Madonna and Child, Metropolitan Museum of Art, detail

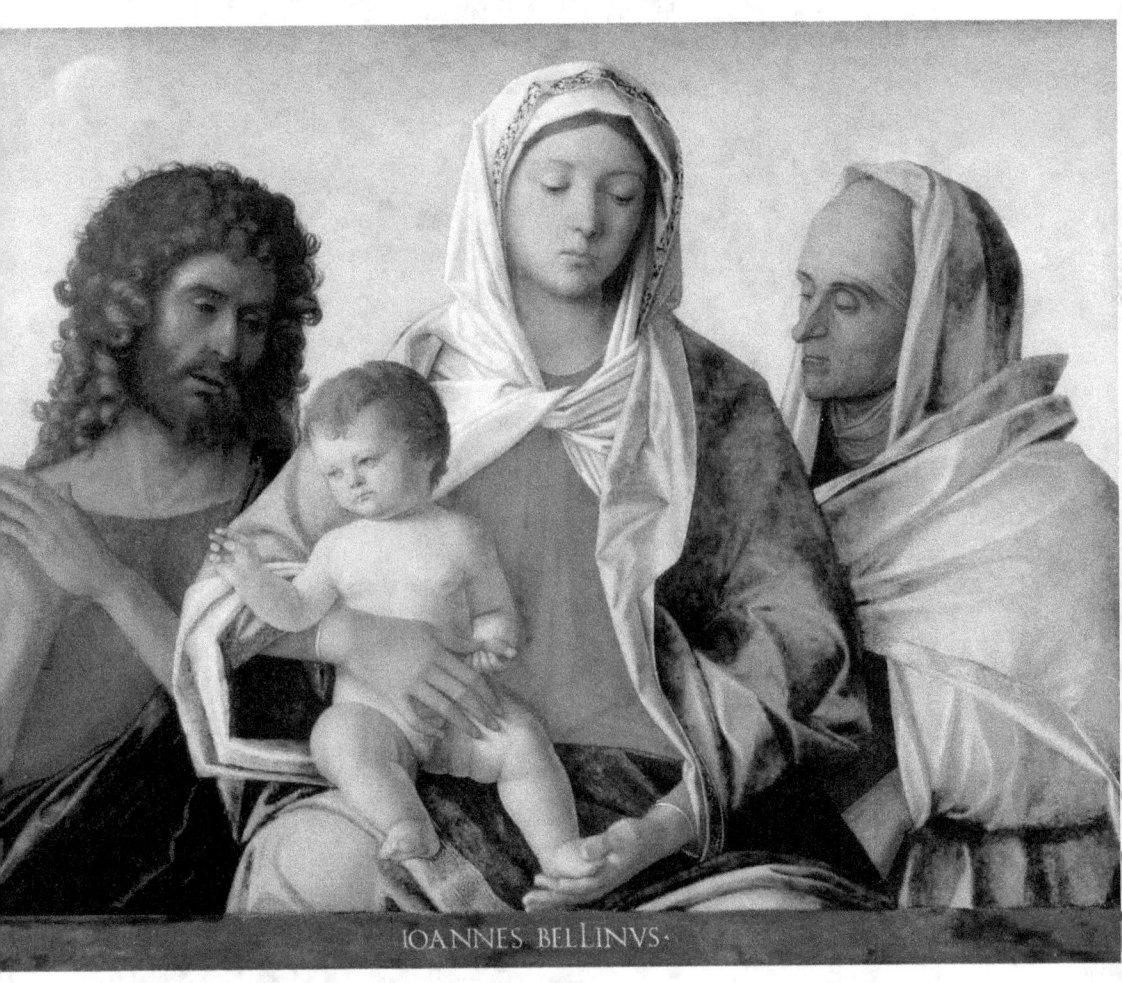

IOANNES BELLINVS·

Giovanni Bellini and workshop, Madonna and Child With St John the Baptist
and Elisabeth, Städel

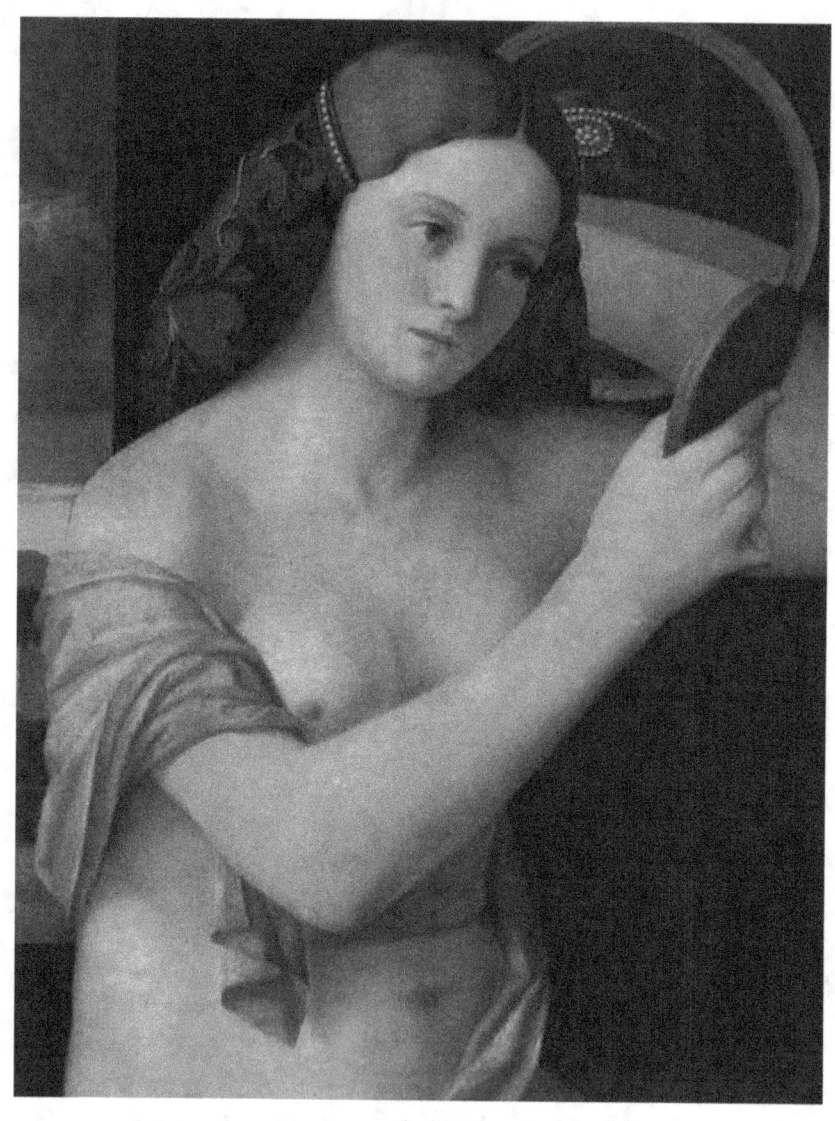

Giovanni Bellini, Young Woman With a Mirror,
1515, Vienna

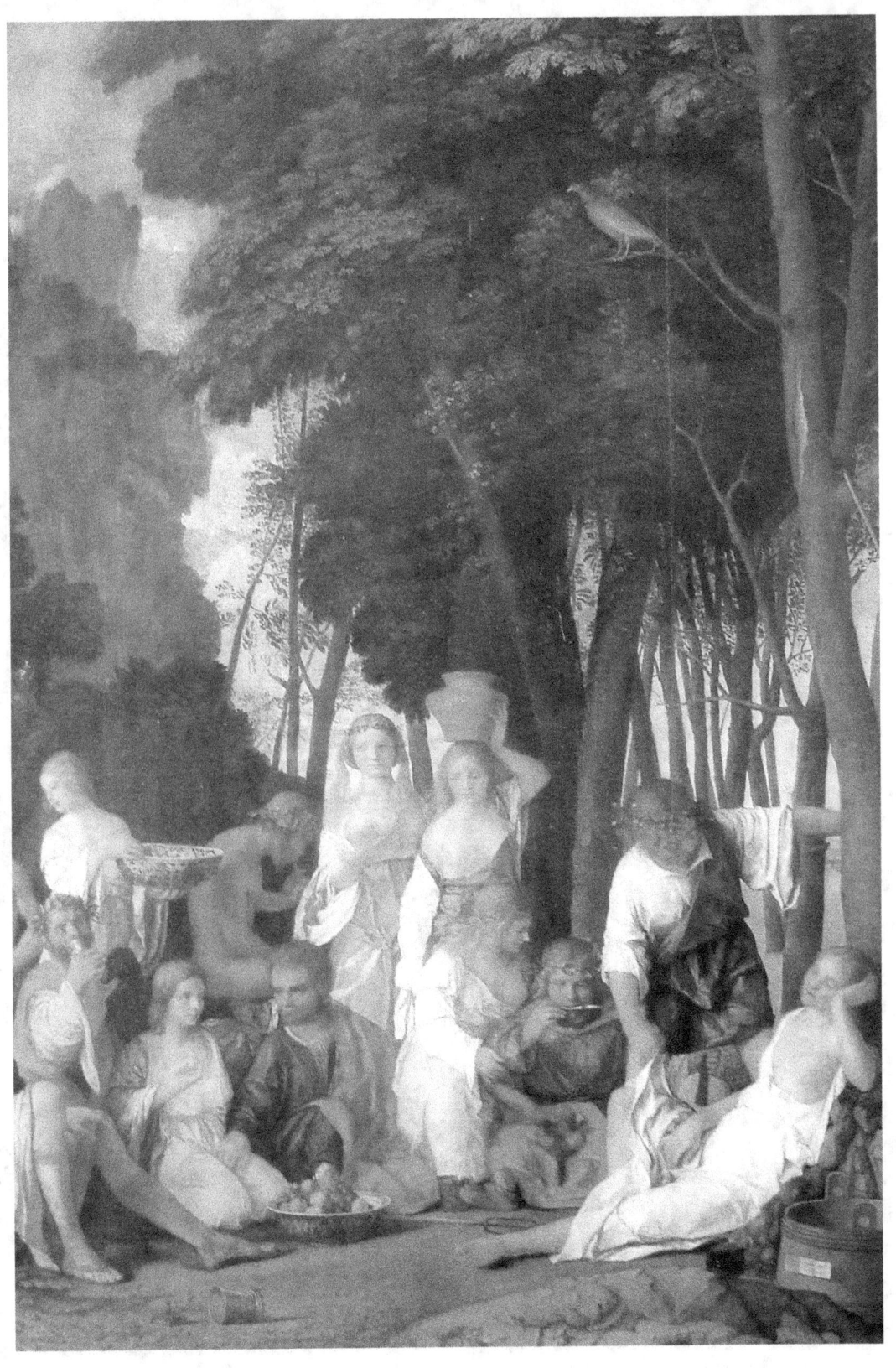

Giovanni Bellini, The Feast of the Gods, 1514, National Gallery of Art, Washington

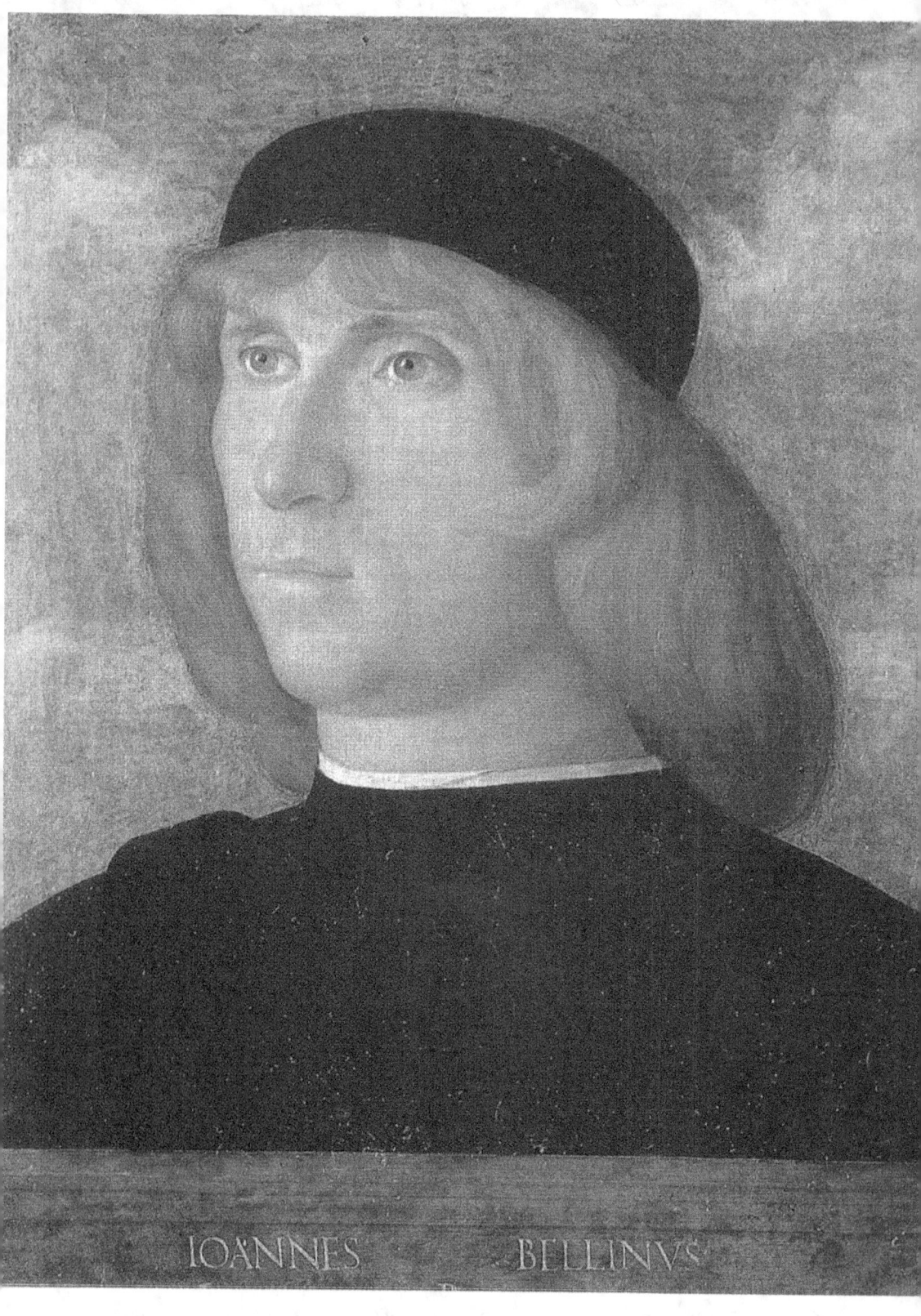

Giovanni Bellini, Self-Portrait, c. 1500, Capitoline Museum

INTRODUCTION

From the standpoint of the biographer, it is to be regretted that more of the great Italian artists of the fifteenth century were not associated with the Church. In the days of the most interesting activity of painters and sculptors, the capacity to write was rarely met beyond the monasteries and few people took the trouble to record any impression of notable men in the early years of their career. We are apt to forget that, for one artist whose name is preserved to us to-day, there are a score of men whose work has perished, whose very names are forgotten. In middle life, or in old age, when commissions from Popes or Emperors had attracted the attention of the world at large to the best men of the time, there might be some chronicler found to make passing but invaluable reference to those of his contemporaries whose names were common in men's mouths, but such notes were made in very haphazard fashion, they were not necessarily accurate, and might be founded upon personal observation or rumour, or even upon the prejudice that was inevitable when Italy was a congerie of opposing states. Latter-day historians grope painfully and conscientiously after the scanty records of great painters, searching the voluminous writings of men who have little to say, and very little authority for saying anything about the great personalities of the art world of their time. It is not surprising, under these circumstances, that despite much search the record of many lives that must have been fascinating cannot be found. We learn more of the man from his work than we can hope to learn from any written record and, as the taste for studying pictures grows, so all the internal evidence of a man's thought and ways of life accumulates and the message that underlies canvas and stands revealed in colour and line to the trained eye, is translated for the benefit of a curious generation. We learn to know what manner of man the painter was from the models he chose, the portraits he painted, the qualities and nature of his landscape, the expression of his joy in light and air, his feeling for flowers and birds. By a process of synthetical reasoning we come to see, though it be as in a glass, darkly, the picture that every man paints, from the years of his activity to the last year of his sojourn among mortals – that is the portrait of himself. Doubtless we are often misled, because as each critic, artist or layman, finds in the picture a reflection of what he takes there, it remains difficult to arrive at definite conclusions upon which all men can agree about any painter. Happily the effort pleases our own generation, and as there are many great men who flourished in the fifteenth century and have left their pictures to be their sole monument, there is no lack of work. Naturally in this curious and inquisitive age there are some who would rather discover a well authenticated story about an artist's life than an unexpected masterpiece from his hand, but then the appeal of letters is always more widespread than that of paint. It is always pleasant to endeavour to supply a want, but it is only fair to remember that in writing about people whose life story was not preserved by their contemporaries, the path is strewn with pitfalls.

In dealing with the Italians from the days of Cimabue to Clovio, it has been the custom to depend very largely upon the works of Giorgio Vasari, and to rely for later and more accurate information upon the volumes written by Crowe and Cavalcaselle, passing from them to Morelli and Berenson.

Vasari, to whom the students of Italian art, down to the middle of the sixteenth century, are so deeply indebted, was born in 1512, and lived for more than sixty years. He was a painter and architect, related to Luca Signorelli, and engaged for a great part of his life upon work in Arezzo. He was a great copyist, a painstaking writer, and never did critic wield a milder pen if he chanced to be writing of Florentine art, or a more prejudiced one if he dealt with things of Venice. He was first a patriot and then a critic. One night, he tells us, a friend of Monsignore Giovio expressed a wish to add to his library a treatise on men who had distinguished themselves in the arts of design, from the time of Cimabue down to the year of the conversation. Vasari undertook the work and founded it, he says, upon notes and memoranda which he had made from the time when he was a boy. The compilation was finished about the year 1547, it was written at a time when the painter was very busy with commissions. He did his best in a certain prejudiced fashion, and the result for all its defects is very valuable. Naturally enough Vasari had not too large a share of the gifts required for his task, nor had he the necessary facts before him for writing really reliable history. Much that he wrote was accepted *faute de mieux*, but modern researches have necessitated a revision of very many estimates that Vasari formed for us, together with a considerable portion of his facts, and we have learned to understand something of the source and direction of his prejudices.

The literary union of Crowe and Cavalcaselle, who started their joint work in the latter half of the nineteenth century, with better equipment of facts and a larger measure of critical insight, has been far more valuable, and a complete popular edition of their work revised by sympathetic and well qualified writers is greatly to be desired; but in no case can we regard a volume devoted to the biographies of scores of artists as being altogether reliable. The spirit of study is abroad, to-day men will devote more time to the life story of a comparatively obscure artist than they would have given fifty years ago to half-a-dozen painters of European reputation. It is not easy, one might almost say it is not possible, to tell succinctly the story of men who have left no clear record and were not regarded by their contemporaries as fit and proper subjects for a biography. At best we can study the available sources of information, and use such measure of judgment as is in us to construct a reasonable and likely narrative. To delve in all manner of likely and unlikely places, to study and make allowances for the prejudices of the time, to rely upon the painted canvas to confirm or confute the printed word – these are the tasks of the conscientious biographer who must not be ill content if, after sifting an intolerable amount of chaff, he can find a few forgotten grains of corn.

I

GIOVANNI BELLINI'S YOUTH

Giovanni, or Gian Bellini as he is generally called, the subject of this brief record and appreciation, is one of the most fascinating painters of the fifteenth century.

He has left many a lovely picture to the world, but alas he was no diarist, he had no Boswell, and there are gaps in the history of his life that will never be filled up. In the vast and unexplored region of Italian archives there may be some facts that research will bring to light, but at present we know very little, and can only be grateful that the story of his life is not shrouded altogether in the mist that obscures so much of the personal history of eminent Venetians in the fifteenth century.

"When zealous efforts are supported by talent and rectitude, though the beginning may appear lowly and poor, yet do they proceed constantly upwards by gradual steps, never ceasing nor taking rest until they have finally attained to the summit of distinction." In this fashion Giorgio Vasari, who in those admirable but unreliable "Lives," seldom fails to speak kindly and enthusiastically of artists whom neither he nor his friends had occasion to dislike, begins his account of the house of Bellini. He passes on to deal in detail with Jacopo Bellini, the father of that

Giovanni with whose life and work it is proposed to deal briefly in this place. Of the father little is known, but he is said to have lived in the shadow of St. Mark's great Cathedral in Venice, and to have worked under some of the Umbrian masters in the Ducal Palace. He must have served and studied in the studio of Gentile da Fabriano in days when Fra Angelico had not reached the Convent of San Marco; there is evidence, too, that he travelled and painted portraits. The date of his death is as uncertain as the year of his birth. It is said that the new paganism held more attractions for him than the old faith, and that the most of his commissions were from the great and flourishing secular institutions of the Republic. Little is left of his pictures, but a few delightful sketches are preserved in Paris and London and, but for the larger fame of his sons, Jacopo Bellini would doubtless have been forgotten to-day, and such work as is left would be attributed by leading critics to different masters.

Gentile Bellini seems to have been born between 1425 and 1430 and the date of Giovanni's birth is not known definitely. It may be associated with the year 1430.

At this time it must be remembered that Venice was on the road to her ultimate decline. Costly wars with Milan and Florence had seriously damaged the Exchequer, the fratricidal sea-fights with Genoa had cost a wealth of human life and treasure and, although Venice had annexed nearly a dozen provinces in half a century, the outlay had been out of proportion to the results. At the same time, the Venetians did not know that their splendid state was on the downward road. The new route to India was unknown. Columbus and Diaz had yet to withdraw the sea-borne commerce of the world from Venice to Spain, and so bring about the commercial ruin of the Republic, and the Republic, with her maritime trade and her wealth of spoils from the East, could furnish endless material for the artists who were rising in her midst. Everywhere there was colour in abundance, the "Purple East" cast a broad shadow upon the Adriatic. Then, again, it is worth remarking that the Venetian painters did not concern themselves, as their Florentine brothers did, with matters lying beyond the scope of their canvas, they did not dally with architecture or sculpture in the intervals of picture painting. In short, pictures represented the tribute of Venice to the arts, and this concentration was not without its influence upon the work done. Literature did not flourish, because the city reared few literary men and the tendency of the citizens was towards pleasure rather than study. All could admire a picture at a time when few could read a book, and the spirit of the Renaissance, fluttering over the Venetian Republic, had done little more than waken its people to a sense of the beauty of the human form. Although in the days when Gian Bellini was a little boy, the terror of the Turkish invasion was upon the eastern end of the Mediterranean, it had hardly reached Venice or, if it had, only through the medium of envoys and kings who came to ask the assistance of the Republic to keep the Turk from Constantinople. To these appeals the response of Venice in those days could not be very efficacious, but the envoys added a more flamboyant note to the city's colouring, and served an artistic if not a political purpose.

Vasari tells us that Jacopo Bellini painted his pictures not on wood, but on canvas. "In Venice," he writes naïvely, "they do not paint on panel, or if they do use it occasionally they take no other wood but that of the fir, which is most abundant in that city, being brought along the river Adige in large quantities from Germany. It is the custom then in Venice to paint very much upon canvas, either because this material does not so readily split, is not liable to clefts, and does not suffer from the worm, or because pictures on canvas may be made of such size as is desired, and can also be sent whithersoever the owner pleases, with little cost and trouble." Perhaps Vasari overlooked the effect of sea air upon open frescoed walls, although that effect was clear enough to the Venetians. But Jacopo, for all that he painted upon canvas, and was employed by some of the leading Venetian guilds, makes no outstanding figure upon the page of the art history of Venice. He seems to have lived prosperously, honourably, and intelligently, to have caught the earliest possible reflection of the growing spirit of paganism, thereby incurring the anger and mistrust of the Church party that had regarded painting as the proper intermediary between faith and the general public, to have pleased his state employers in Venice and Padua, and then to have died rather outside the odour of sanctity, leaving an honourable name behind him, and children who were destined to spread its fame far and wide.

Students of Gian Bellini's life and work can see that only a part of the father's teaching fell upon fruitful soil. Jacopo Bellini, as we have seen, was a man in whom the early religious spirit that the Renaissance did much to cloud over was of small account, but the pagan revival that found so many adherents in Florence and Venice, towards the close of the fifteenth century, left young Gian Bellini almost untouched. We shall see that the commissions offered by wealthy patrons, who had no love for sacred subjects, were either rejected, or were accepted and not fulfilled. It is surely permissible to believe that the teaching of early days had a lasting influence upon the outlook of the two Bellinis, and strengthened them in the determination to do work that appealed as much to their heart as to their hand. Certainly they followed conscience where it led them. In the case of Gian Bellini, with whom we are mostly concerned here, it is interesting to see that his long life, passed as it was in the very critical time that embraced the fall of Constantinople and the League of Cambrai, was completely free from cloud. His mind was formed very early. He worked strenuously, carefully, and in the fashion that pleased his conscience, till within a very short time of his death, and the serenity of his spirit, clearly revealed in a series of exquisite pictures, was untouched by all that happened in the world around him.

Changes came thick and fast upon Venice in the years when Bellini was hard at work, and new ideas were receiving acceptance on every hand. The Renaissance, with its revival of pagan thought in the train of learning, scattered new ideas throughout the Venetian studios. Bellini's pupil and successor Titian could depict pagan goddess and Christian Deity with equal facility. Giorgione was travelling along the same paths when death overtook him, but Gian Bellini, while he continued to make progress in his art, refused to make any concession to the pagan spirit, and with one possible exception in the case of the Bacchanals, a picture painted for the Duke of Ferrara, now in the Alnwick Castle Collection, his last pictures were as devout in thought and feeling as the first.

It seems strange, perhaps, to express doubts about a picture that bears the painter's signature, and has been freely accepted as the work of his hands, but we must not forget that the fifteenth-century painters in Italy were the directors of a school as well as the tenants of a studio. The Bellini and Vivarini families were at the head of Venetian painters, and consequently the best students of the time were attracted to their studios, content to mix colours, prepare canvases, and paint the less important parts of a commissioned picture. After a time they even painted pictures, and signed them with the master's name. We have certain facts in connection with the Ferrara picture, and few facts are to be found in the case of any others. It is on record that Bellini took an unfinished picture to Ferrara, completed it under the eye of the Duke, and received eighty-five ducats for it. The question becomes whether this is the picture now at Alnwick that Titian finished, because those who know it say that the background has a landscape of the familiar Titian kind, with glimpses of Cadore and Pieve, where the younger painter was born. We are left, then, with the almost certain knowledge that Titian painted a part of the "Bacchanal" picture, and that the other part is opposed in sentiment to Bellini's theories of art. So the sceptics do not lack a measure of justification.

In the latter days of his life Bellini's studio became something like a factory, and there seems very little reason to doubt that some of his clever pupils like Bondinelli, Bissolo, Marconi, Catena and others were allowed to sign, with the master's name, "Ioannes Bellinus," pictures that had no more than the slightest acquaintance with the master's brush. One of the most distinguished of our modern critics, Mr. Bernhard Berenson, attended an exhibition of Venetian pictures held in London a few years ago, and found that the great majority of the pictures attributed to Bellini were by his pupils. He pointed out then that the signature upon which the unfortunate owners were accustomed to lean was no better than a broken reed. Bellini, of course, was not the only offender in this respect. His great pupil Titian copied the master's fault, and there is on record a letter from Frederic, Duke of Mantua, asking Titian to send out work that has his touch as well as his signature. With these facts before us, it becomes permissible to doubt whether Bellini, in the last years of a long life devoted to sacred work, elected to turn aside, and yield deliberately to the pagan movement he had opposed so long. We can find no other work of his hand that is directly opposed to his theories of religious art, though it is fair to remember that he had a very active mind, and even responded to the influence of his own great pupils Titian and Giorgione.

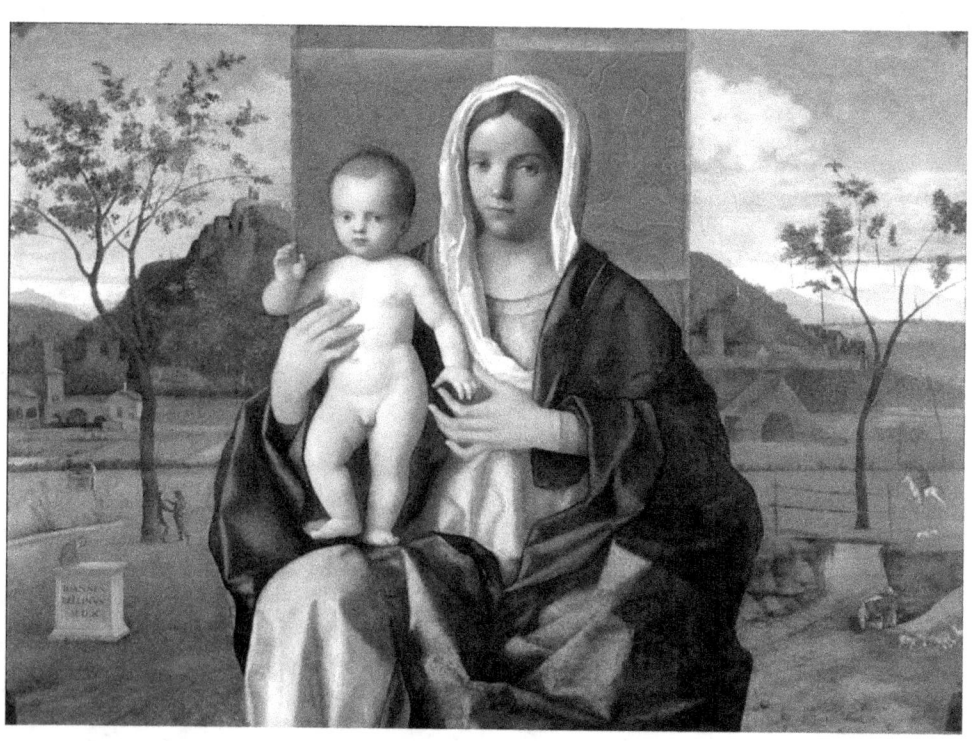

Giovanni Bellini, Brera Madonna, 1510, Milan

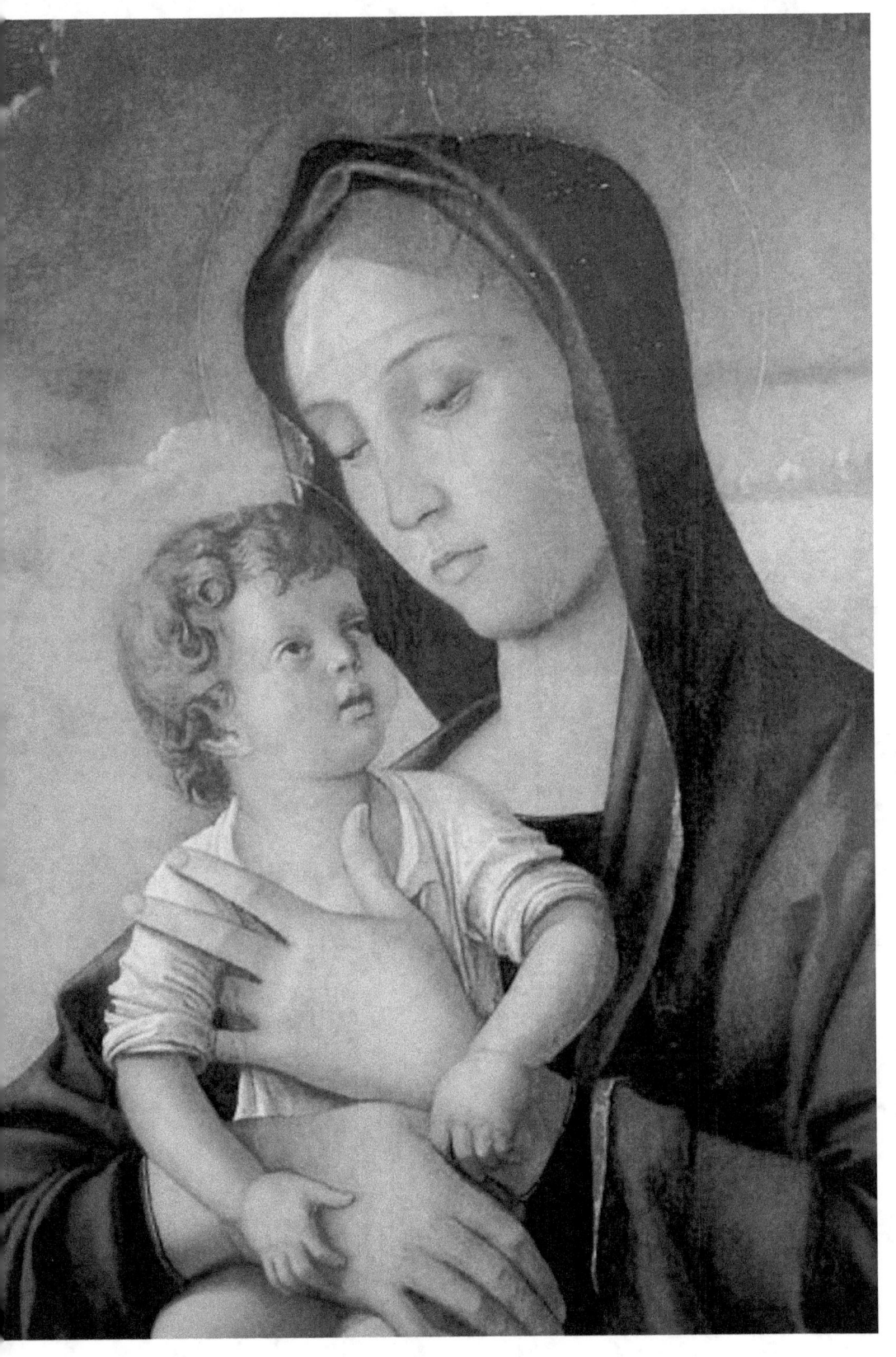

Giovanni Bellini, Madonna and Child, 1475, Castelvecchio Museum

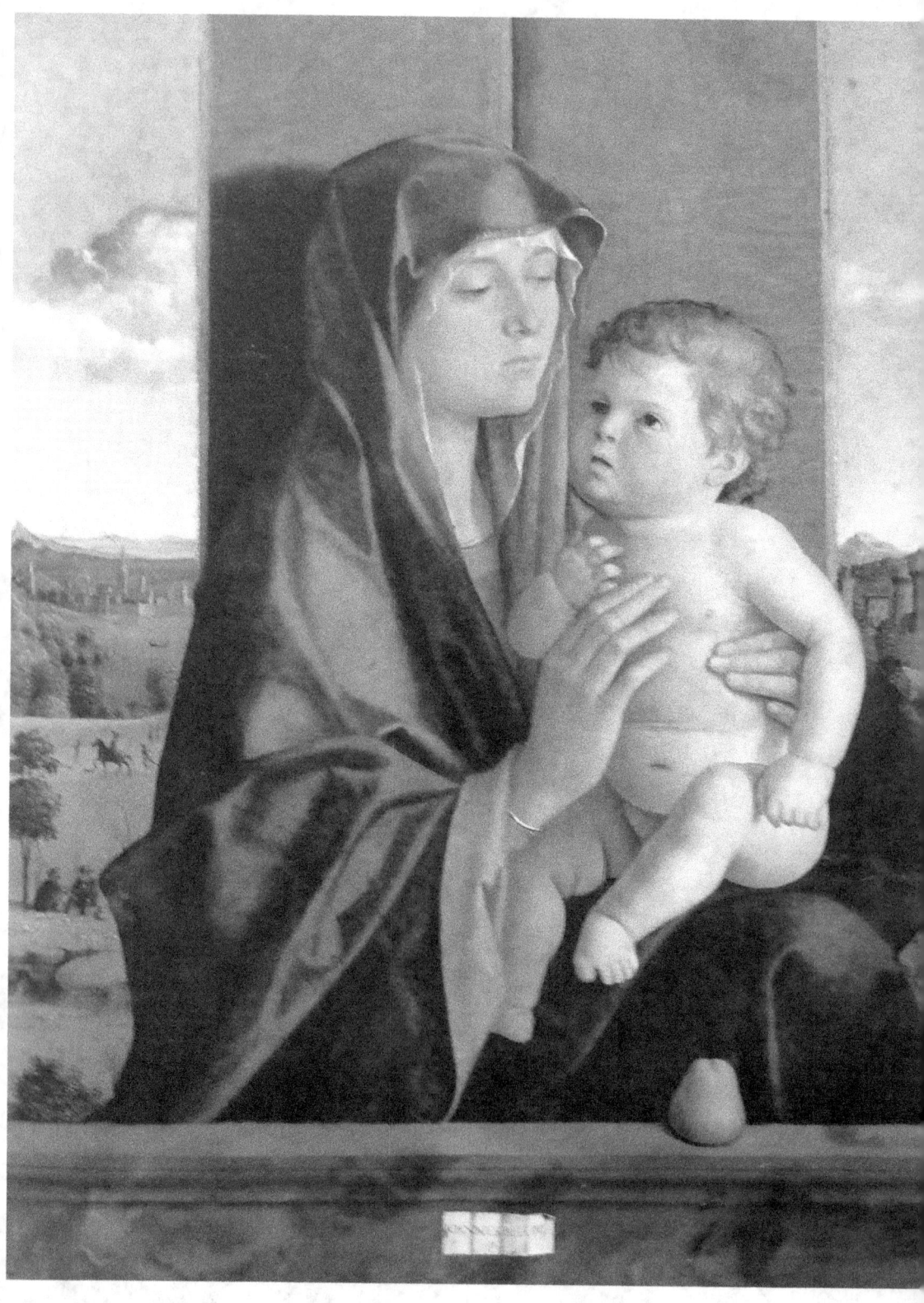

Giovanni Bellini, The Virgin and Child, Bergamo

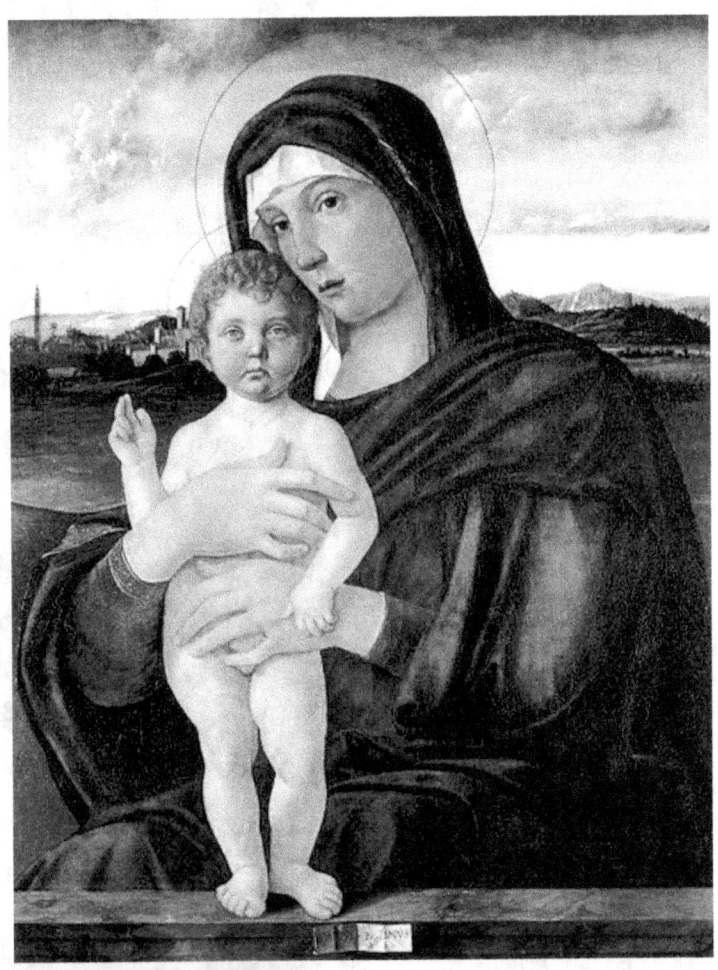

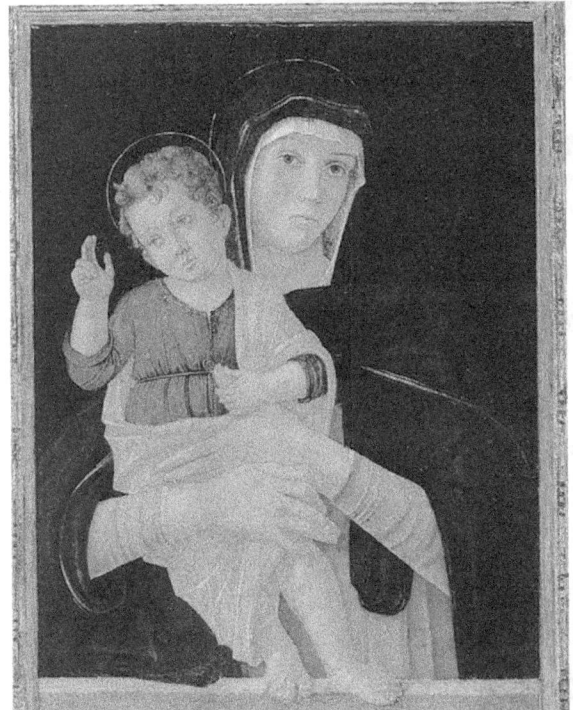

Giovanni Bellini, two Madonna and Child paintings, with Jesus blessing.

1475-80, Venice (above).
1460-65, Venice (left).

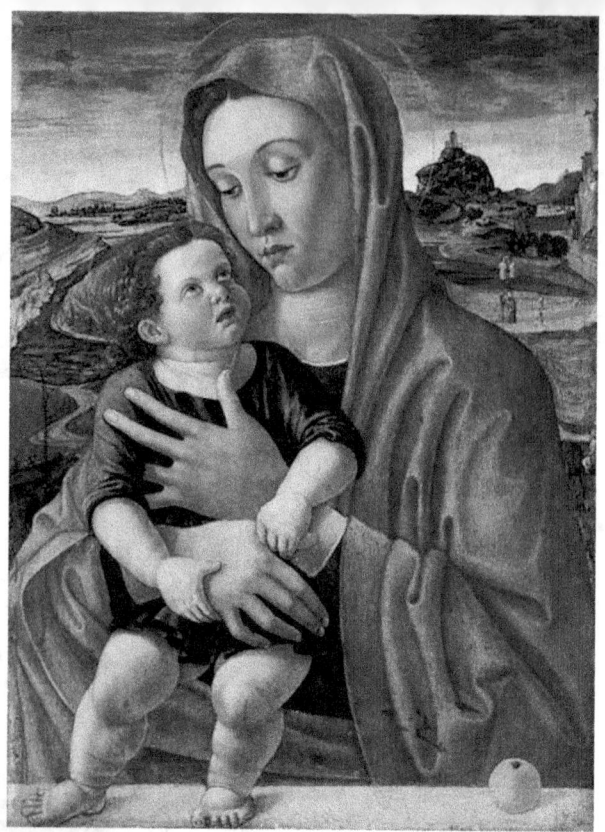

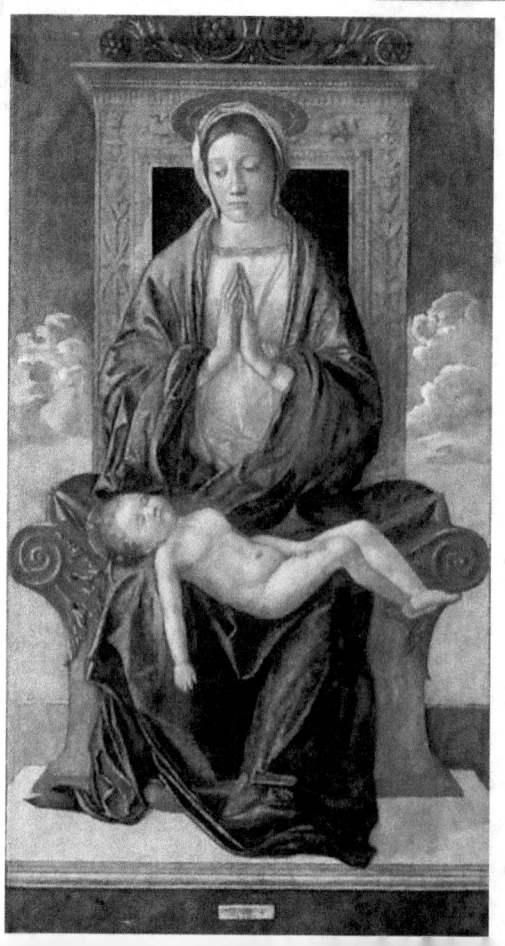

Giovanni Bellini, Madonna In
Adoration of the Sleeping Child,
1475, Venice (left).
Madonna and Child, 1460, Berlin
(above).

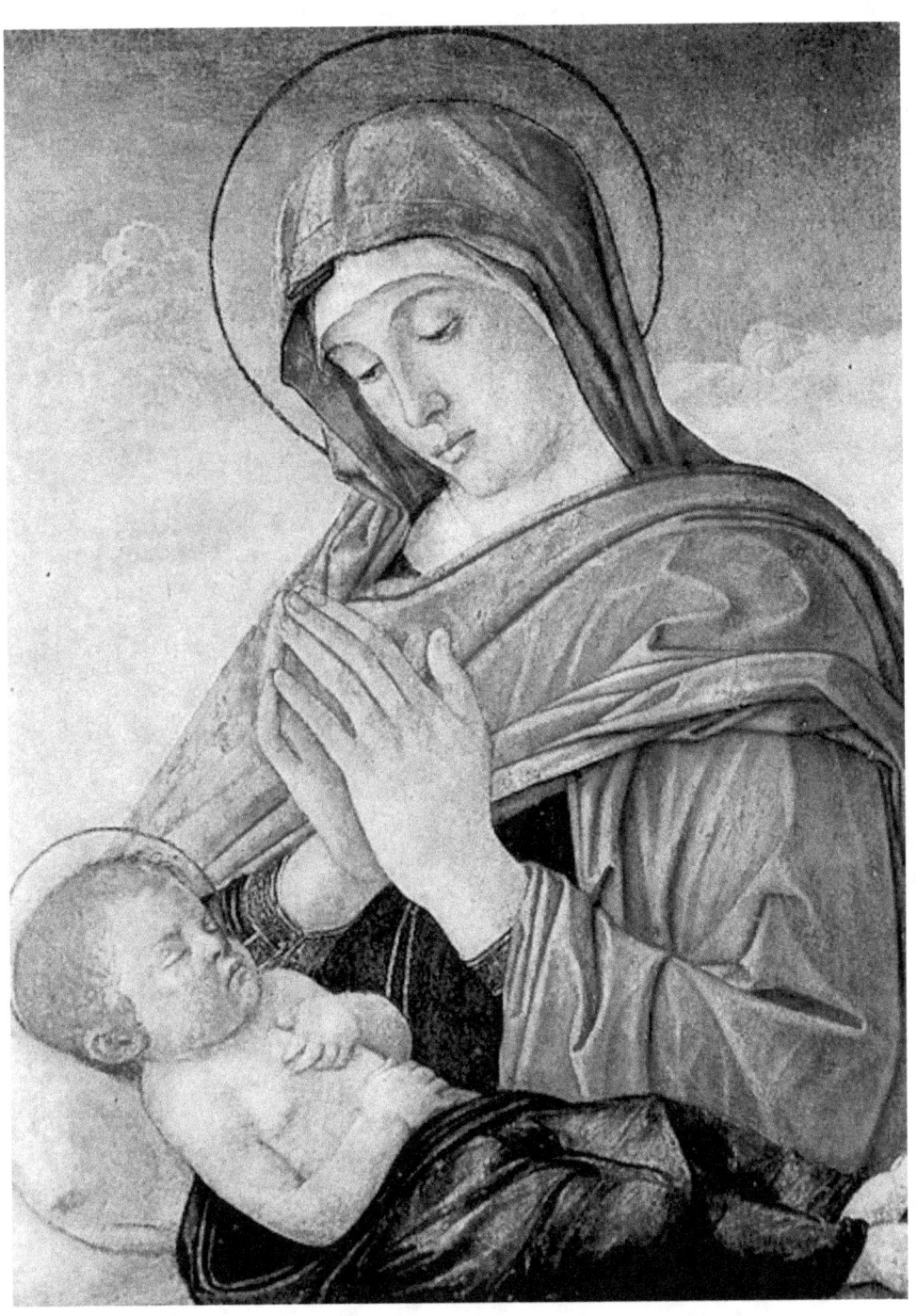

Giovanni Bellini, Madonna In Adoration of the
Sleeping Child, Florence

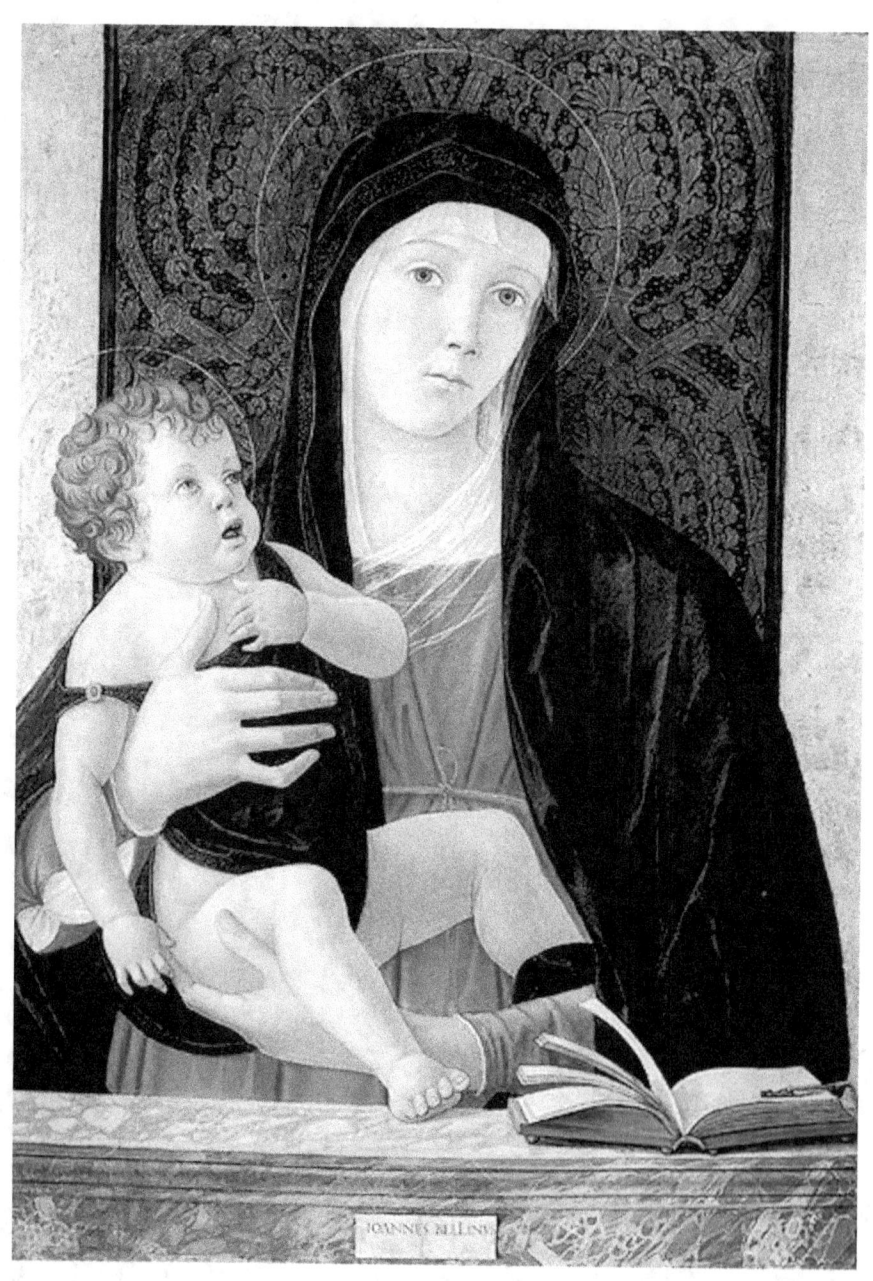

Giovanni Bellini, Madonna and Child, 1460, Kimbell Art Museum

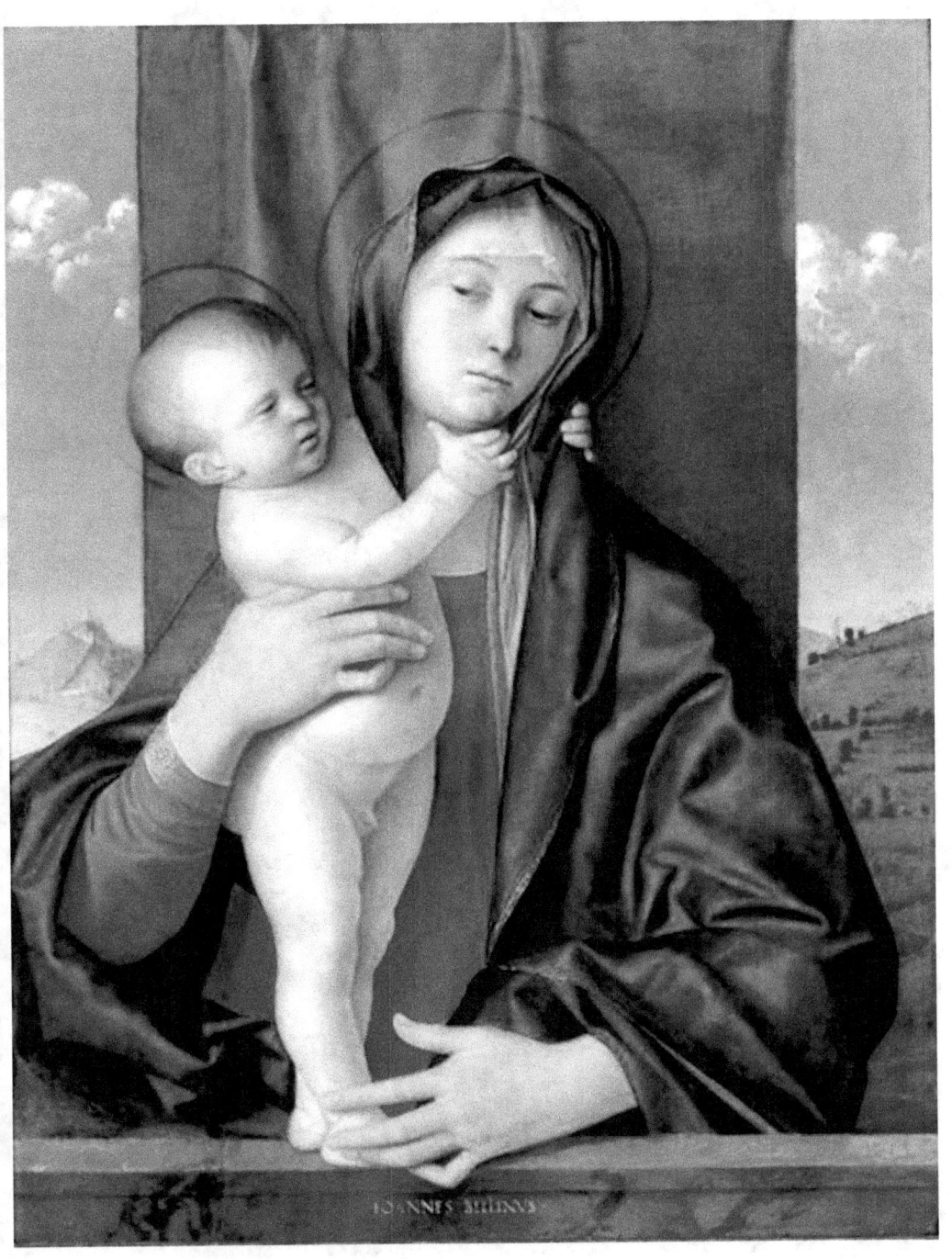

Giovanni Bellini, Madonna and Child, 1480-90, Sao Paolo

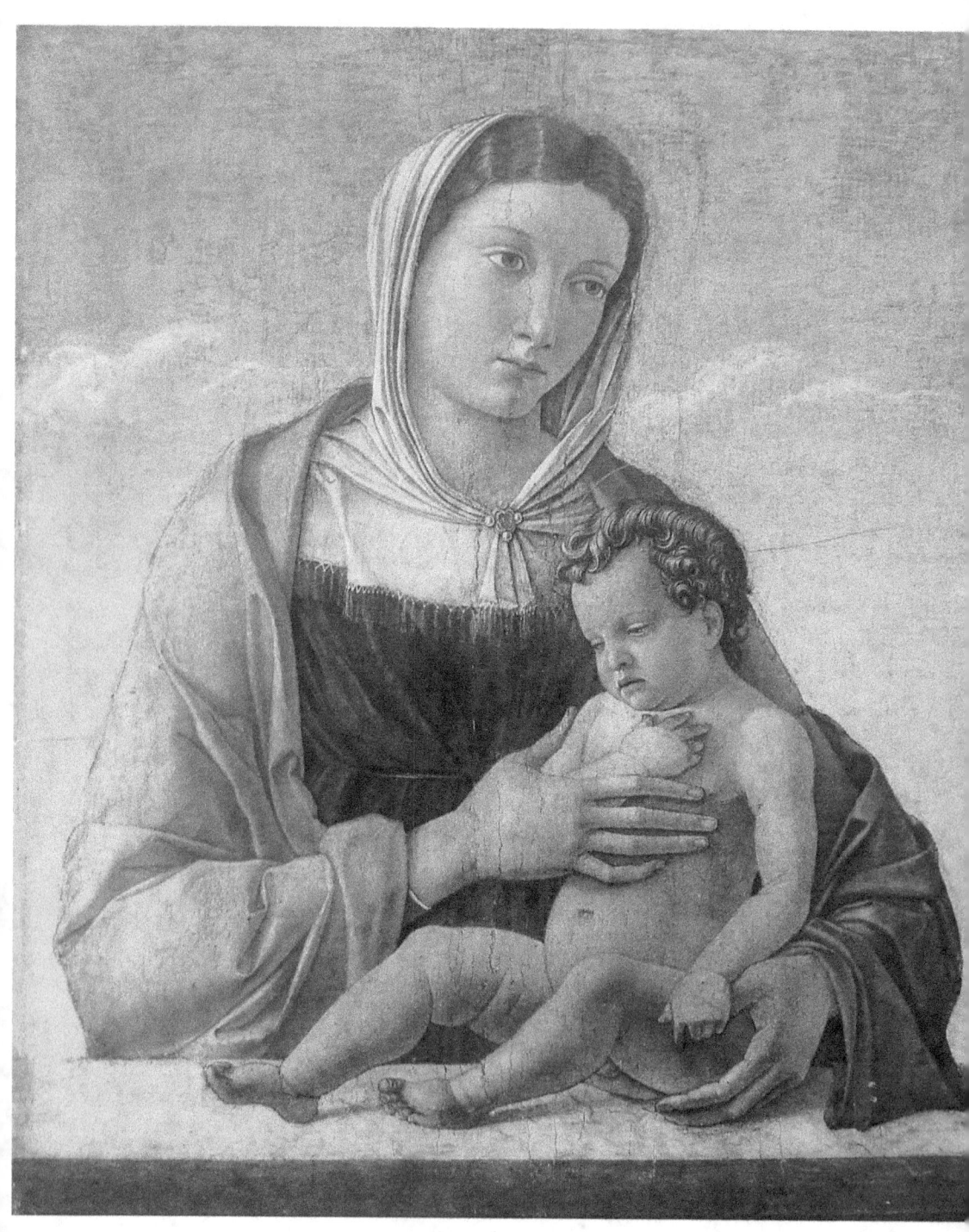

Giovanni Bellini, Madona and Child, Museo Correr e
Quadreria Correr, Venice

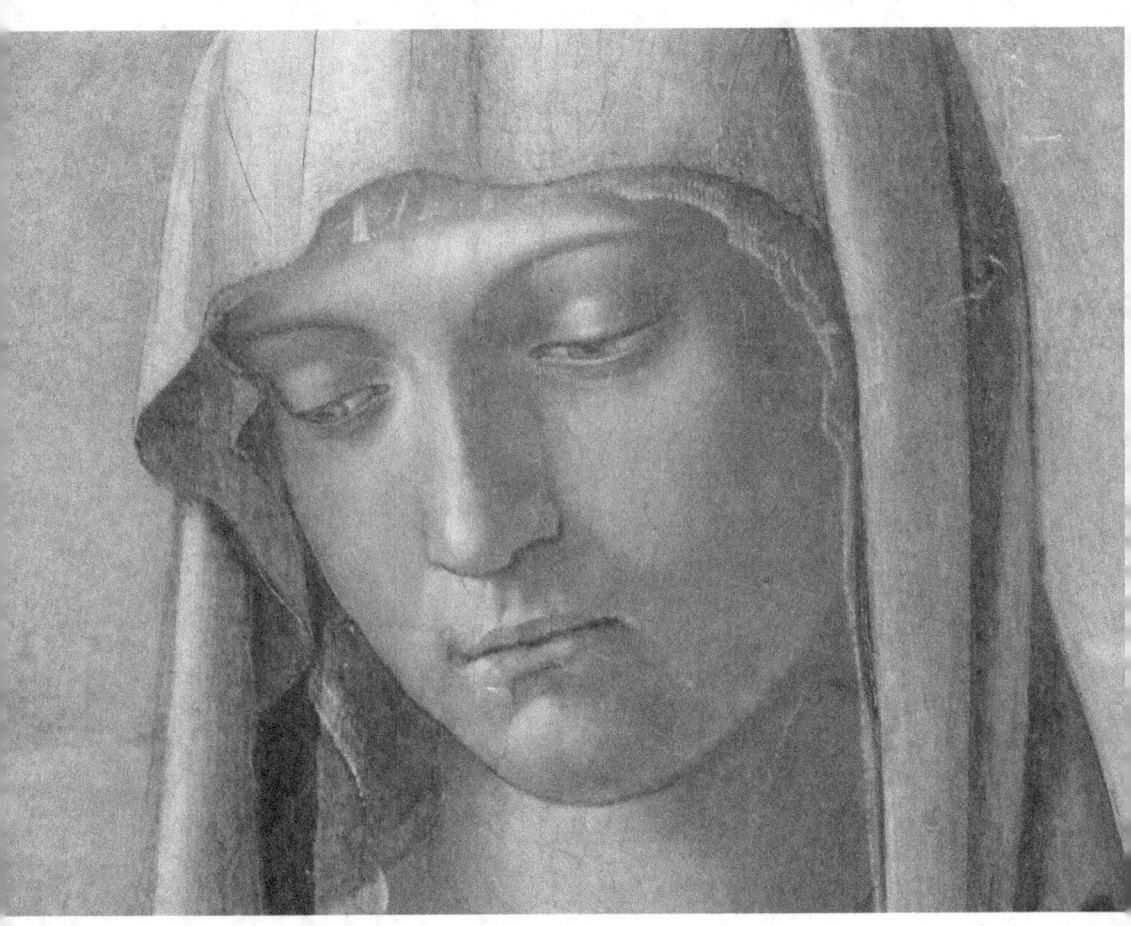

Giovanni Bellini in the Met, New York City, detail

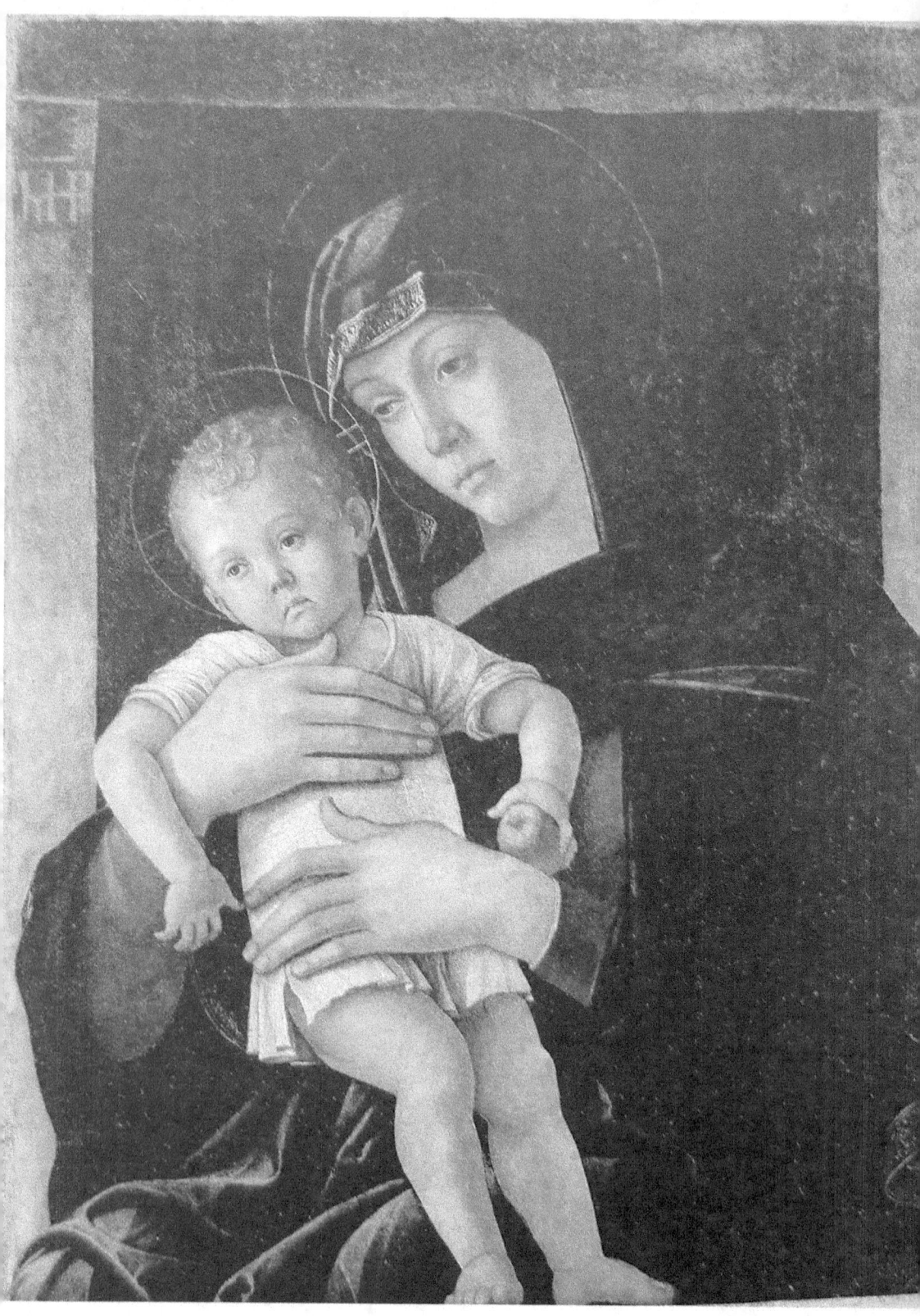

Giovanni Bellini, The Virgin and Child, Pinacoteca de Brera, Milan

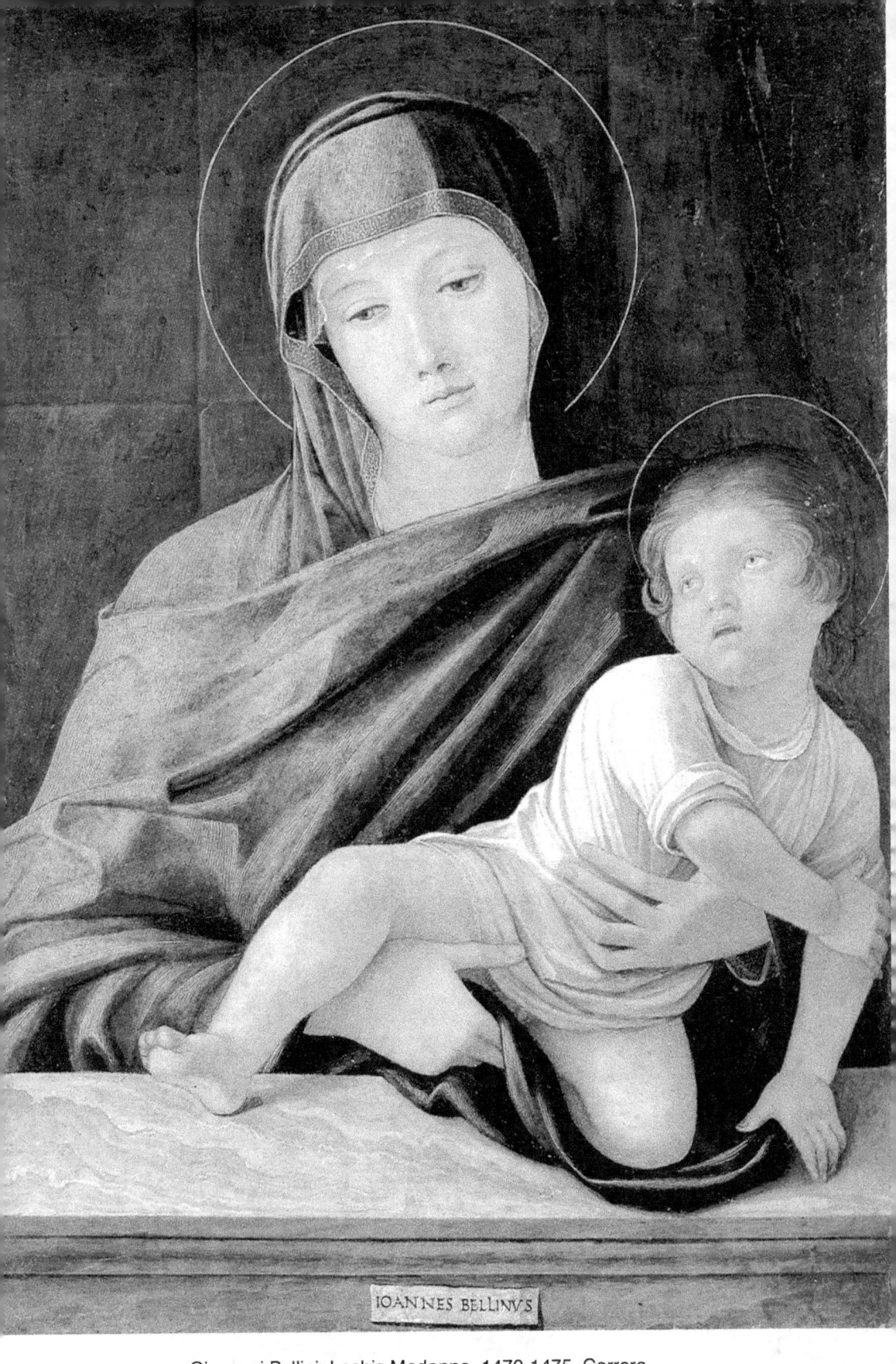

IOANNES BELLINVS

Giovanni Bellini, Lochis Madonna, 1470-1475, Carrara

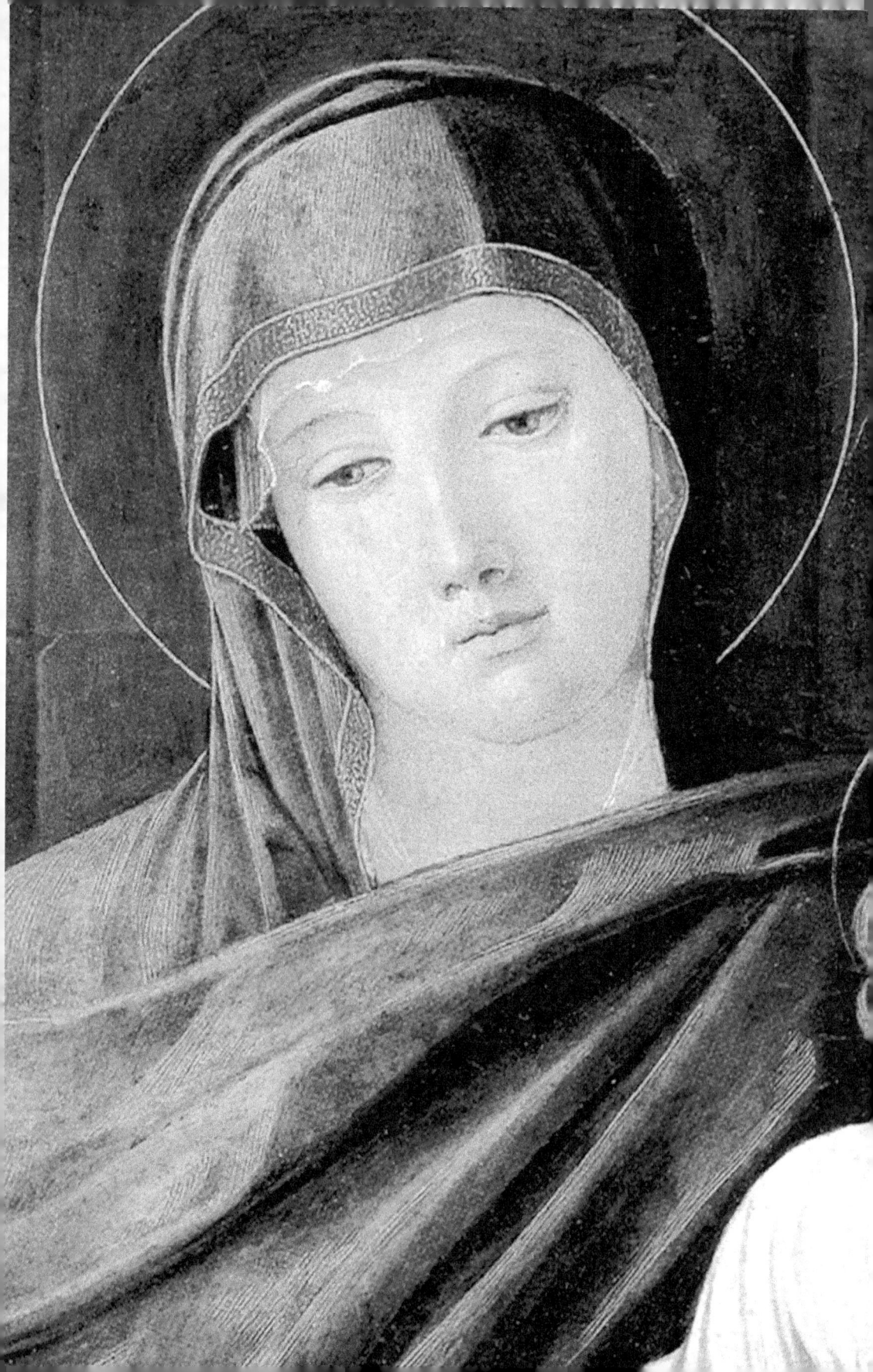

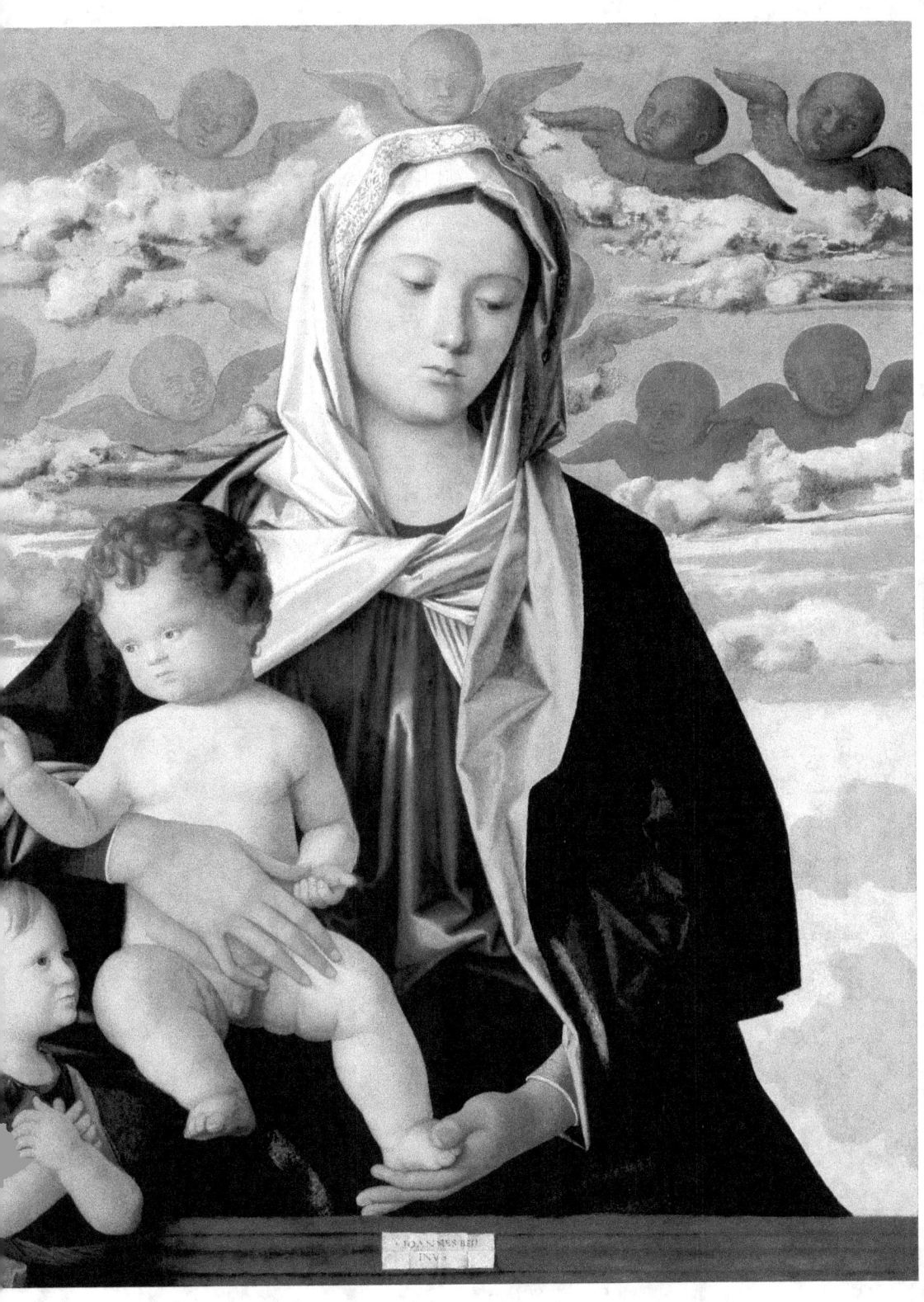

Giovanni Bellini, Madonna and Child With St John the Baptist,
1490-1500, Indianapolis

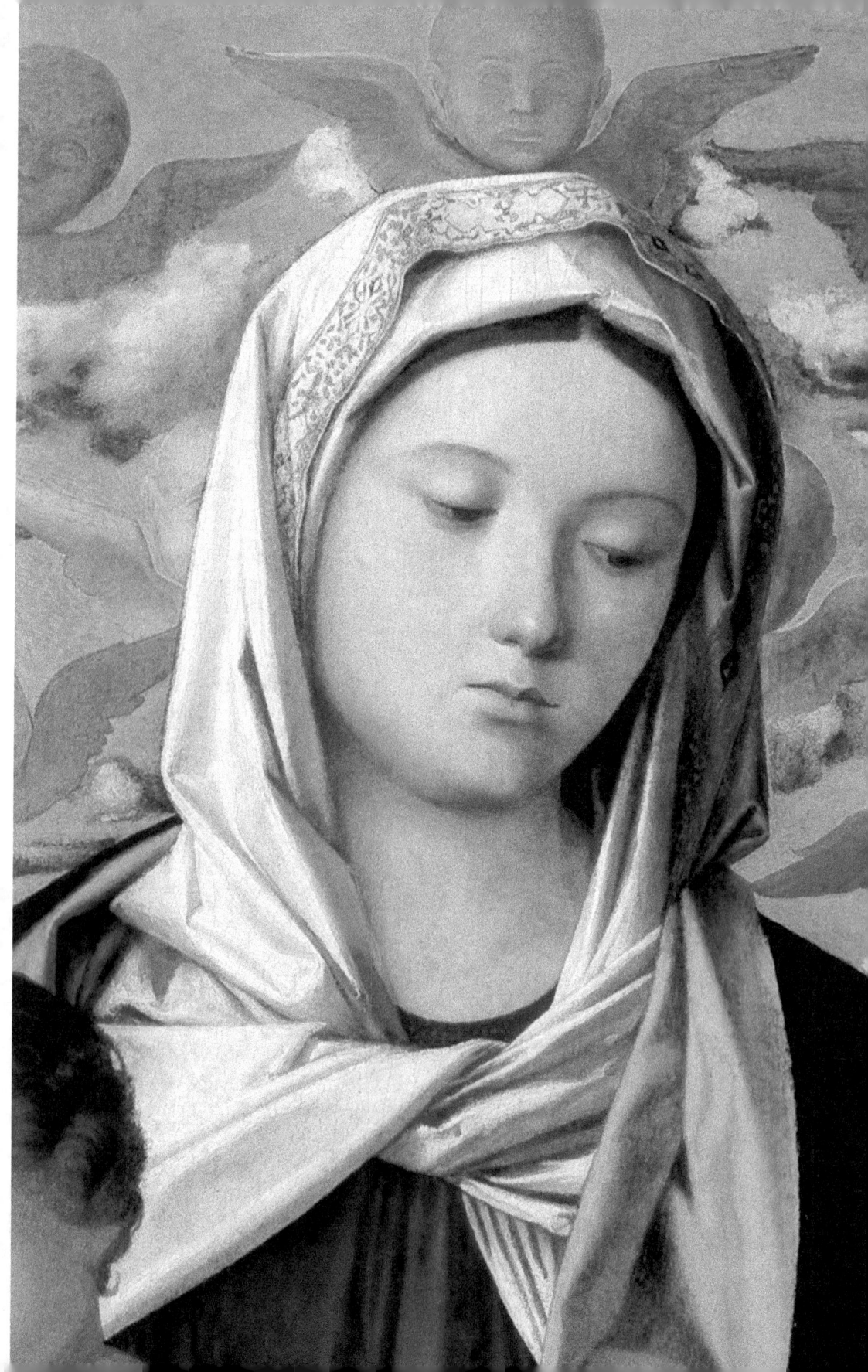

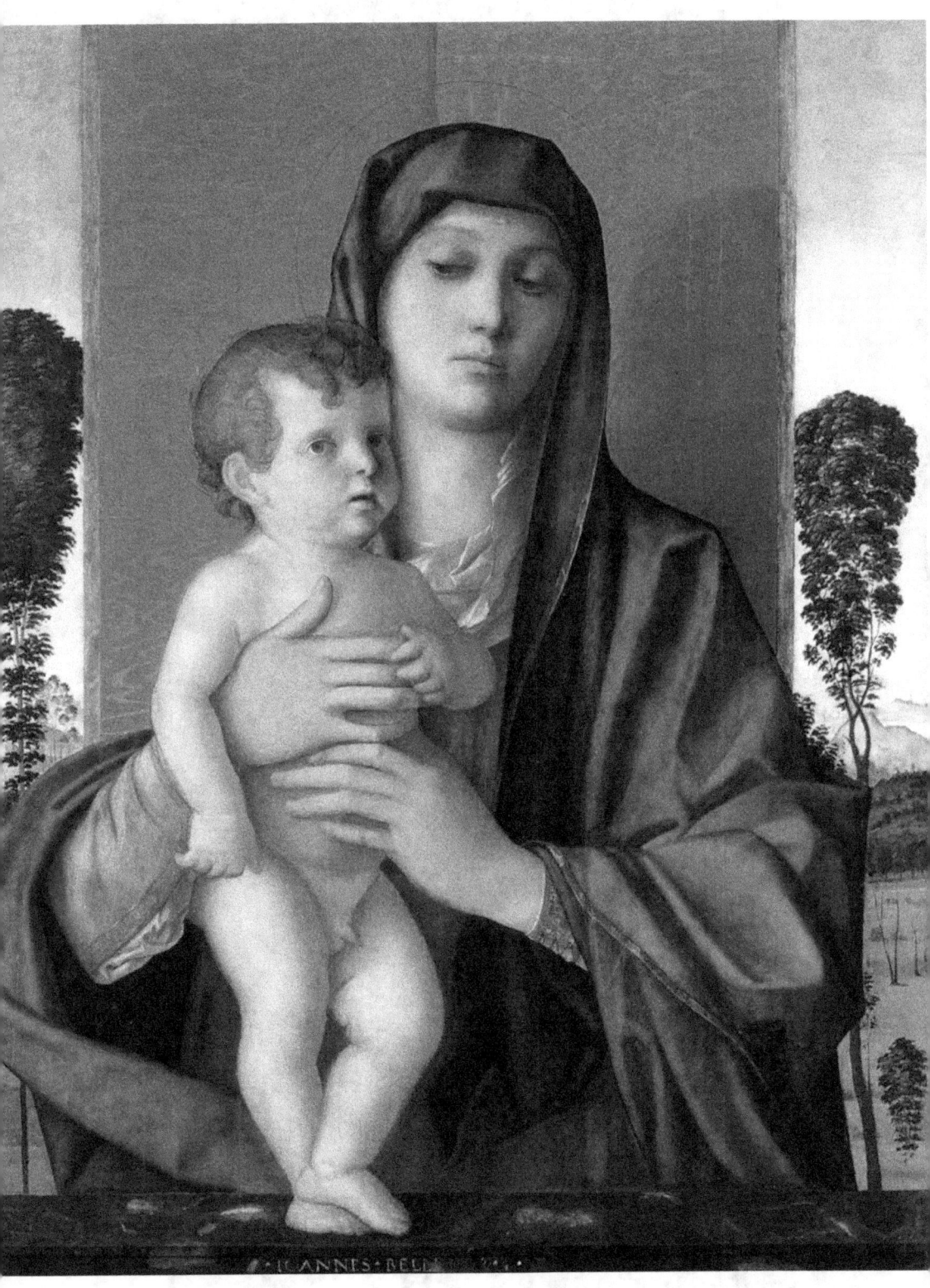

Giovanni Bellini, Madonna degli Alberetti, 1487, Venice

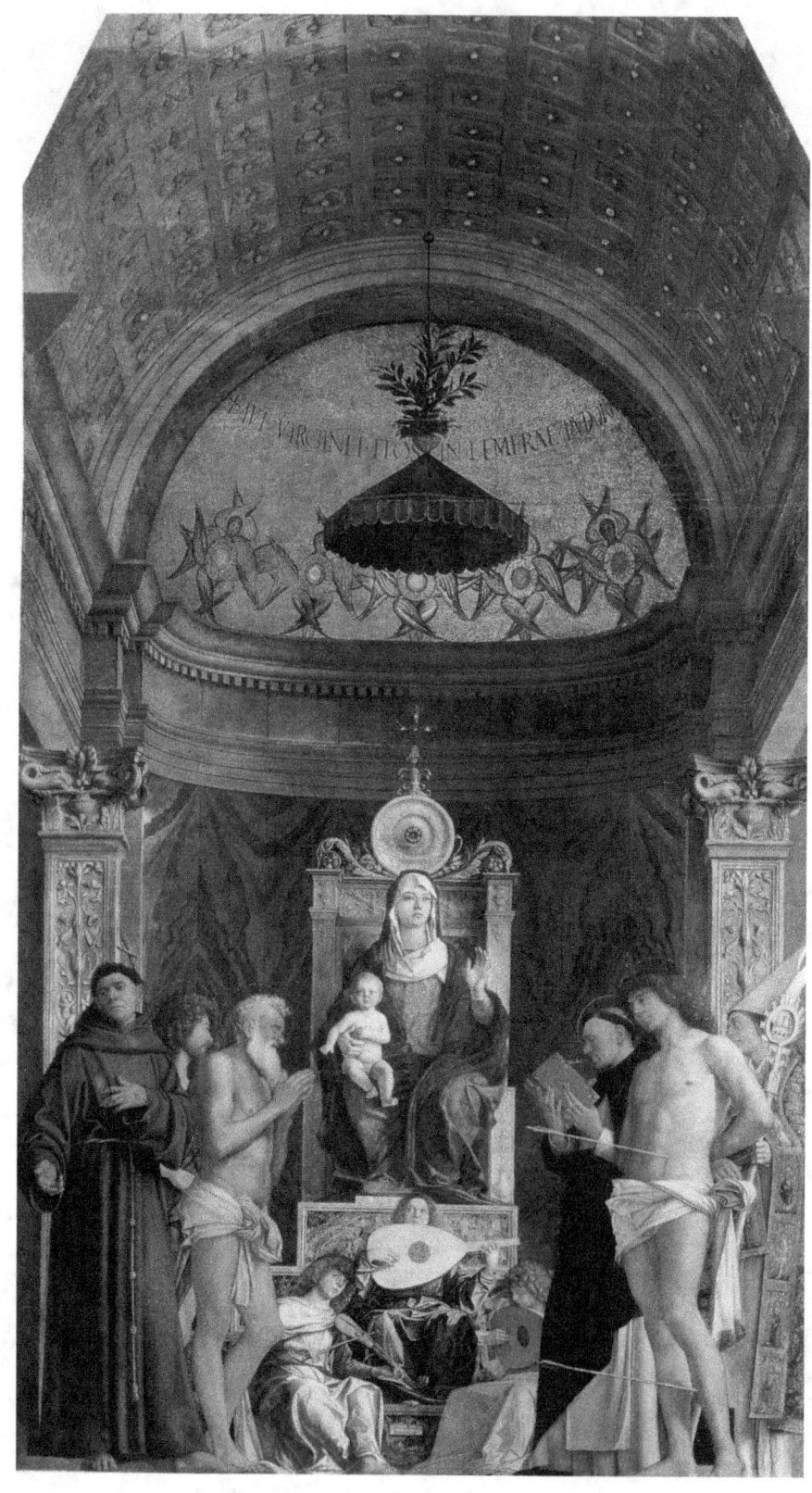

Giovanni Bellini, San Giobbe Altarpiece, 1487, Venice

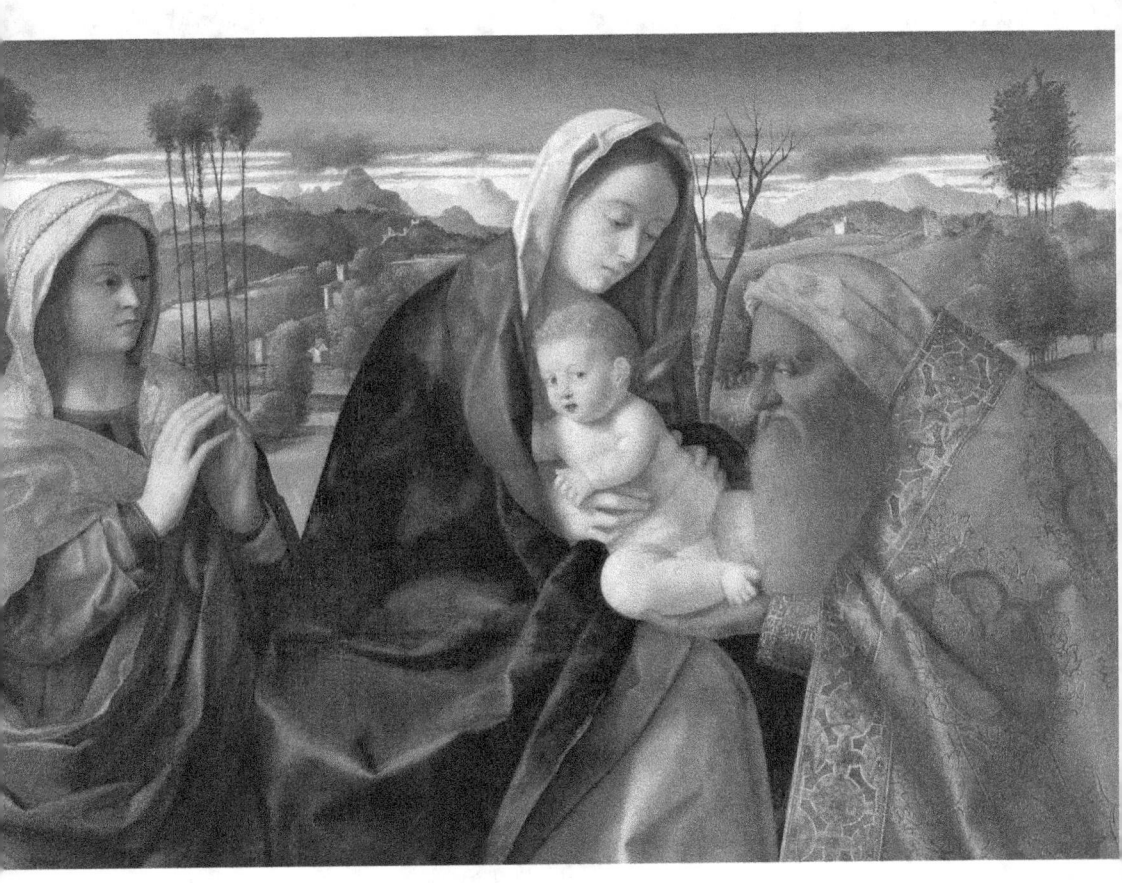

Giovanni Bellini, Nunc Dimittis, c. 1505-1510,
Thyssen-Bornemisza Museum, Madrid.

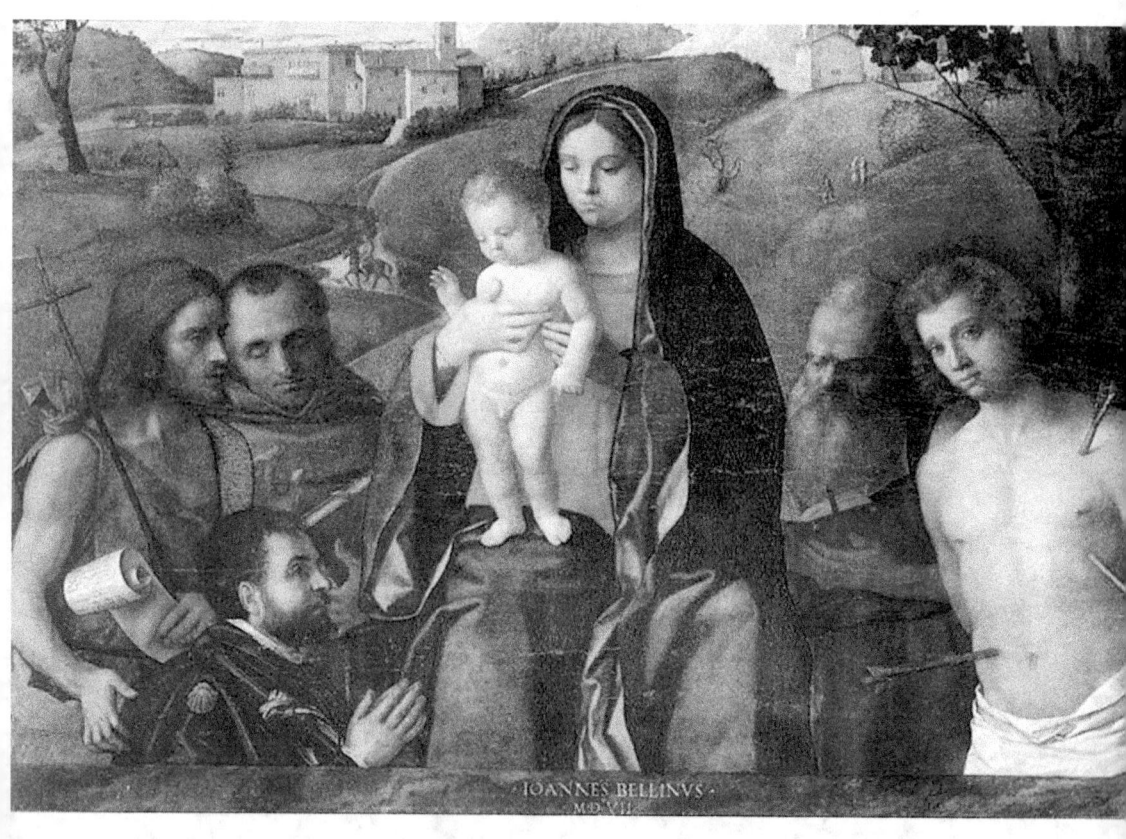

Giovanni Bellini, Madonna and Child With Four Saints and Donor,
1507, Venice

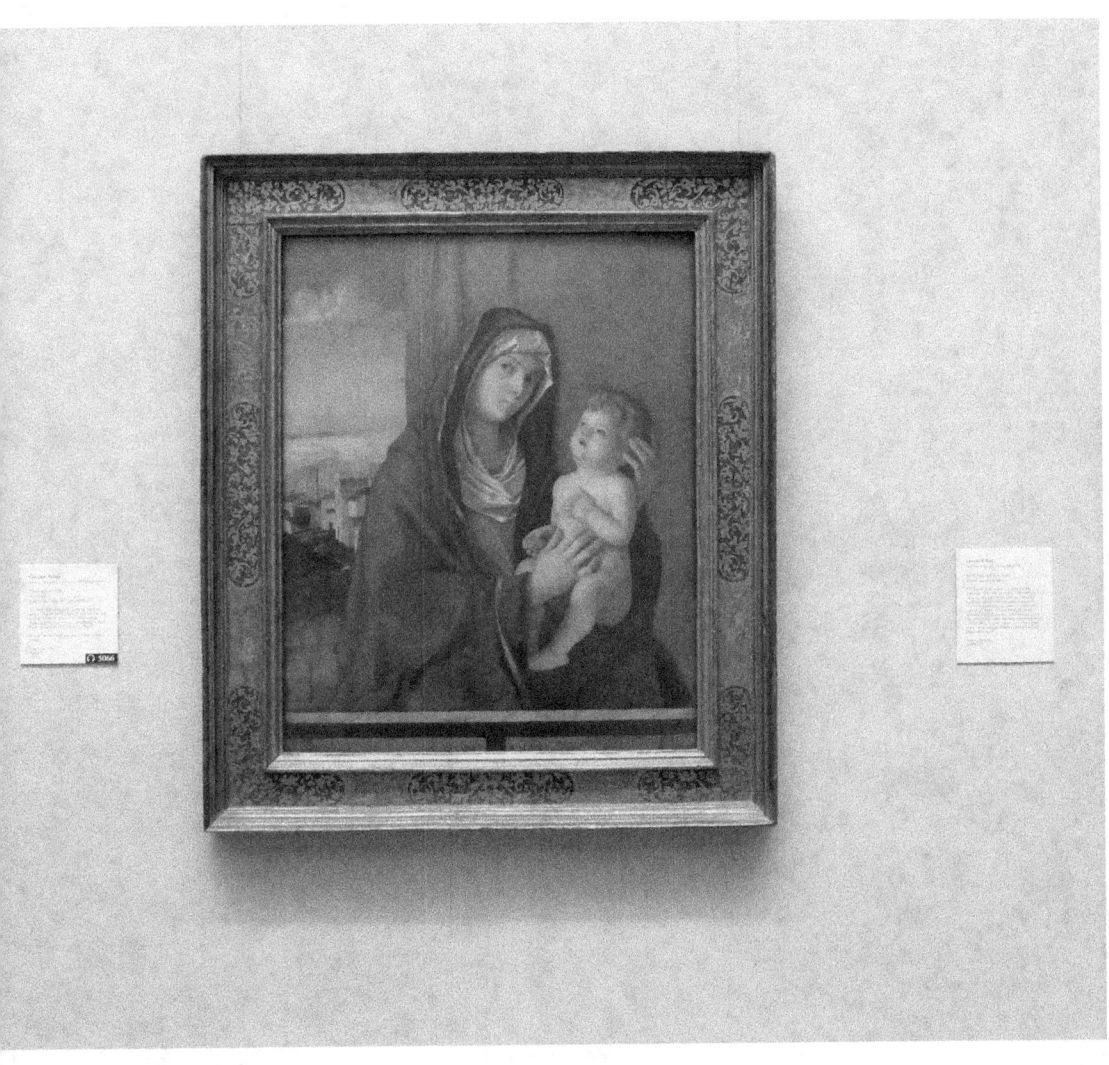

Giovanni Bellini at the Met, New York City

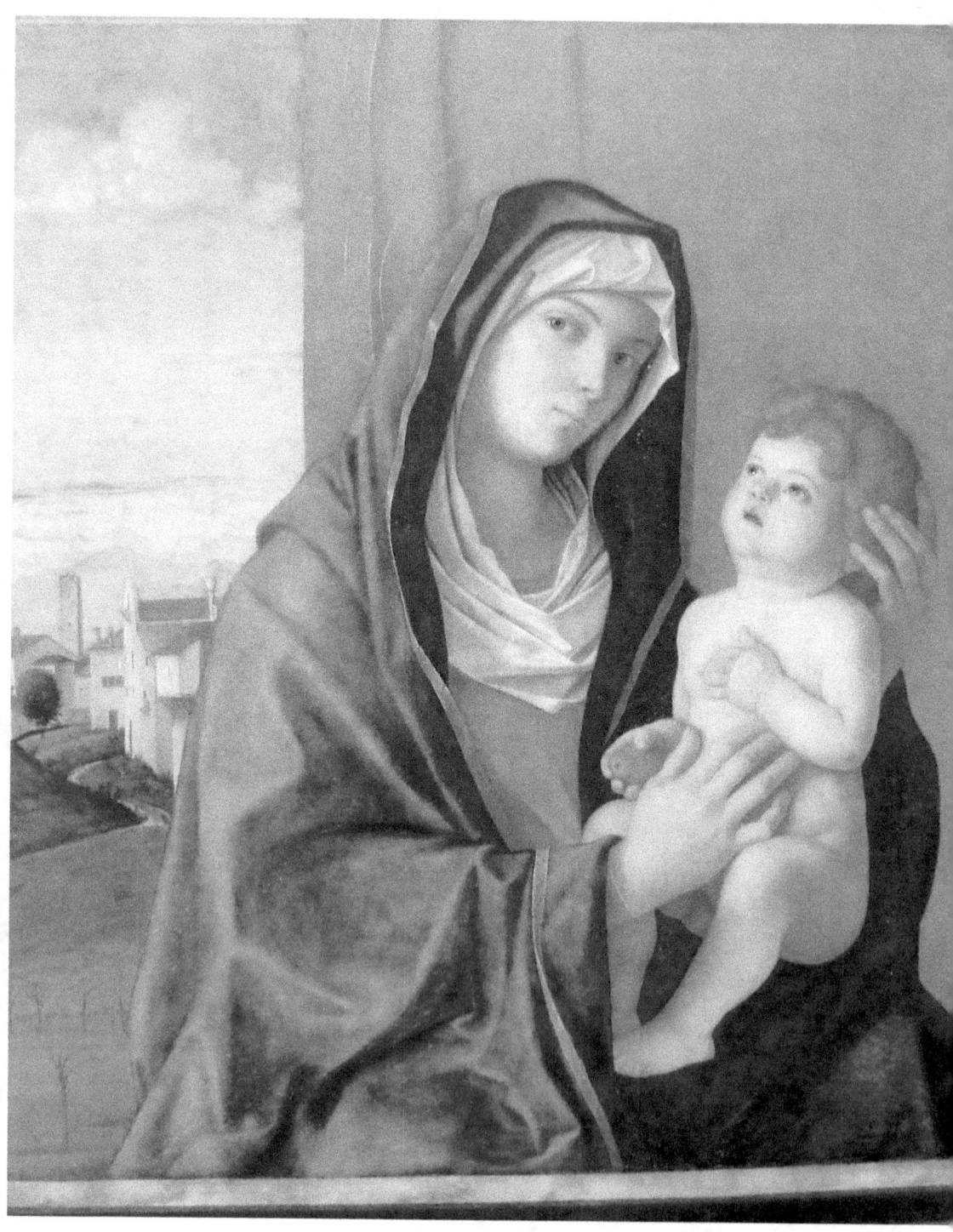

Giovanni Bellini, Virgin and Child, Metropolitan Museum,
New York City

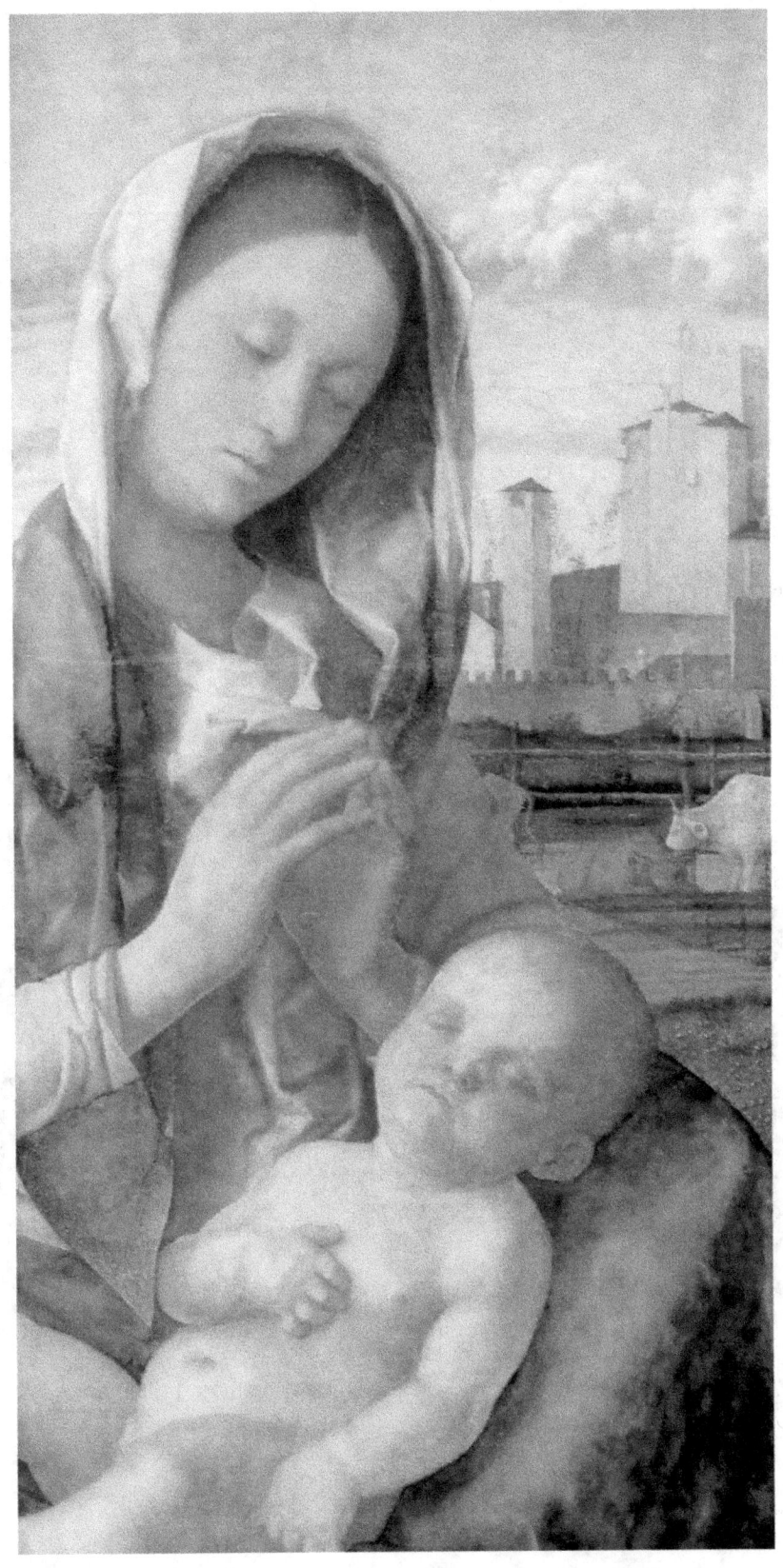

Giovanni Bellini, The Madonna of the Meadow, detail

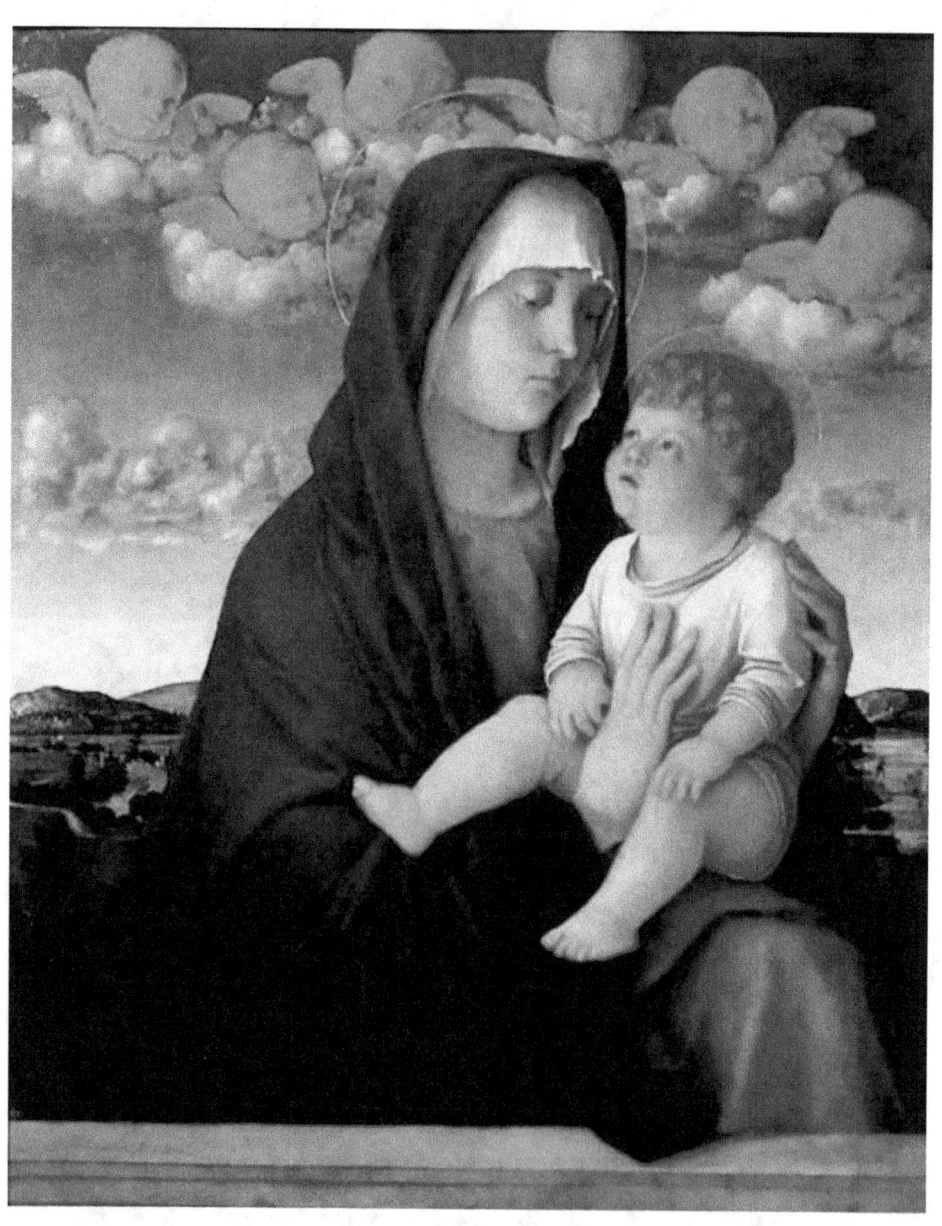

Giovanni Bellini, Madonna and Child With Red Cherubs, 1485, Venice

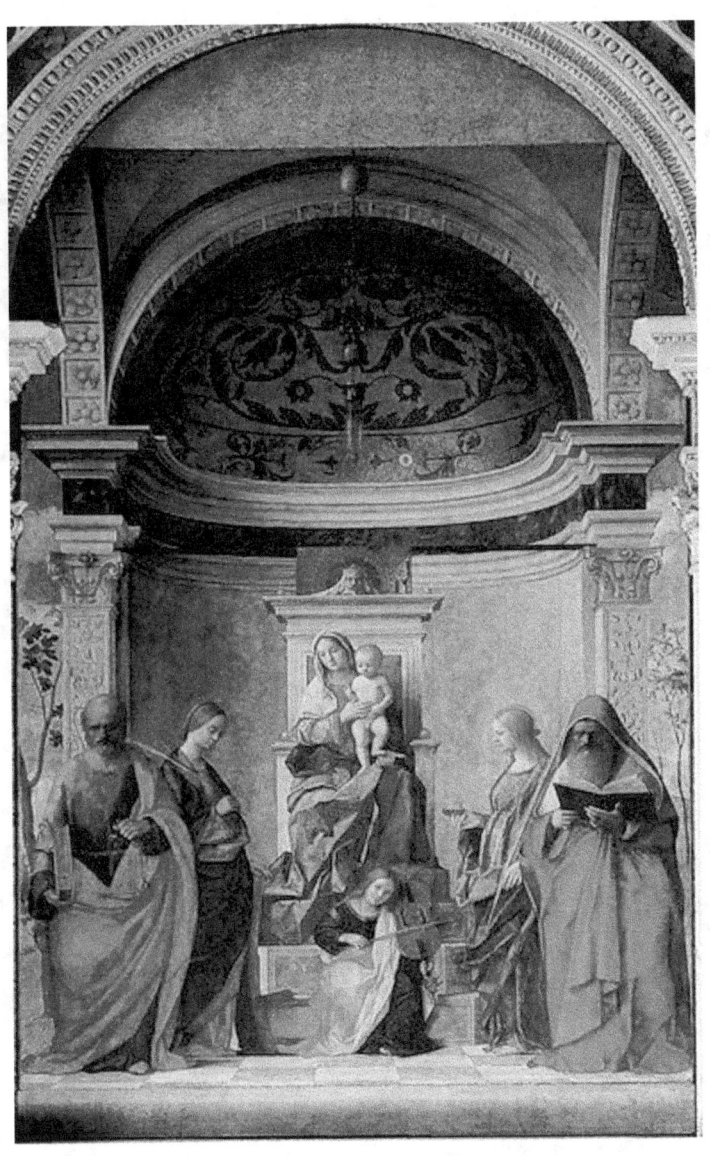

Giovanni Bellini, San Zaccaria Altarpiece

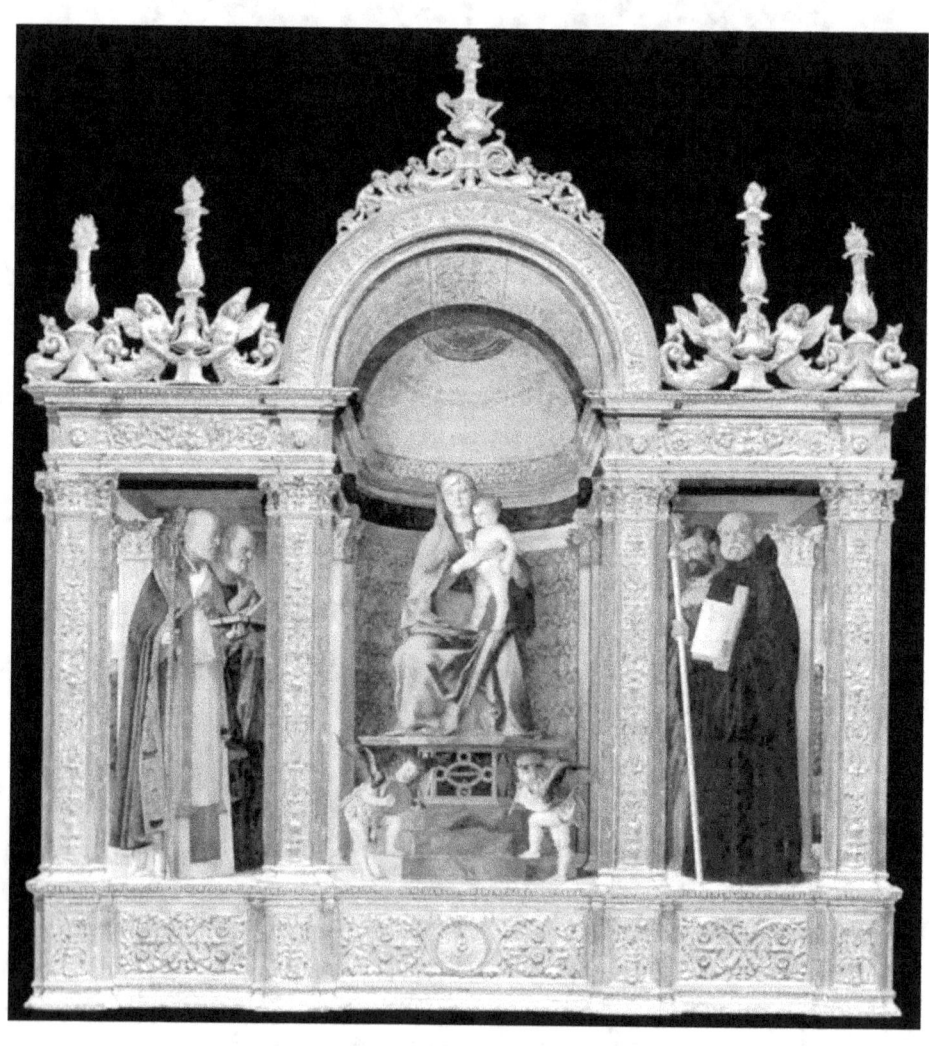

Giovanni Bellini, Friari Altarpiece

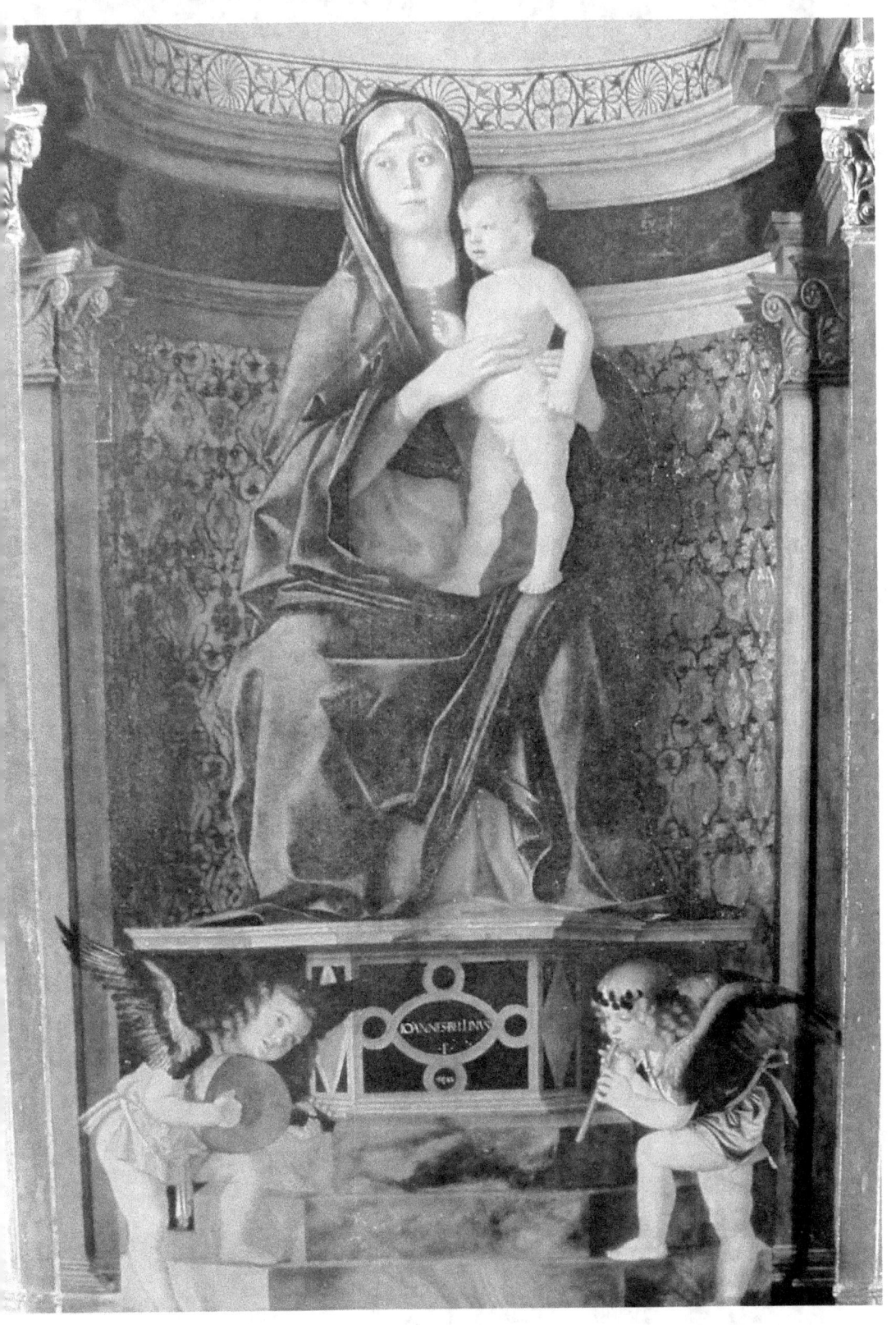

Giovanni Bellini, Madonna and Child Enthroned, 1488, Venice

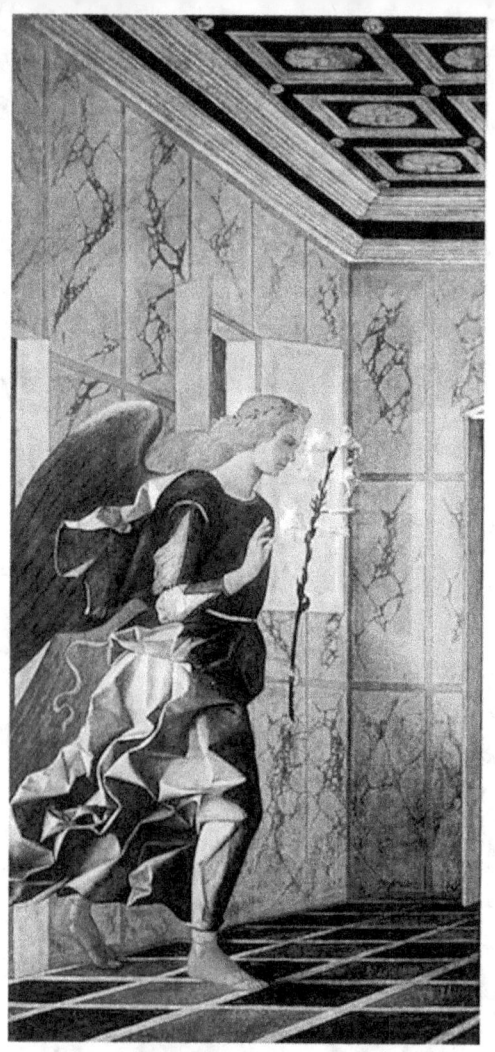
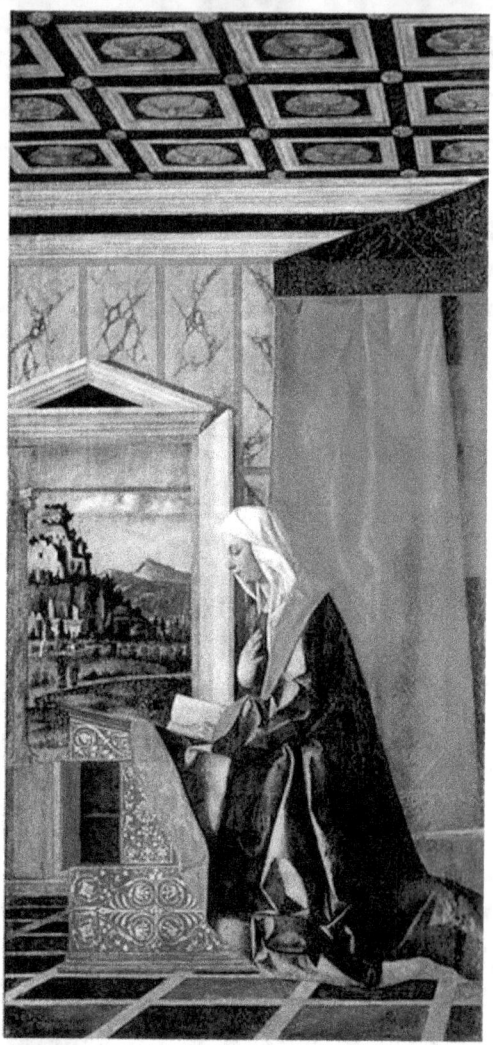

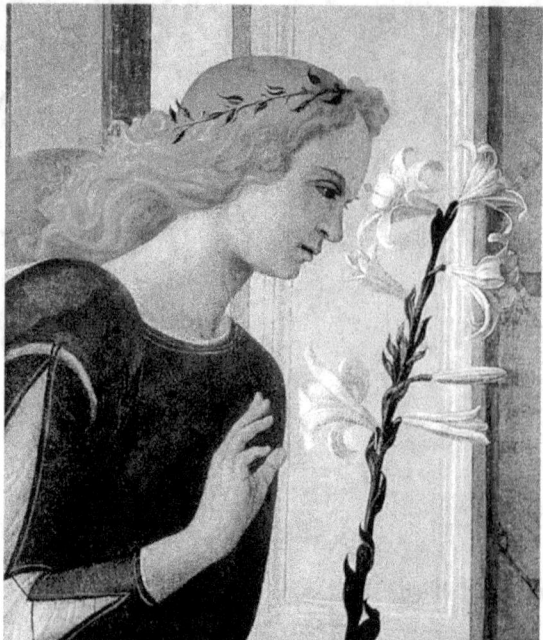

Giovanni Bellini, Annunciation,
c. 1500, Venice (and detail, left).

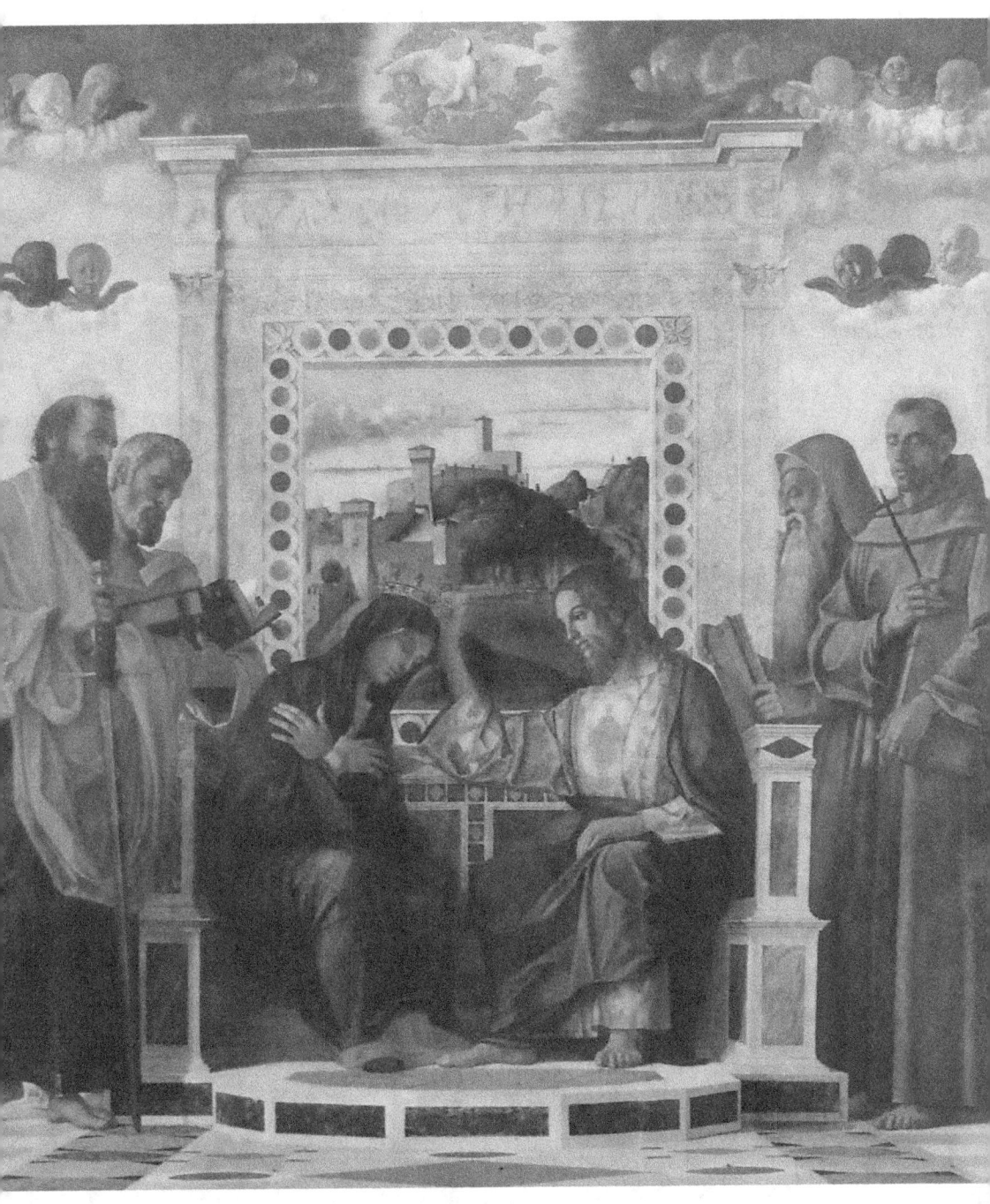

Giovanni Bellini, The Coronation of the Virgin, Pesaro

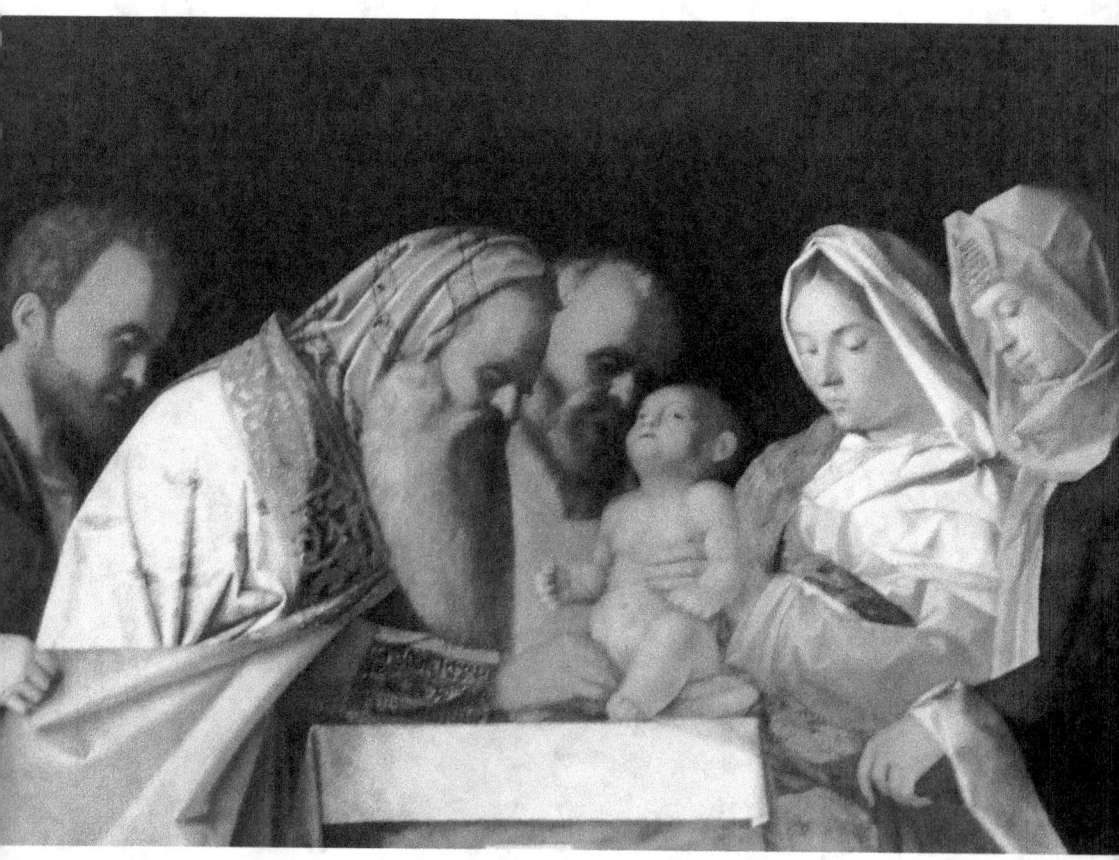

Giovanni Bellini, The Circumcision, National Gallery, London

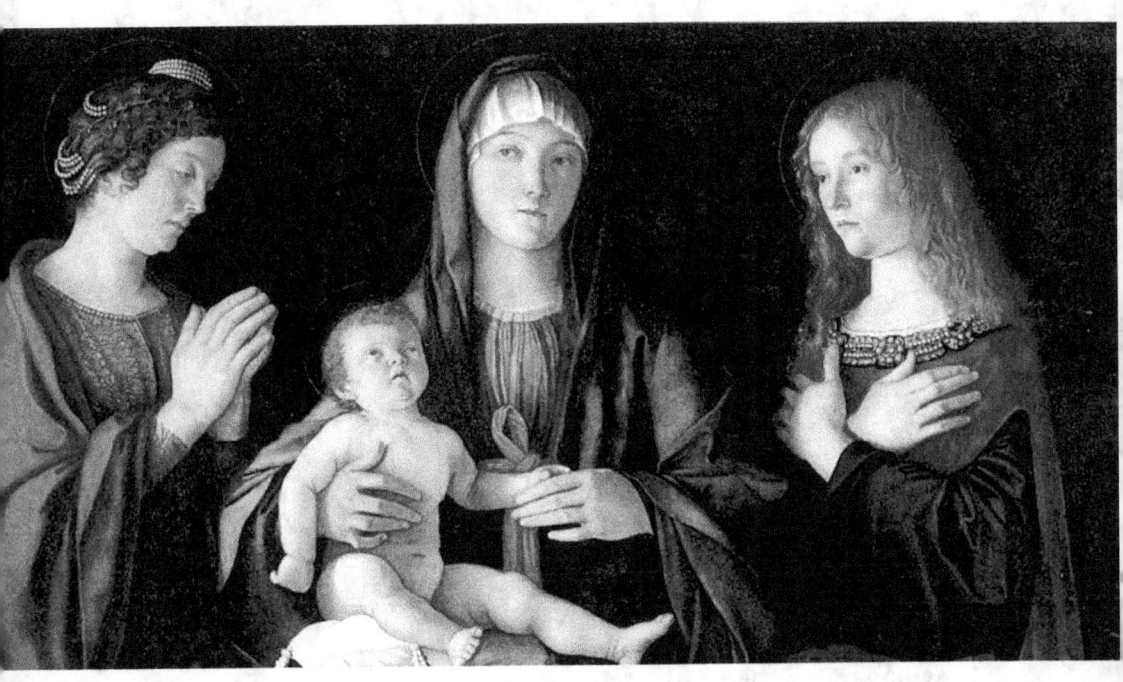

Giovanni Bellini, Sacra Conversazione, 1490

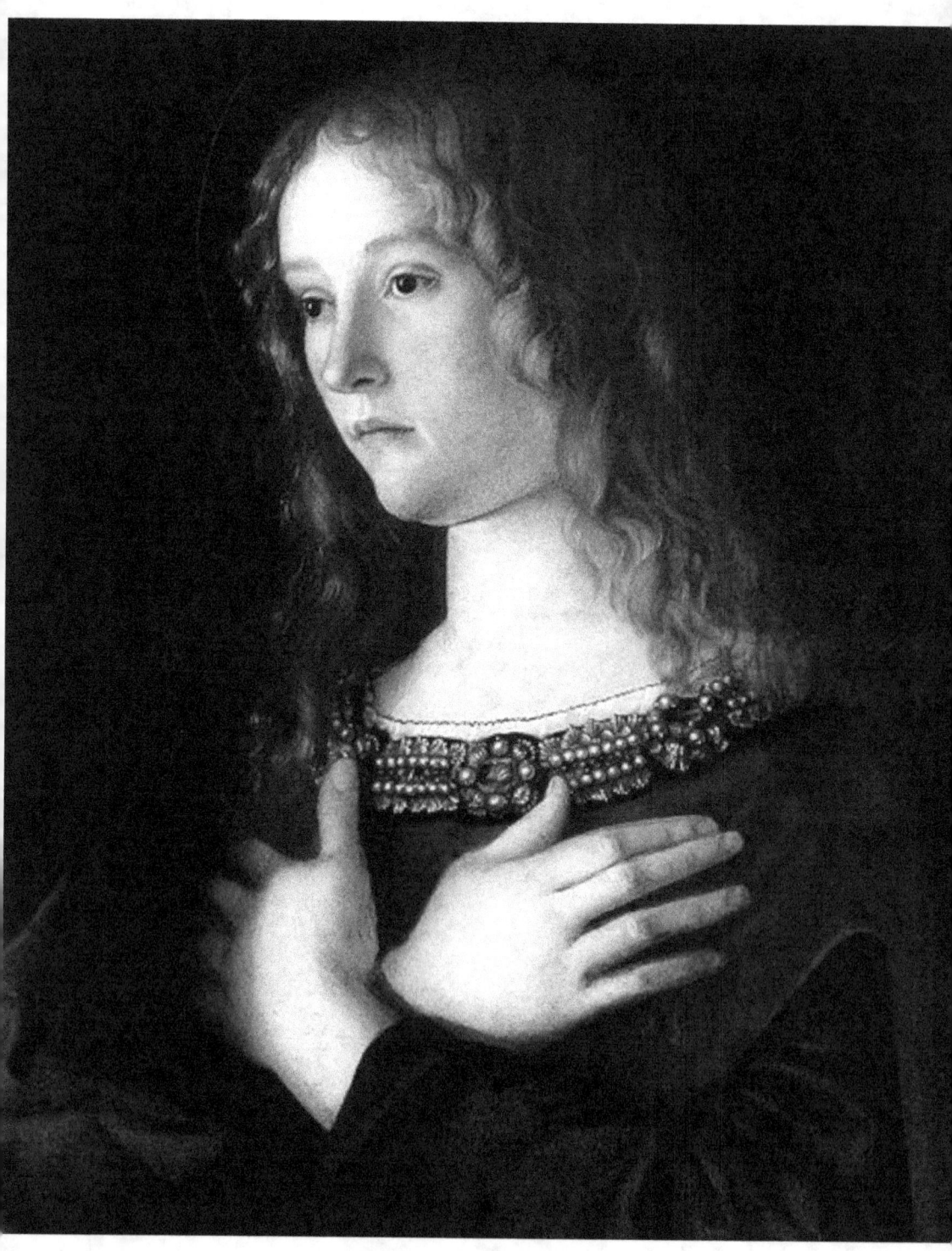

Giovanni Bellini, Sacra Conversazione, detail

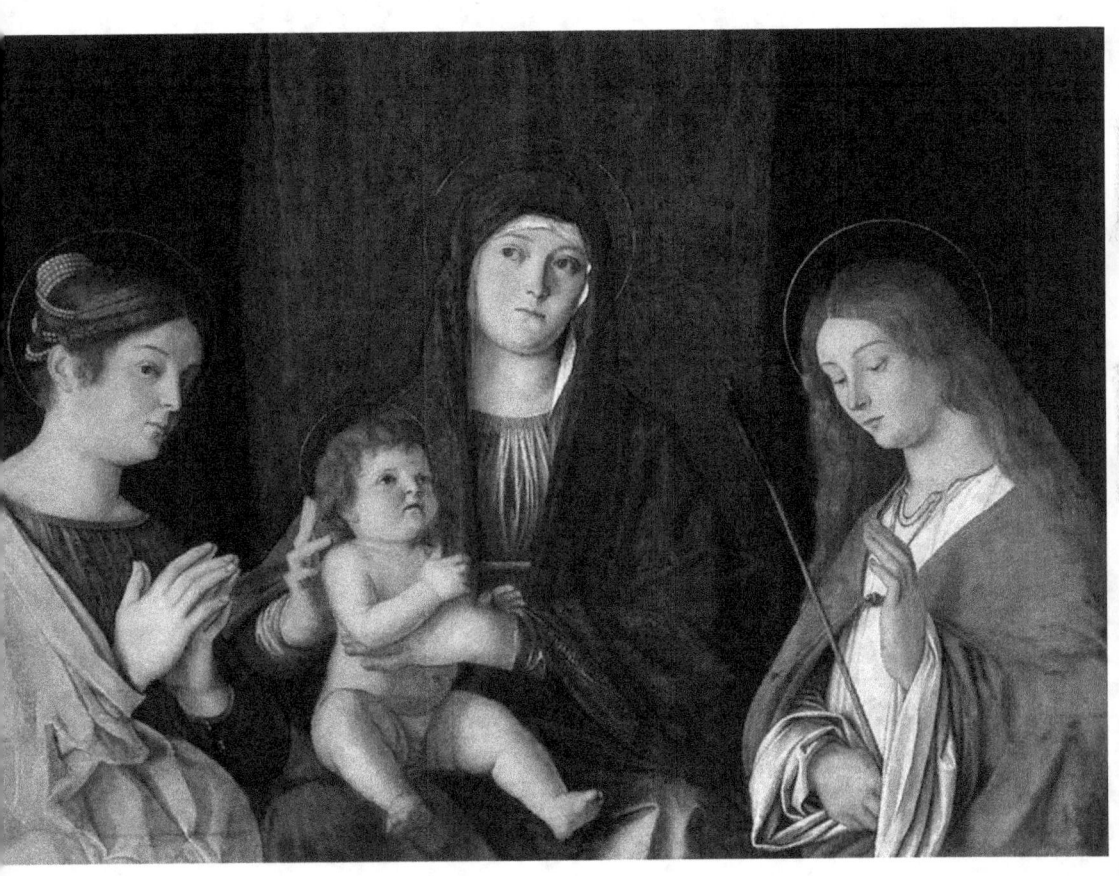

Giovanni Bellini, Sacra Conversazione, 1490, Prado, Madrid

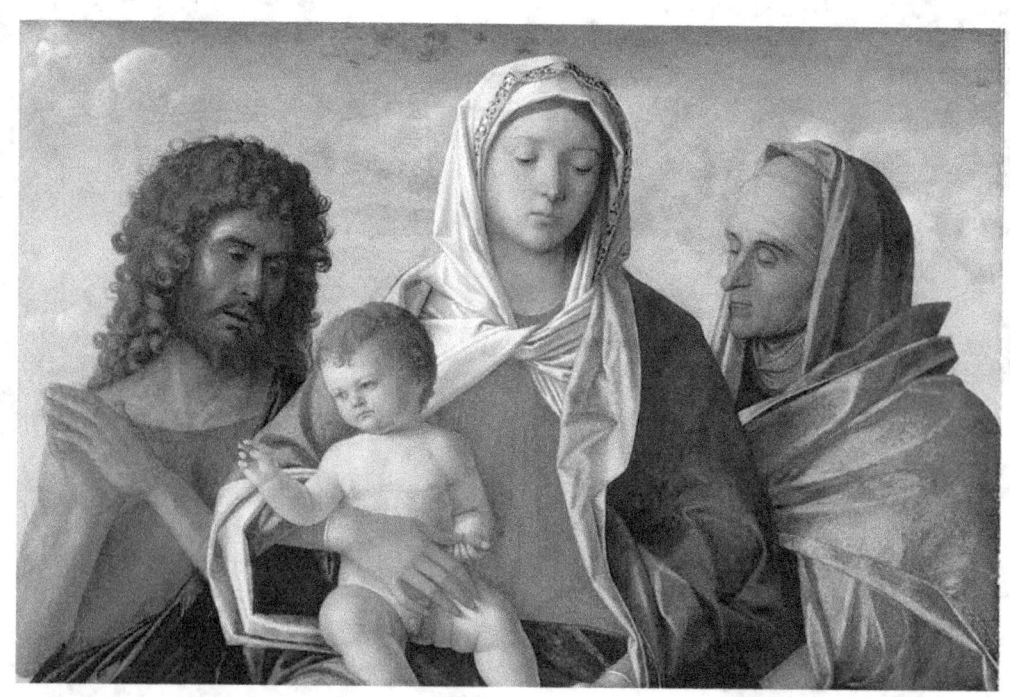

Giovanni Bellini, Madonna and Child, John and Elisabeth, early 1500s, Stadel

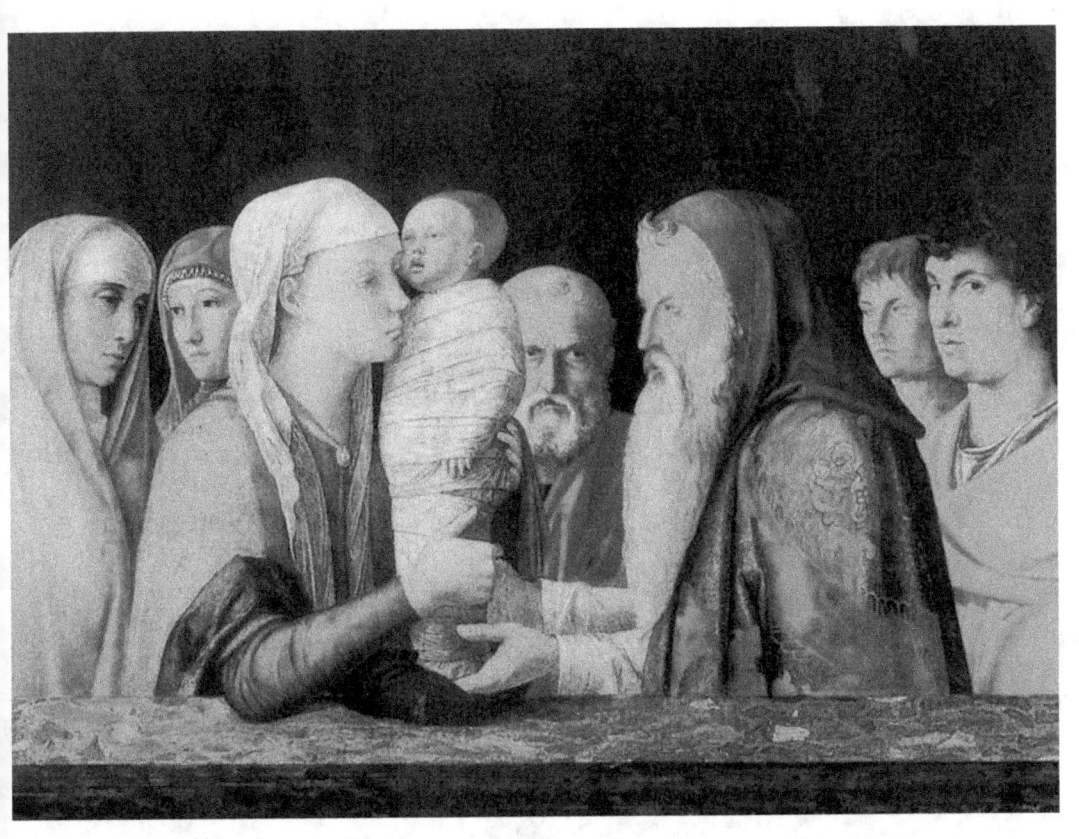

Giovanni Bellini, Presentation In the Temple, c. 1459, Venice

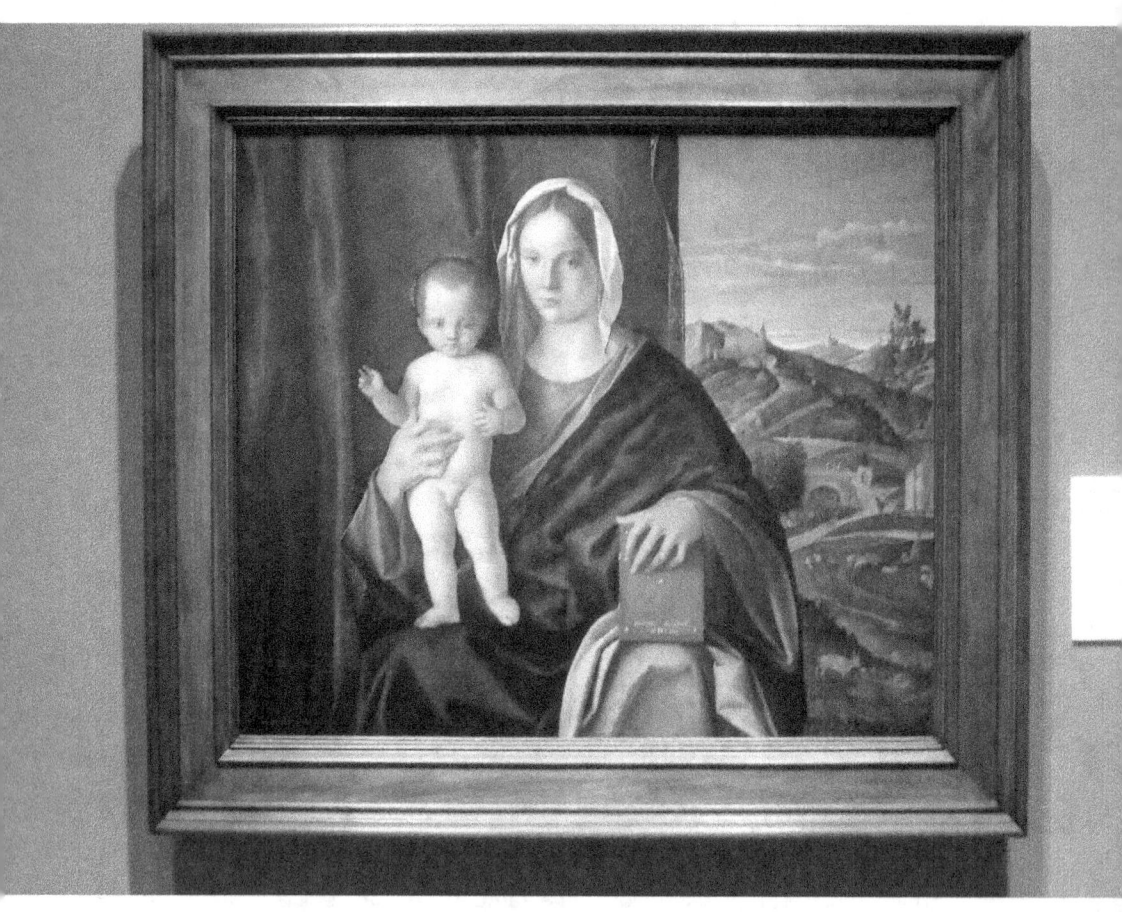

Giovanni Bellini in the Met, New York City

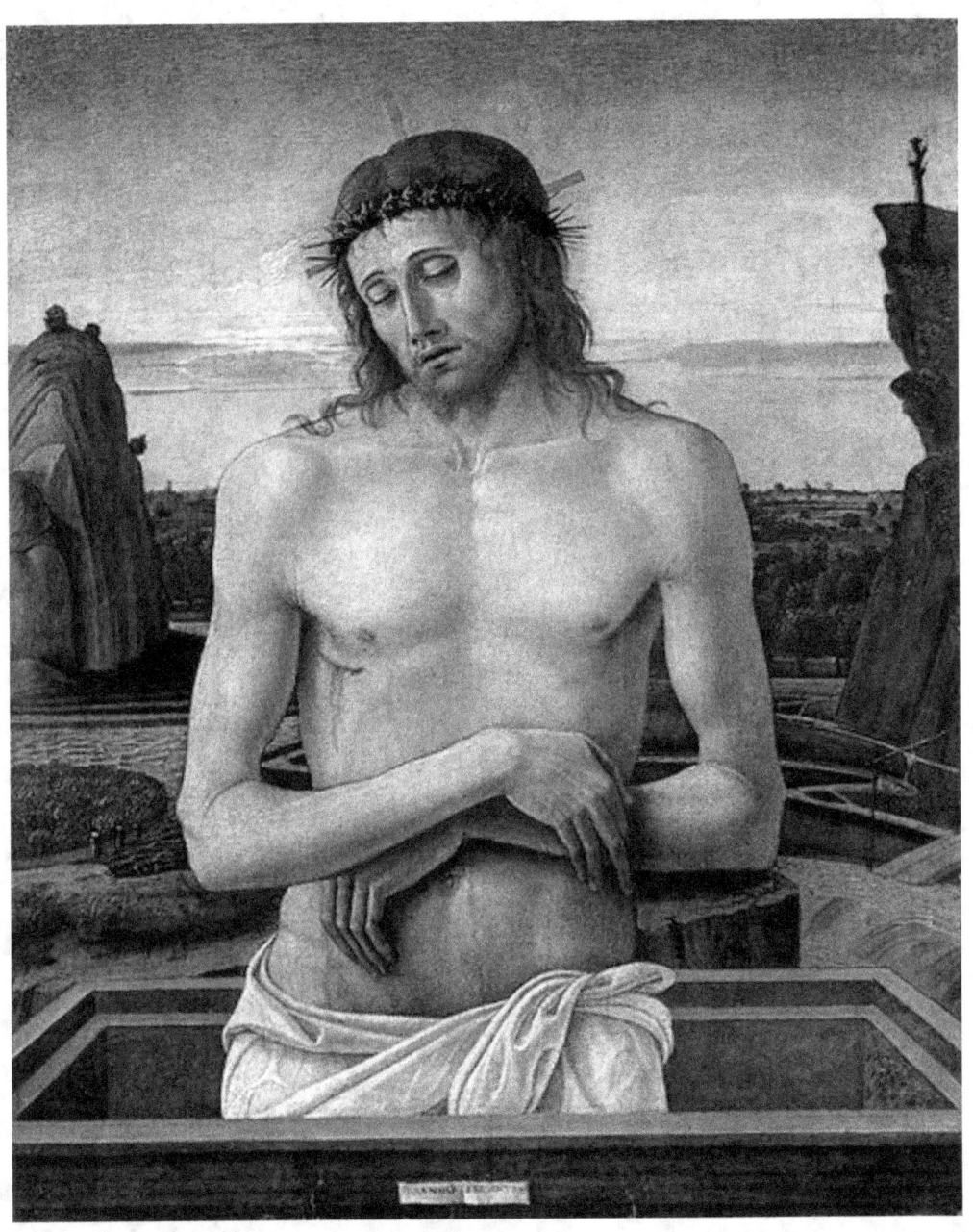

Giovanni Bellini, Pietà, 1460, Poldi Pezzoli Museum

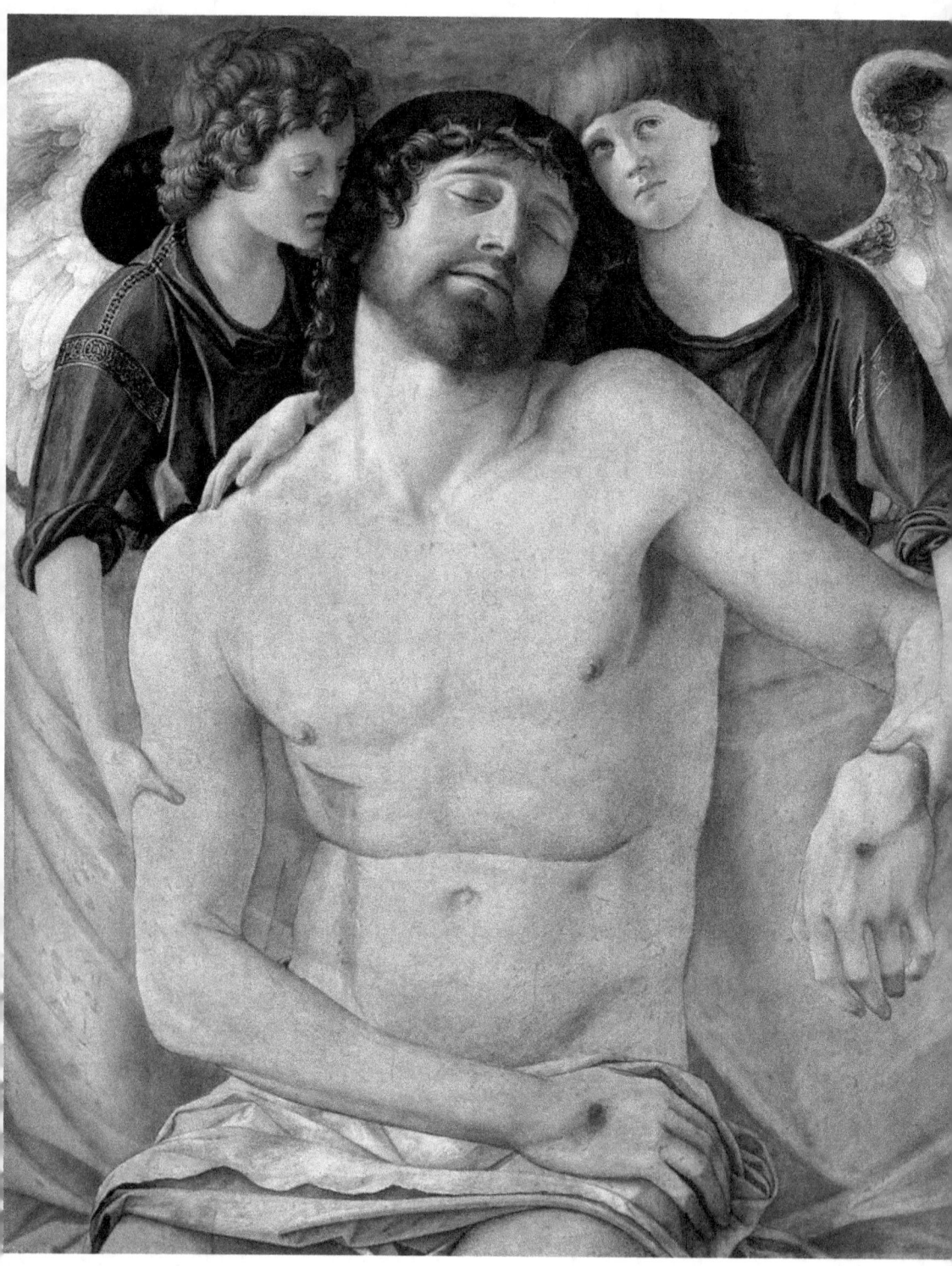

Giovanni Bellini, Pietà, 1485-90, Berlin

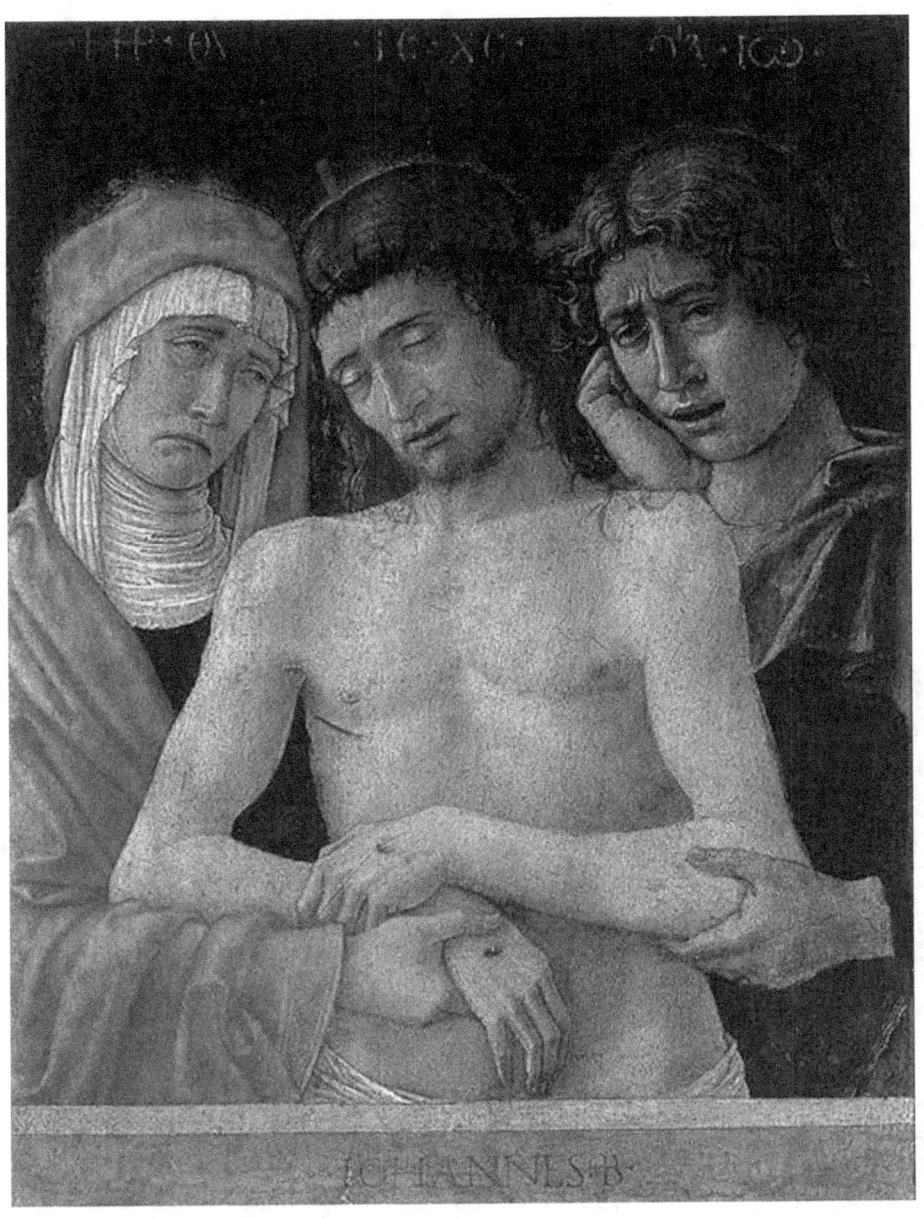

Giovanni Bellini, Pietà, 1455, Bergamo

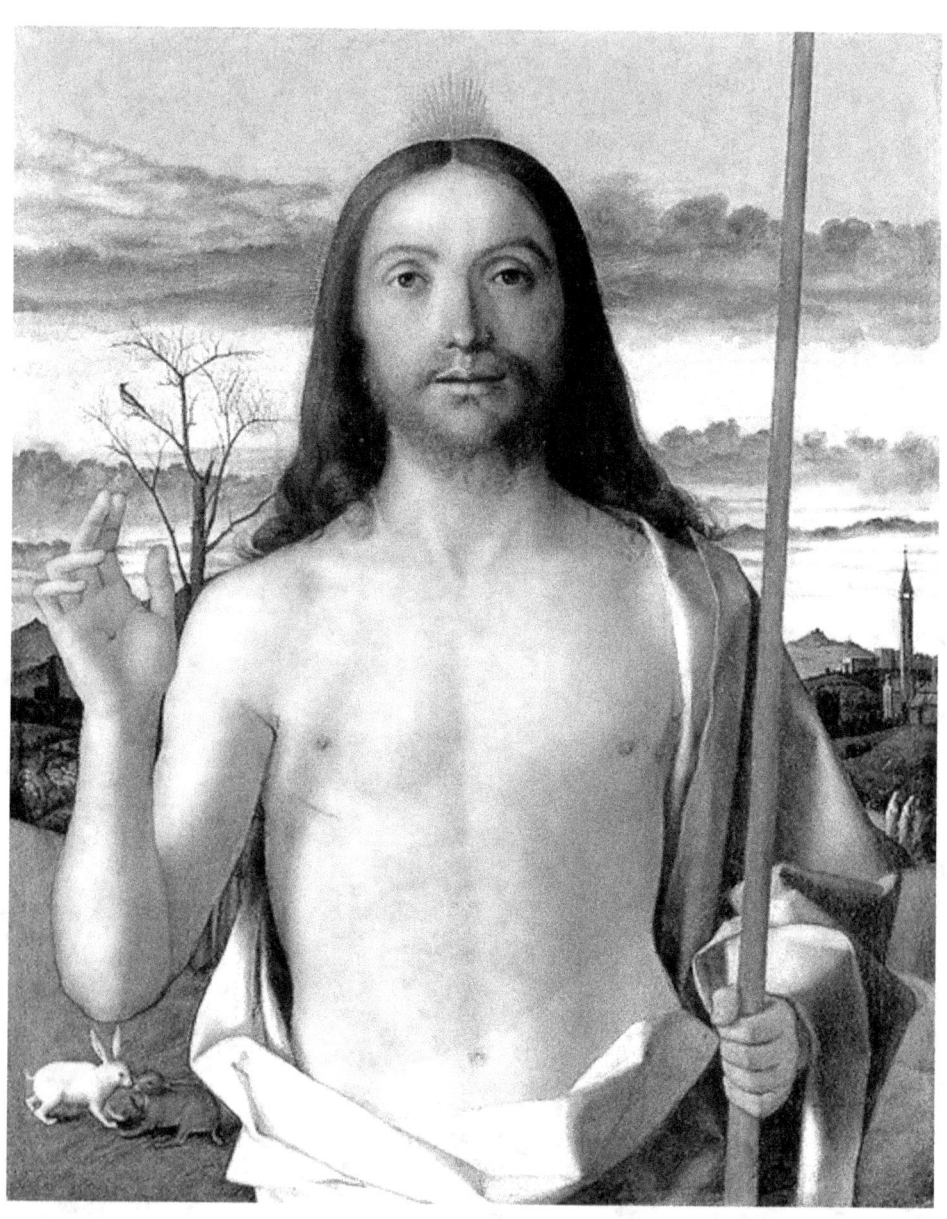

Giovanni Bellini, Christ Blessing, c. 1500, Kimbell Art Museum

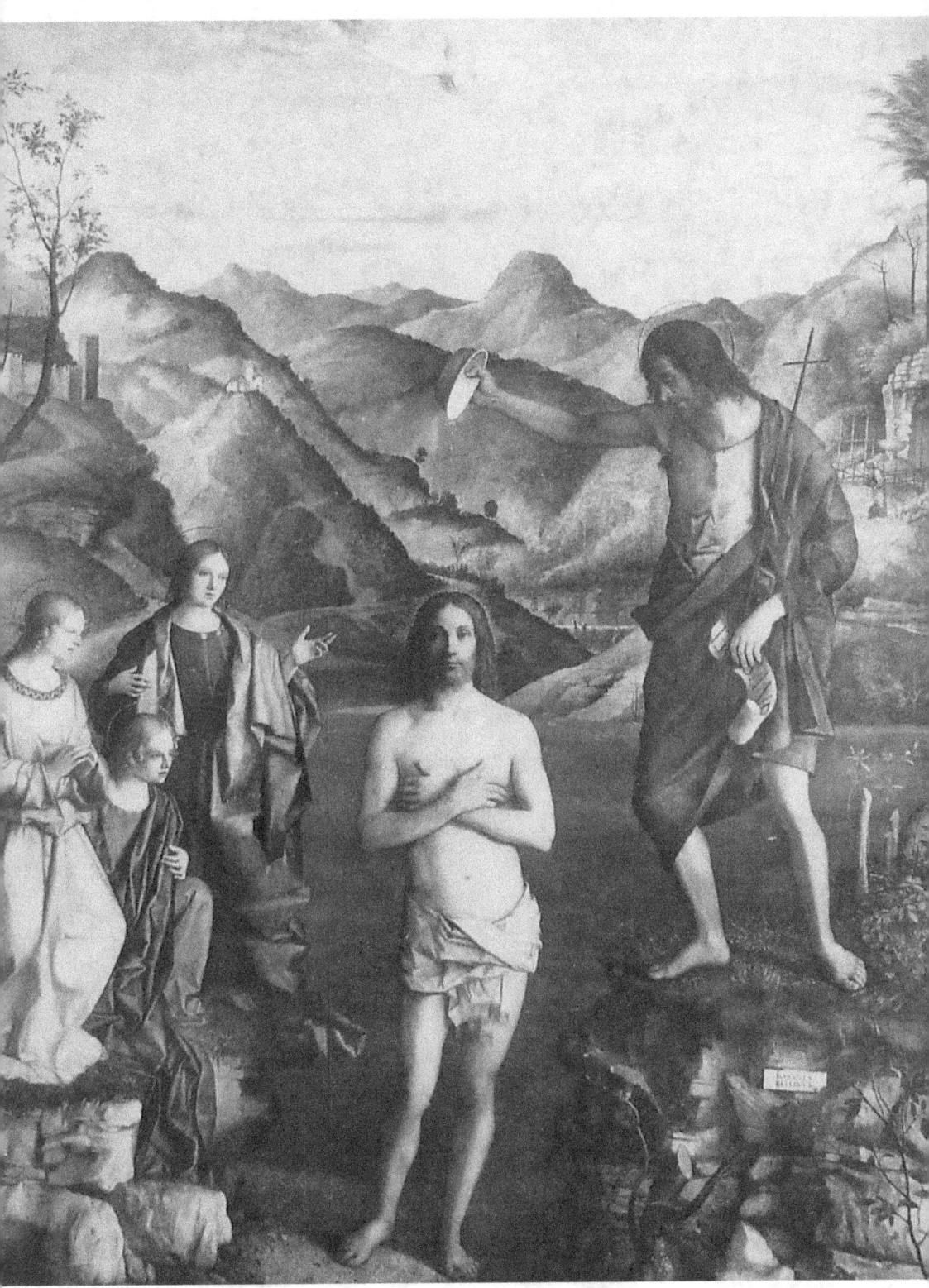

Giovanni Bellini, Baptism, early 16th century

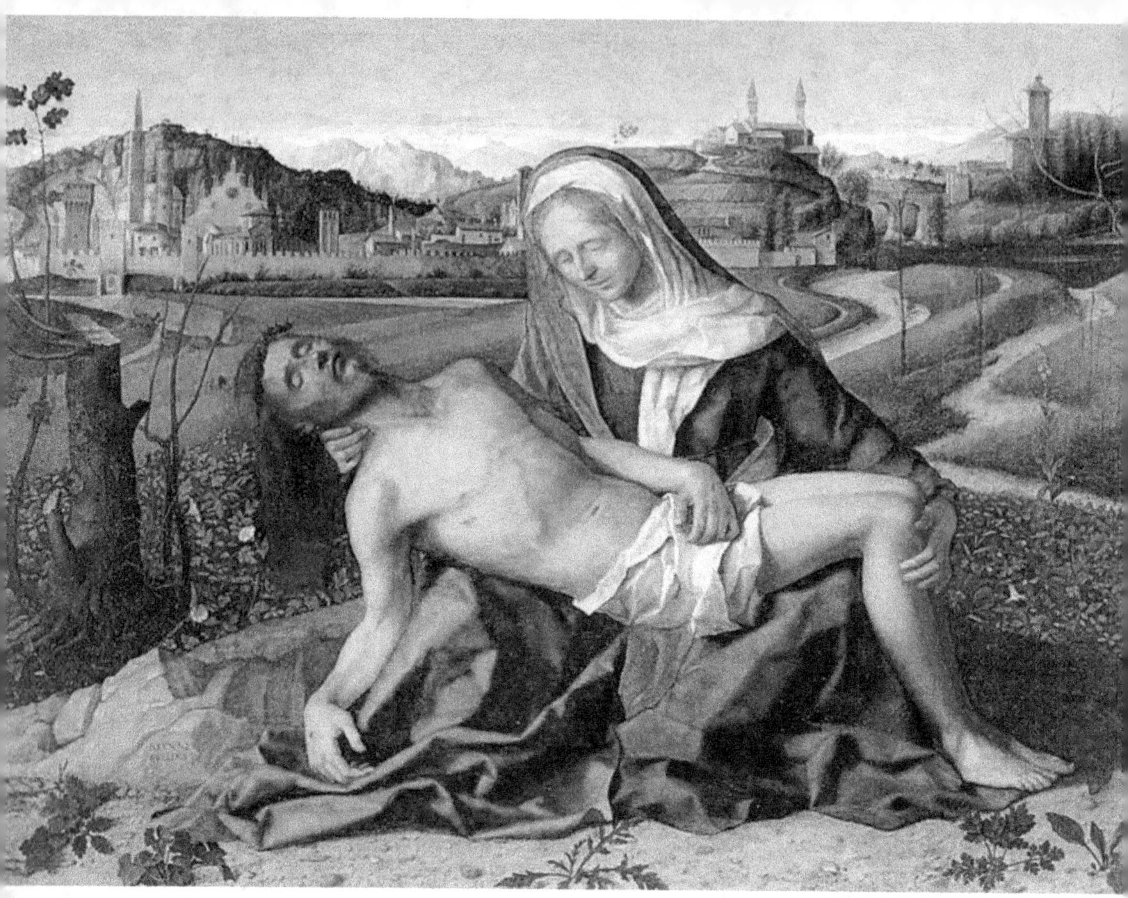

Giovanni Bellini, Pietà, 1505 (above).
Allegory, 1490, Uffizi Gallery, Florence

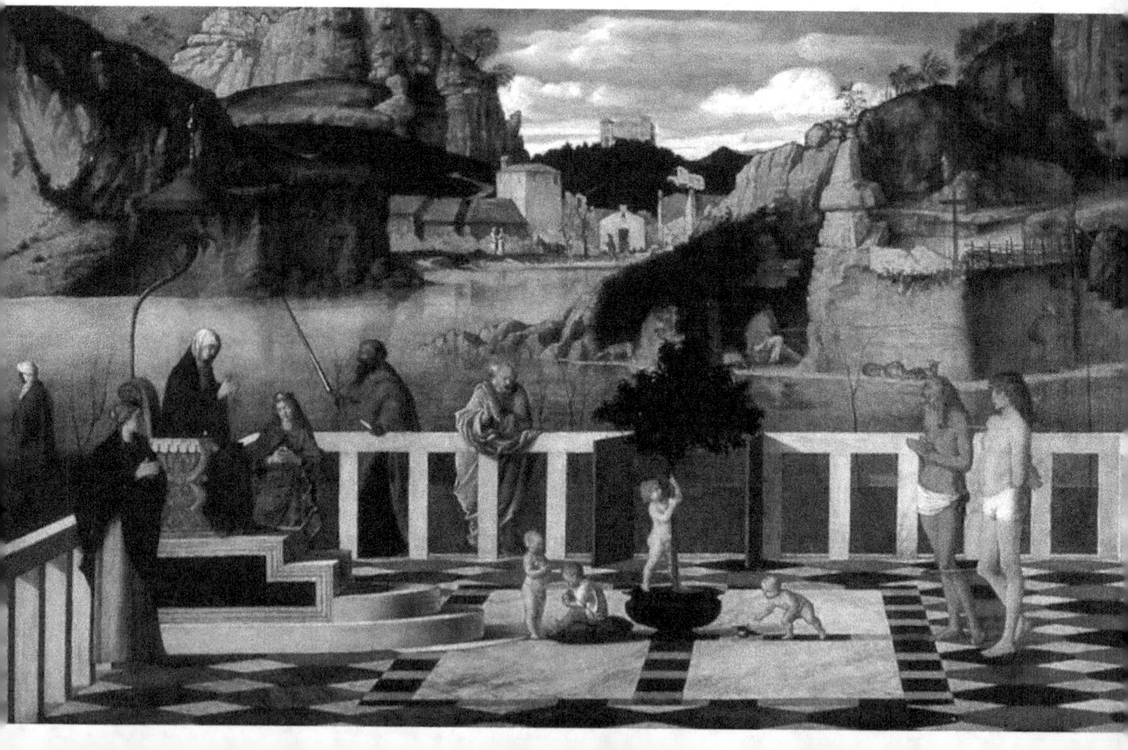

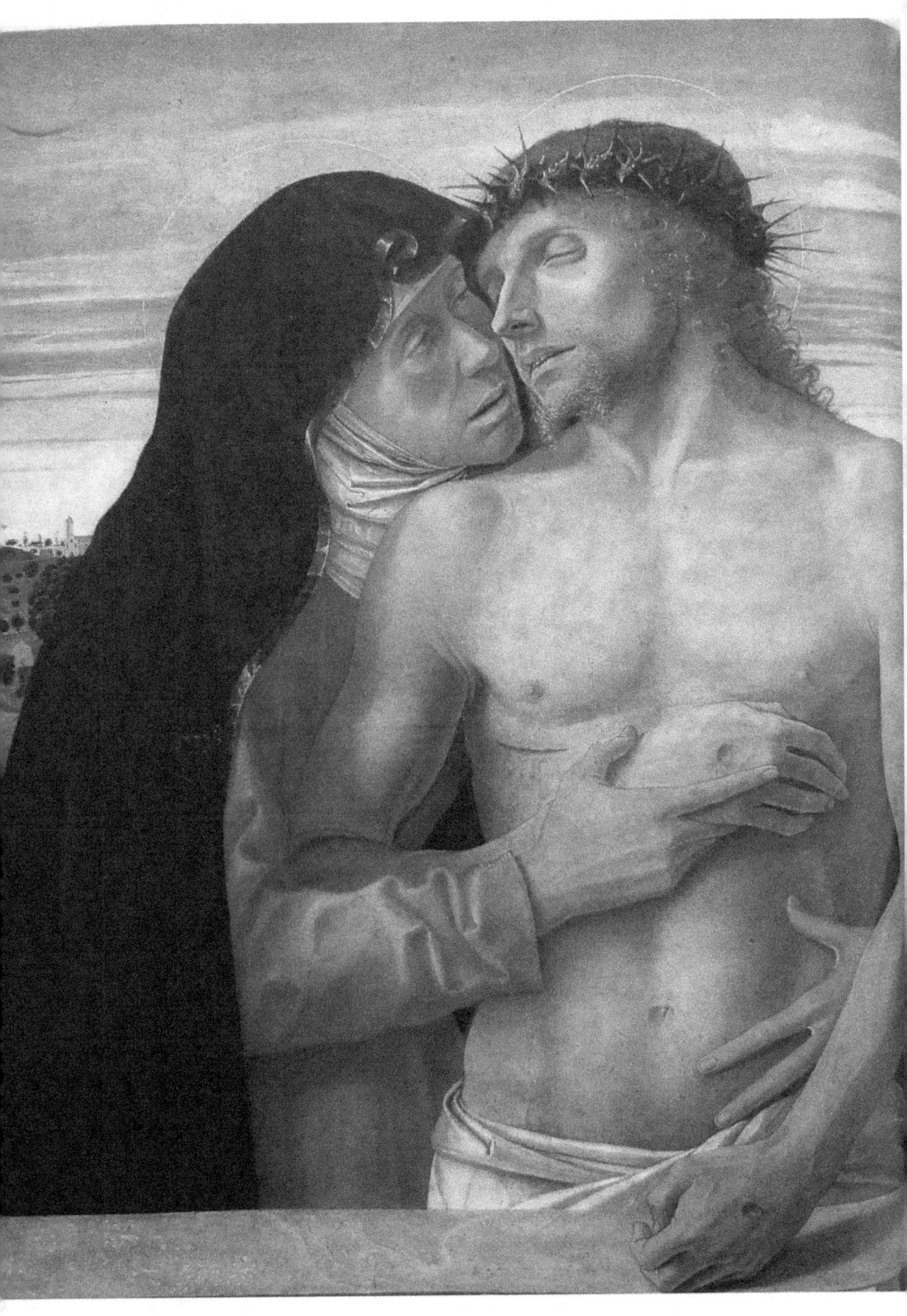

Giovanni Bellini, Pietà, Milan

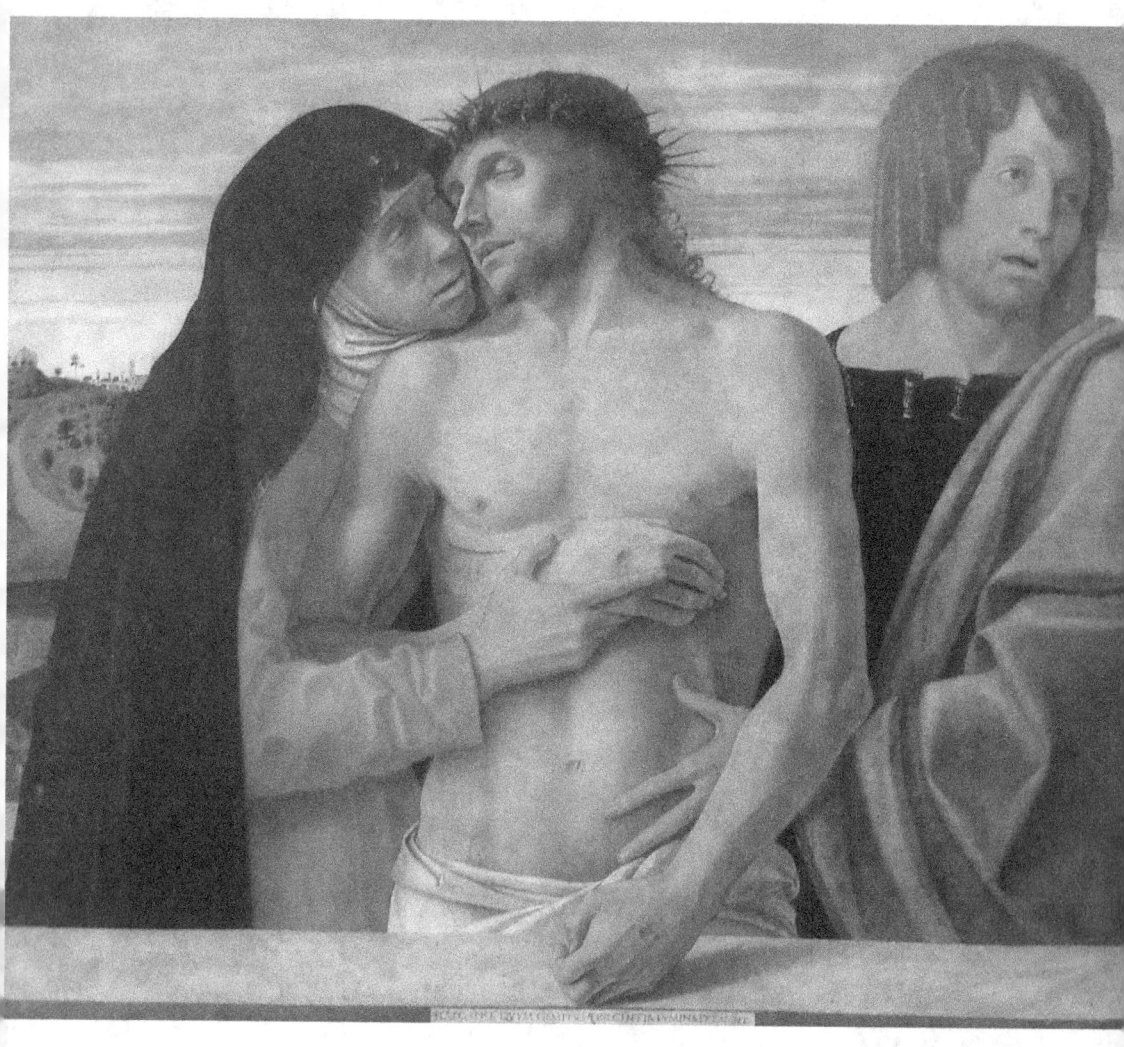

Giovanni Bellini, Pietà, Milan

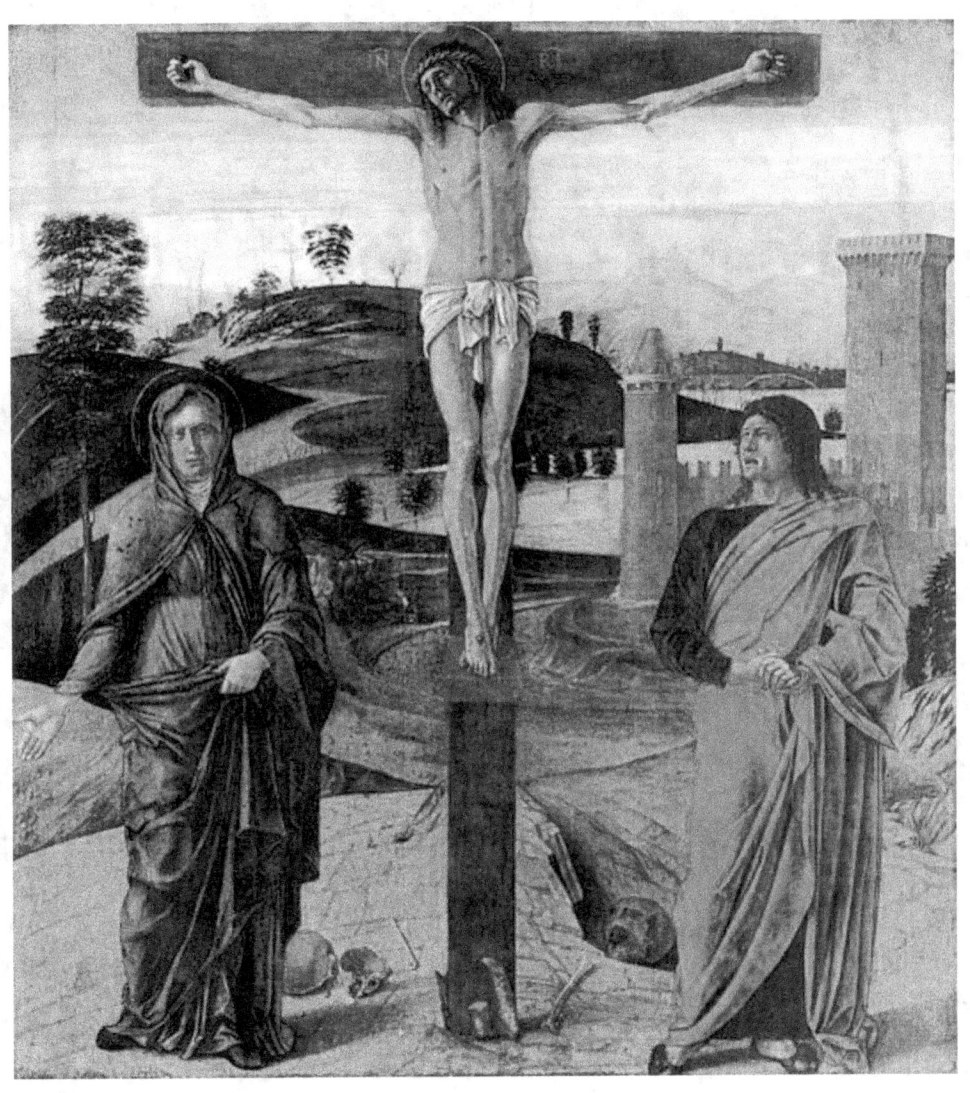

Giovanni Bellini, Calvary, 1465-70, Louvre,
Paris

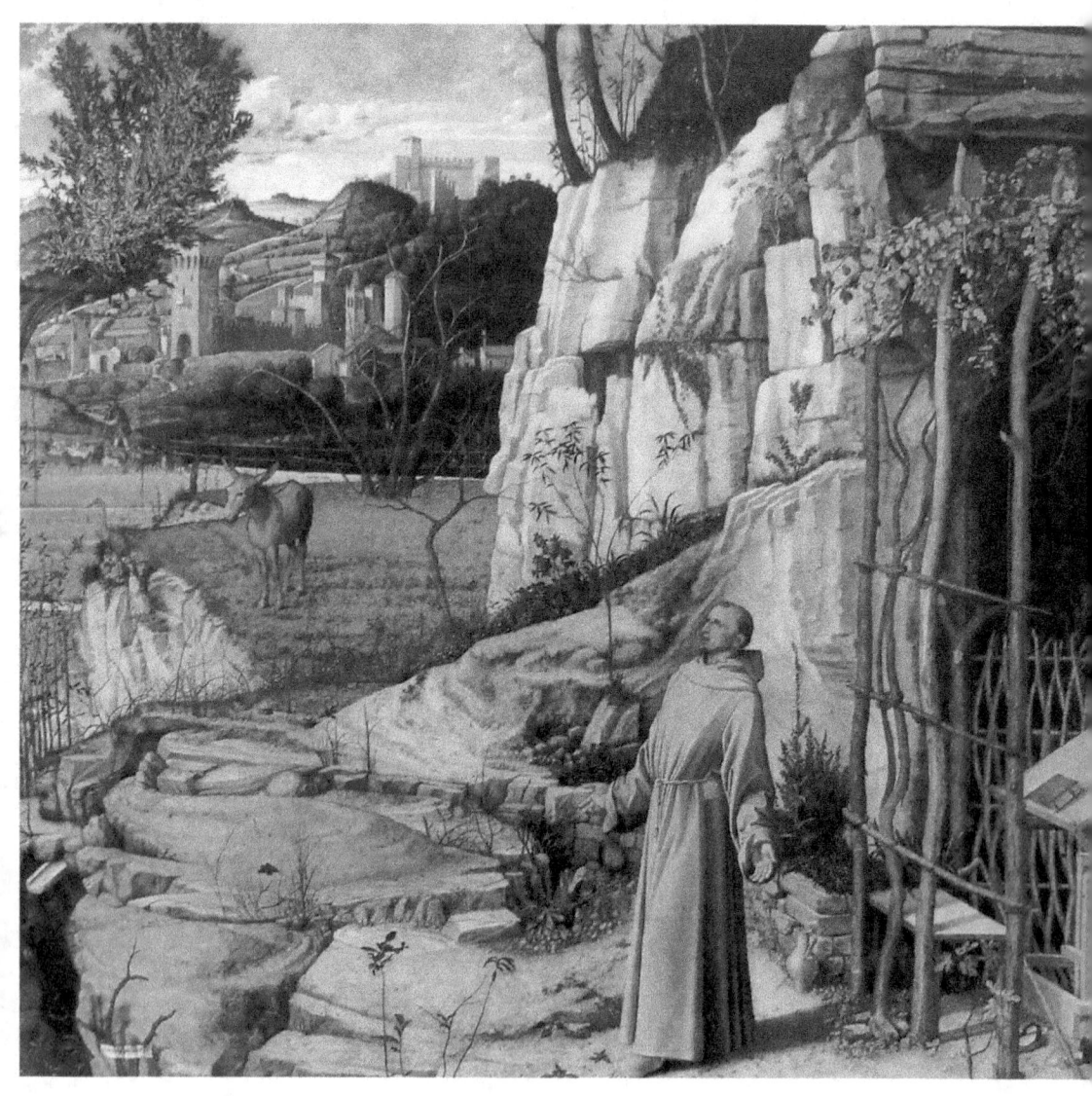

Giovanni Bellini, The Ecstasy of St Francis, Frick Collection, New York

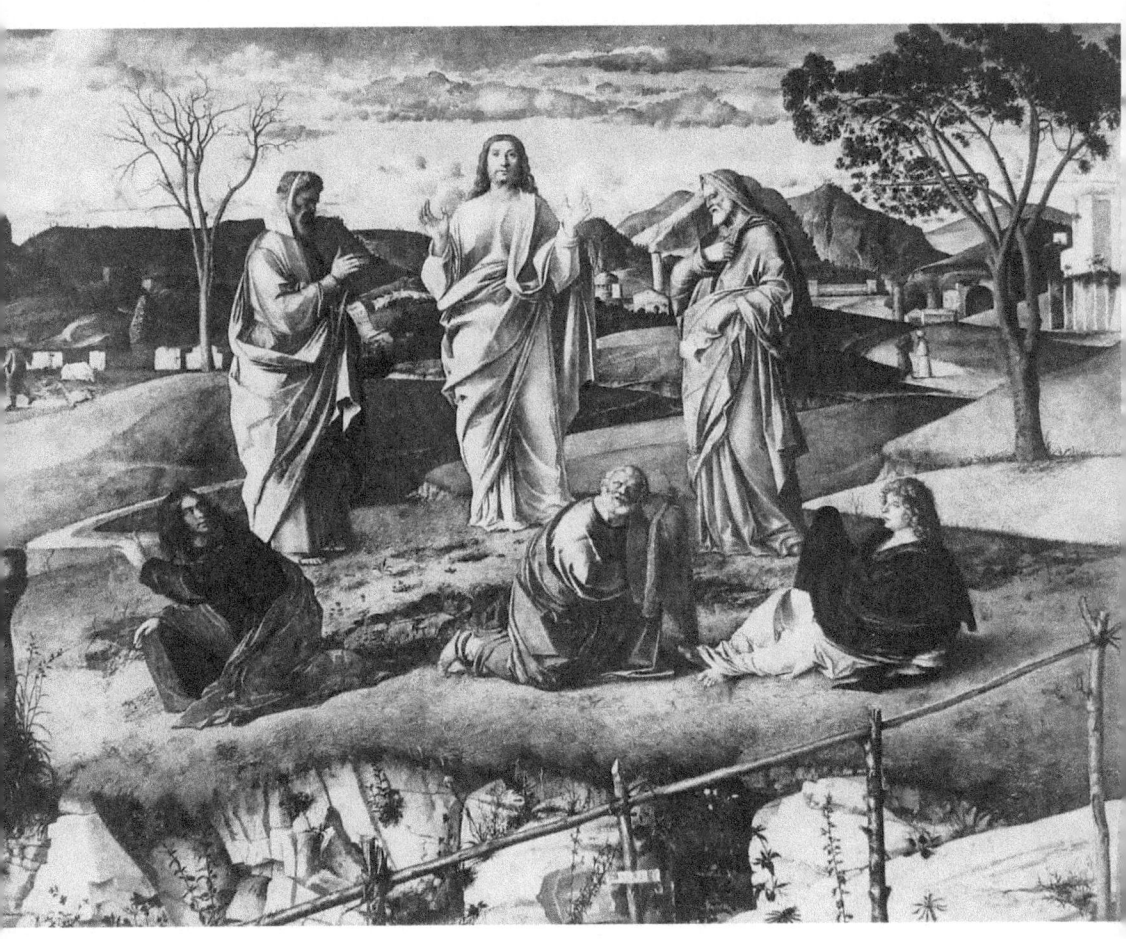

Giovanni Bellini, The Transfiguration, 1485-90

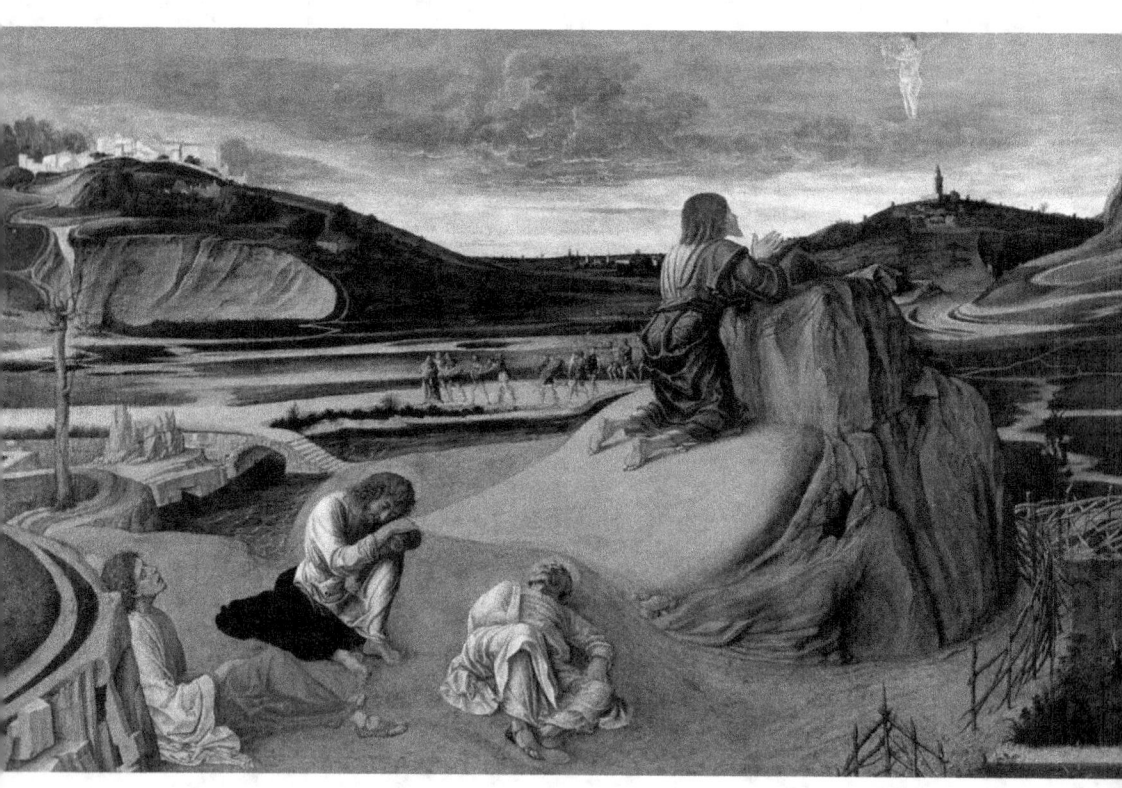

Giovanni Bellini, The Agony In the Garden, National Gallery, London

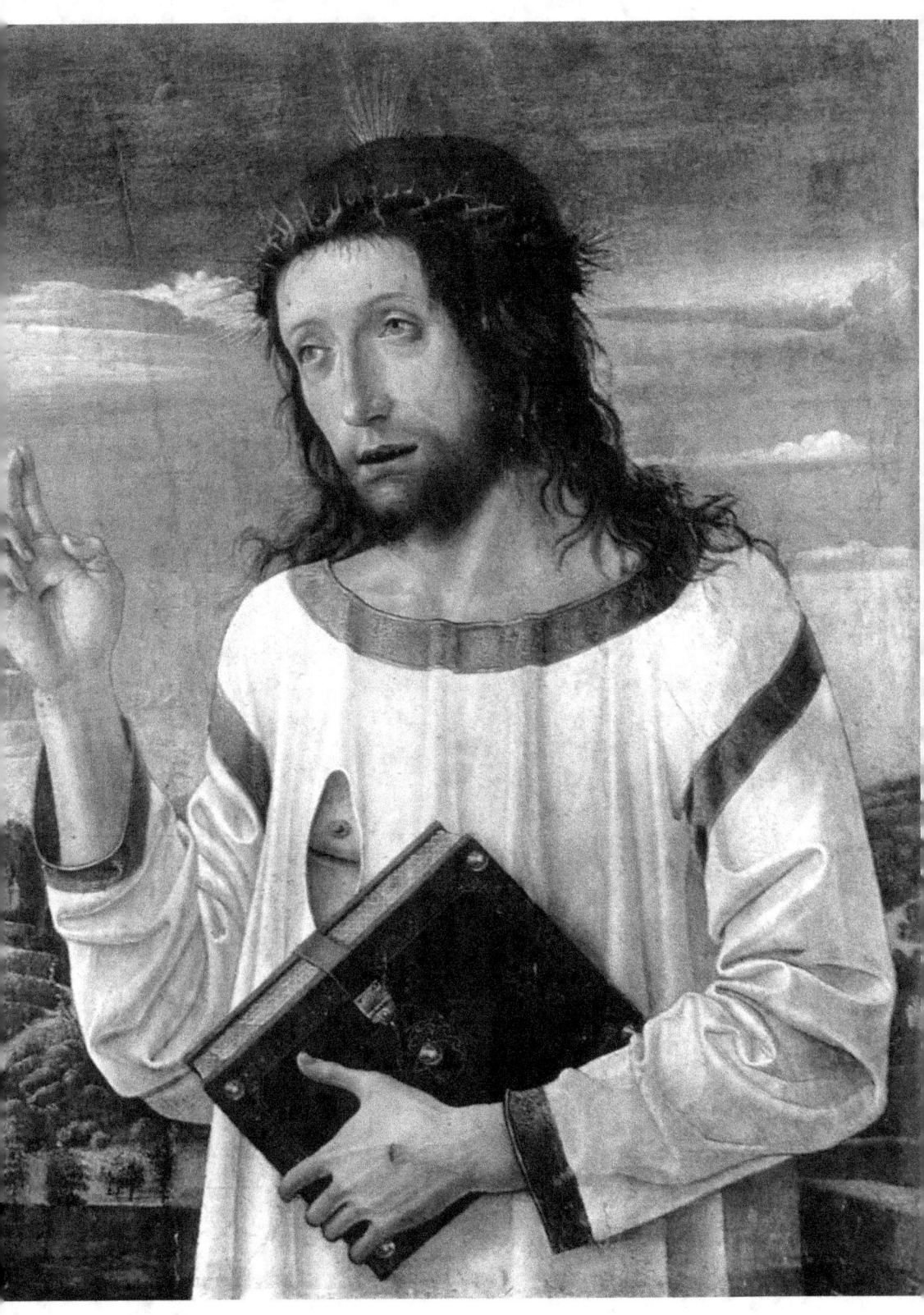

Giovanni Bellini, Christ Blessing, 1460, Louvre

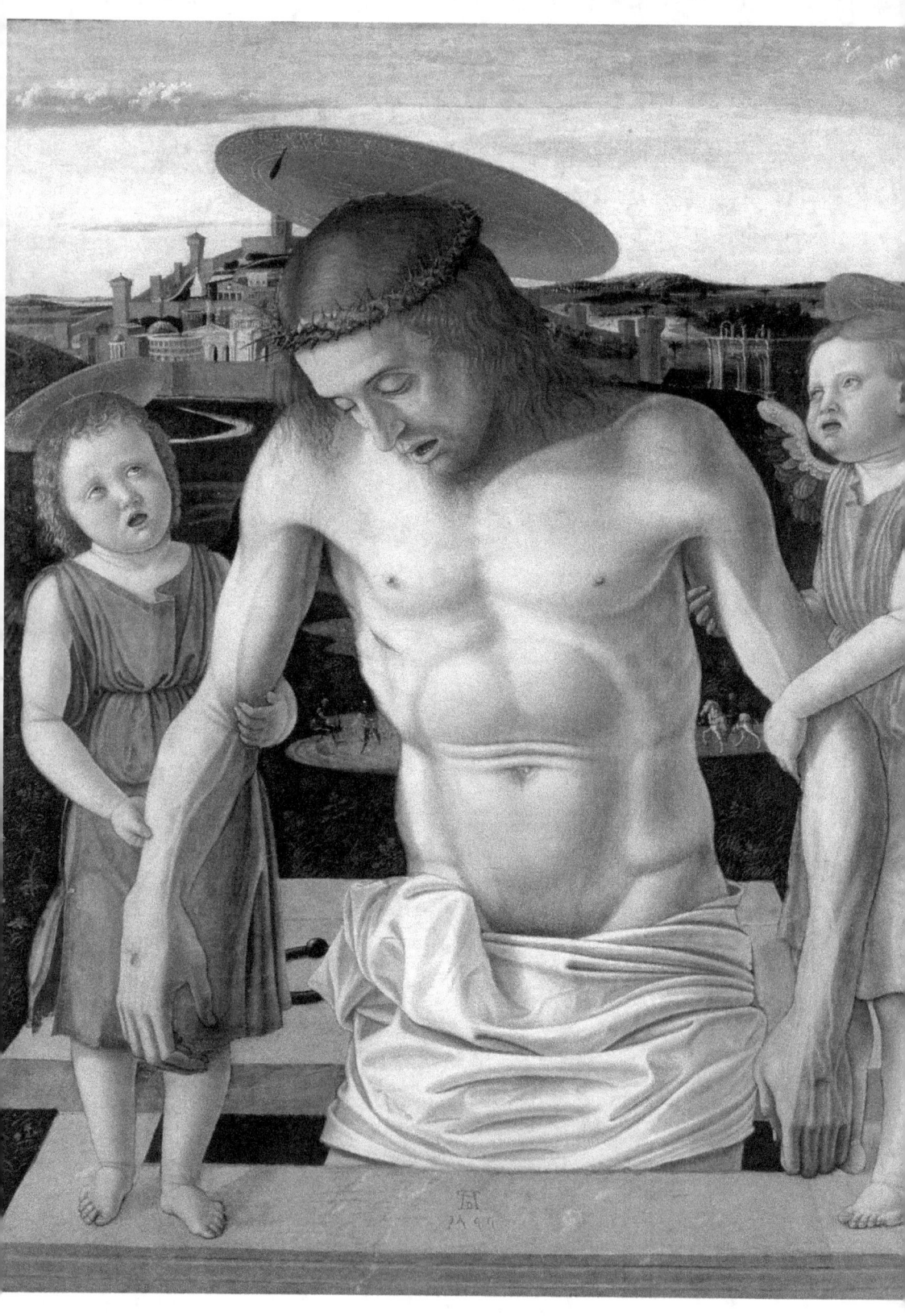

Giovanni Bellini, Pietà, 1460, Venice

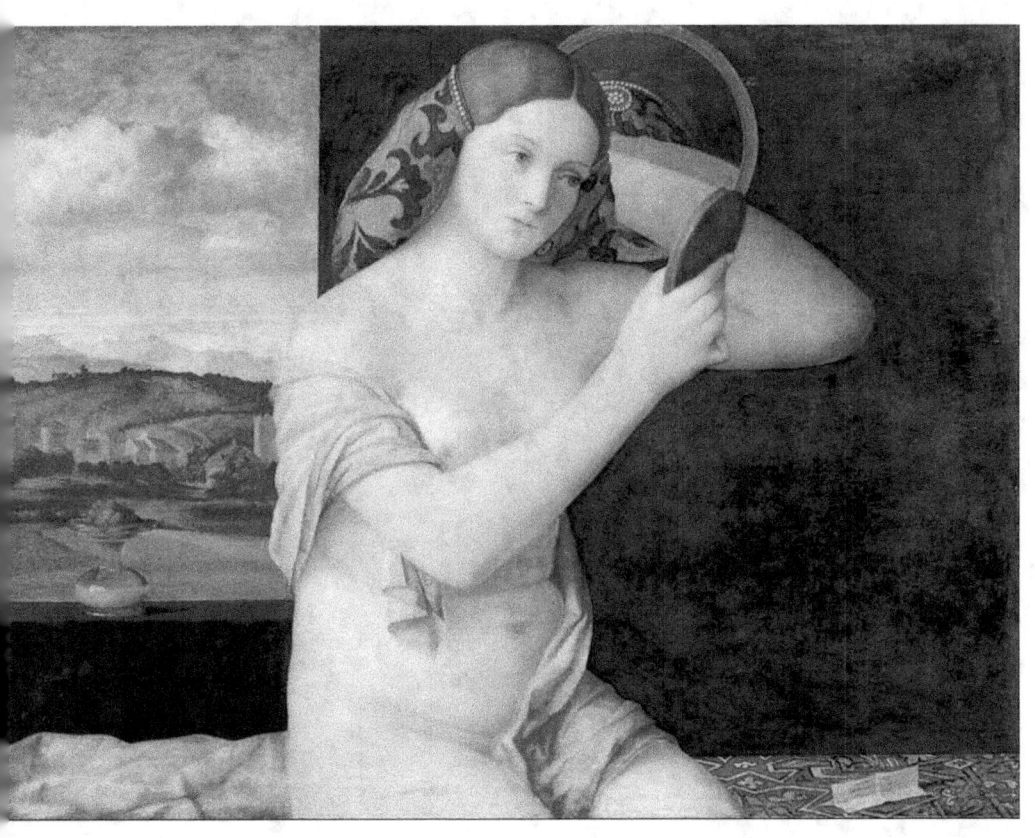

Giovanni Bellini, Young Woman At Her Toilette,
1515, Kunsthistorrisches Museum

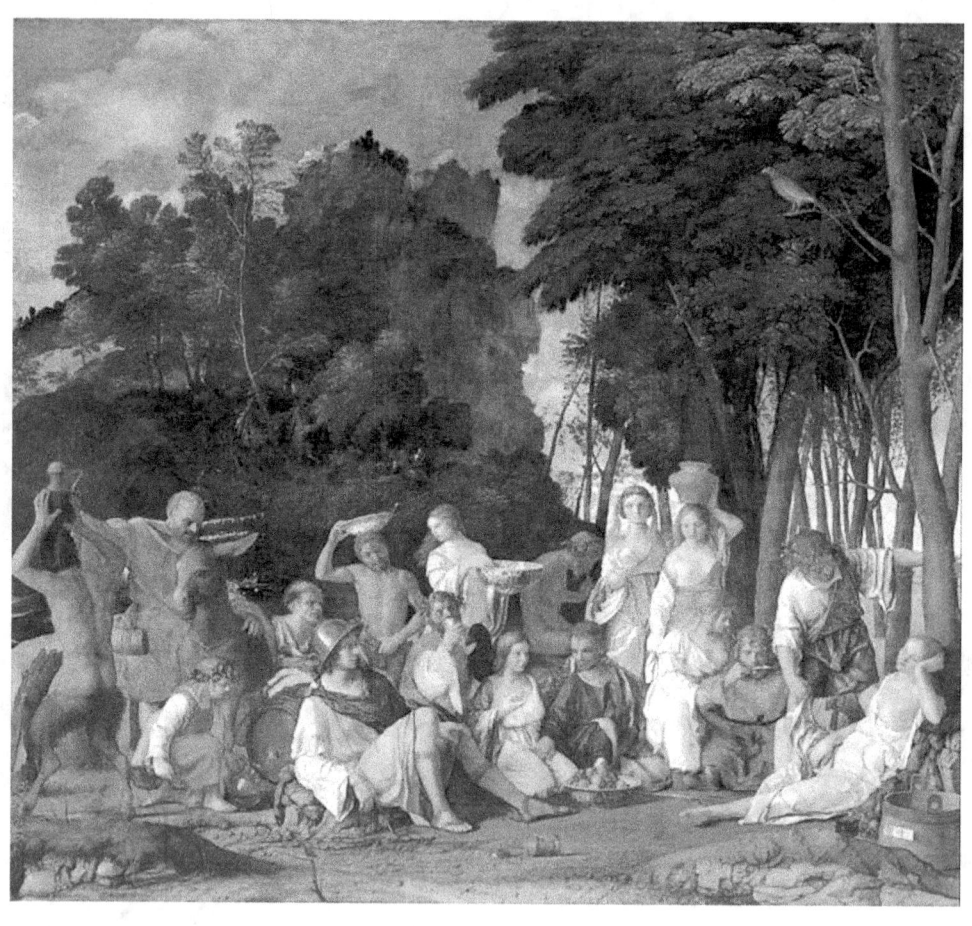

Giovanni Bellini, The Feast of the Gods, 1514,
National Gallery of Art, Washington, DC

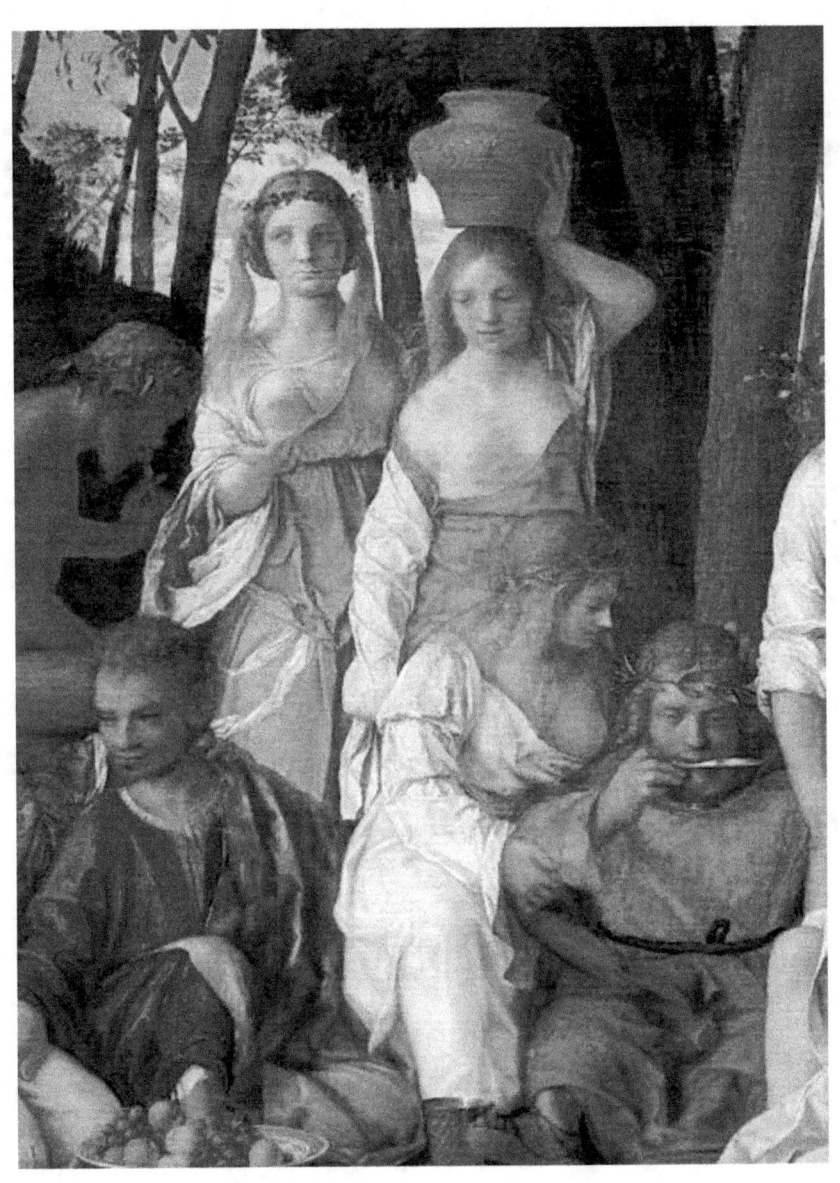

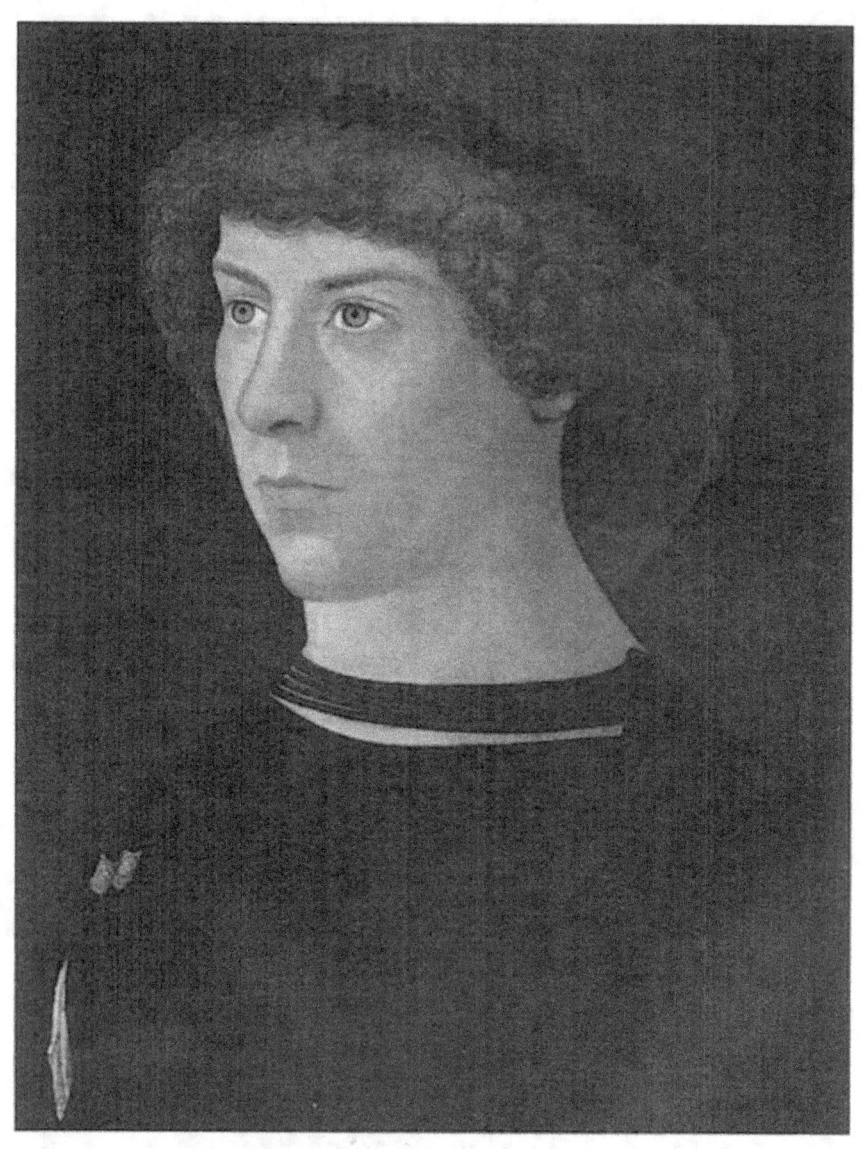

Giovanni Bellini, Portrait of Jeorg Fugger, 1474, Norton Simon Museum

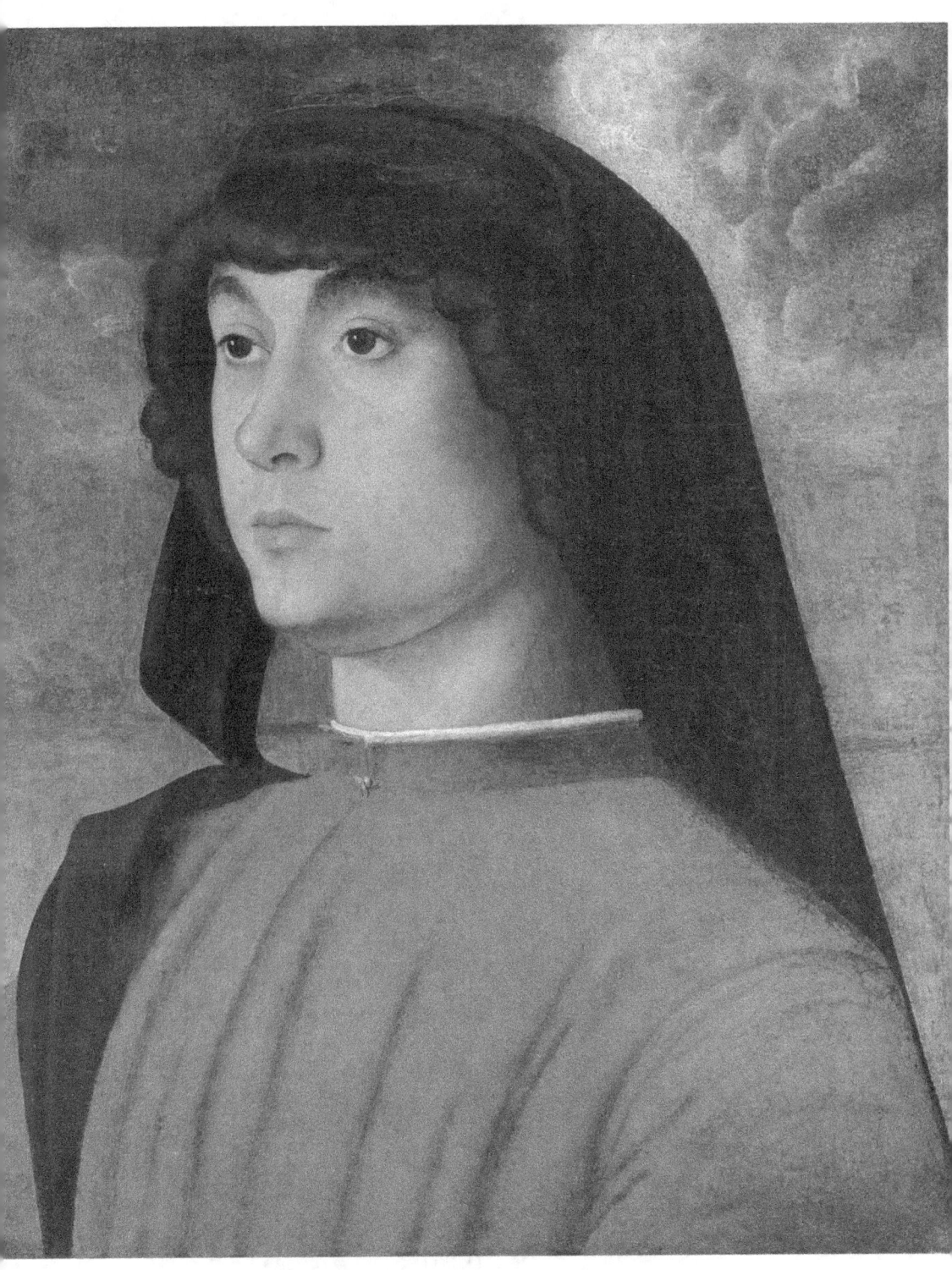

Giovanni Bellini, Portrait of a Young Man In Red,
National Gallery of Art, Washington, DC

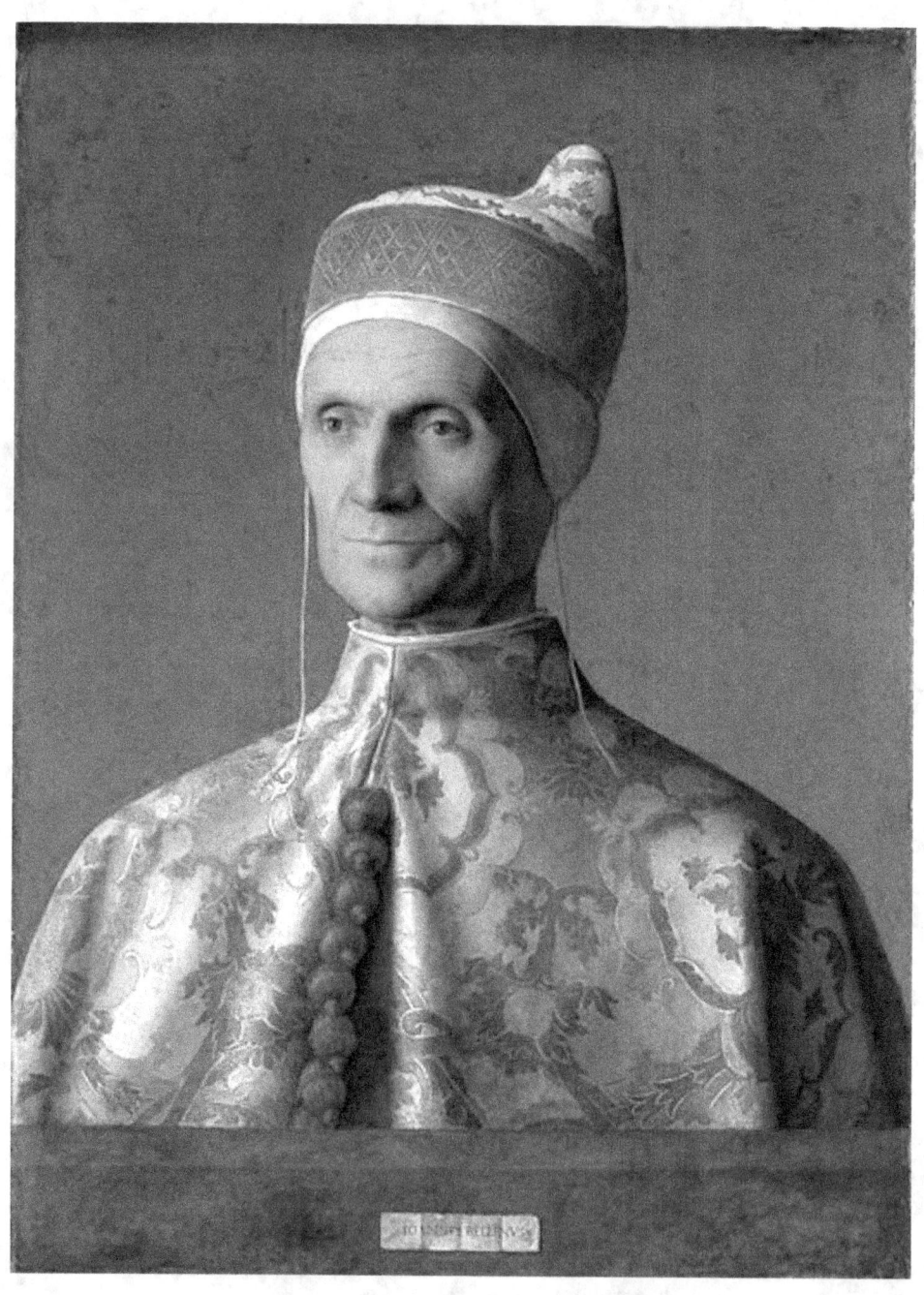

Giovanni Bellini, Portrait of Doge Leonardo Loredan, 1501,
National Gallery, London

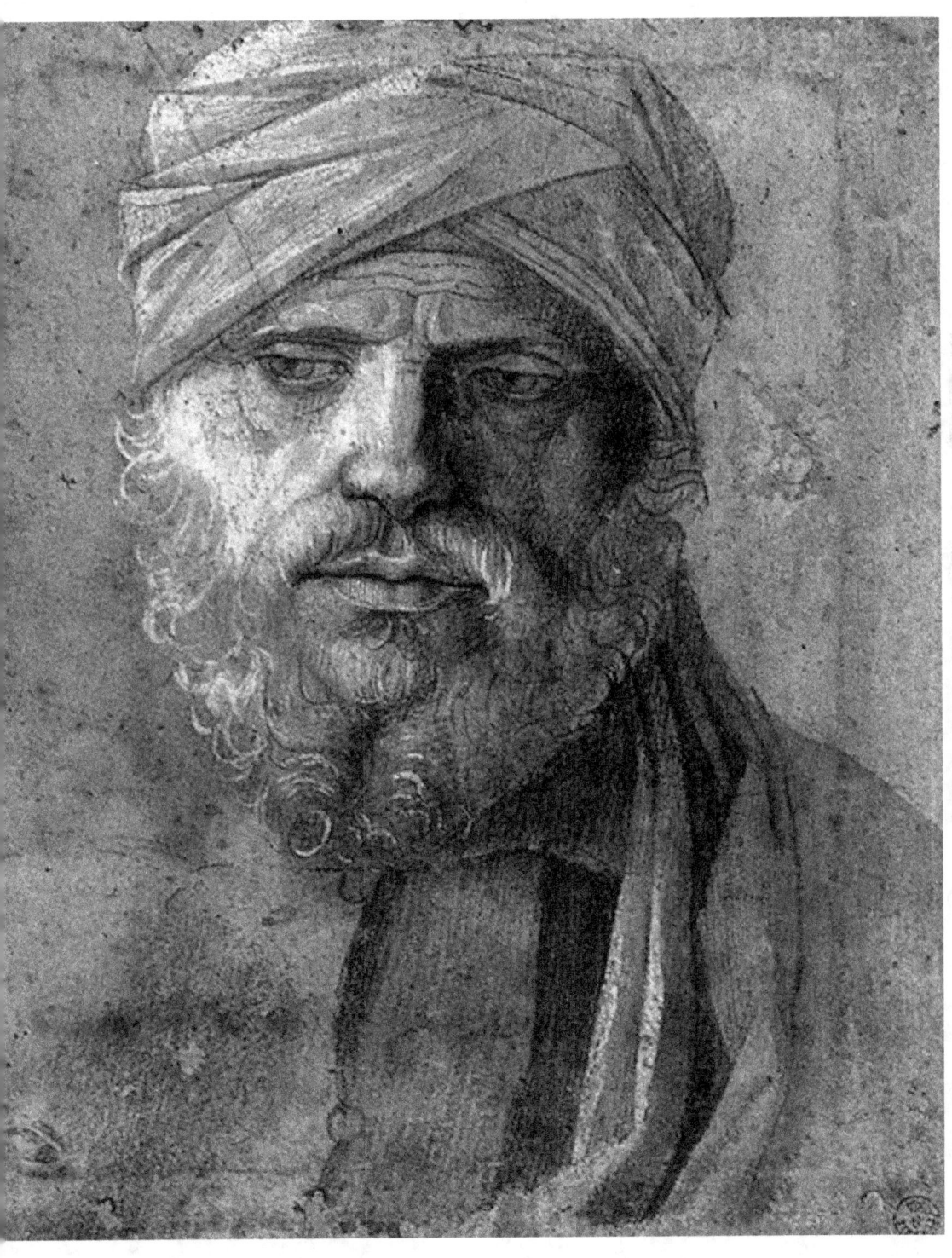

Giovanni Bellini, Man With a Turban, study, 1490s, Uffizi Gallery

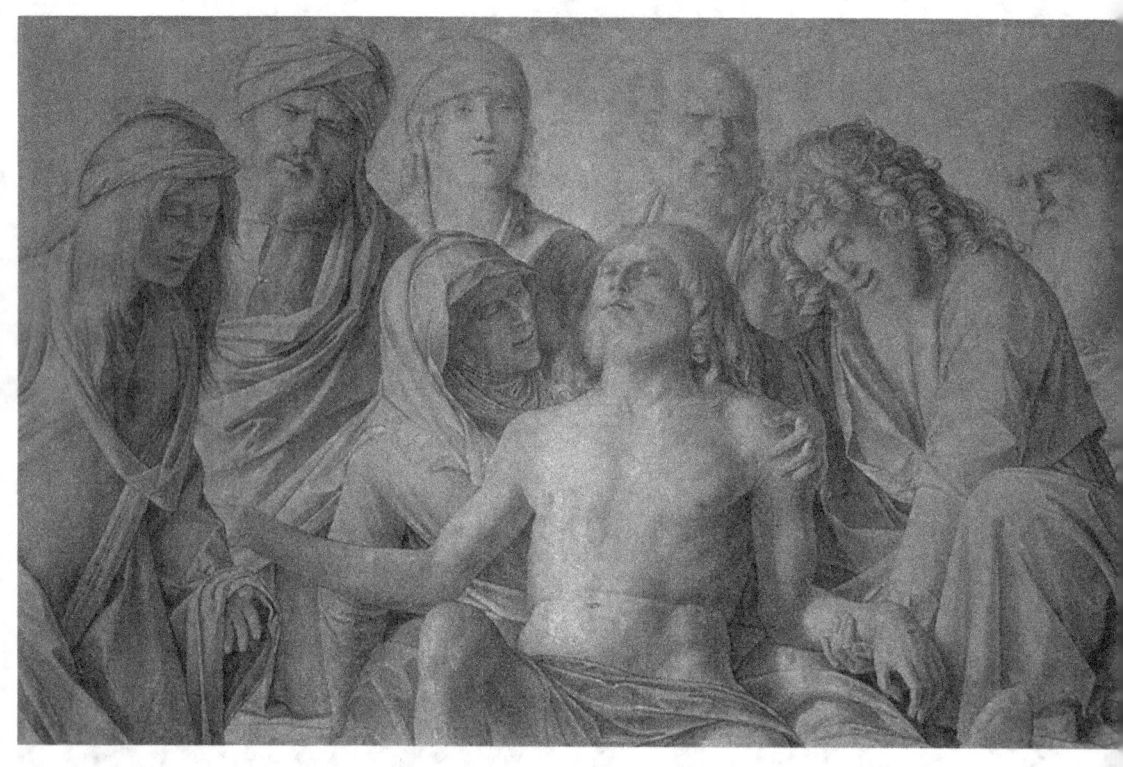

Giovanni Bellini, Descent From the Cross, drawing, c. 1500, Uffizi Gallery

II

MIDDLE LIFE

It is not easy to say how far a great painter reflects his time and how far he influences it. Tradition and surroundings must needs count for much, but their exact value is not easy to estimate. Indeed the influence of a man is often strongest upon the generations that succeed to his own, for no hints are left of the doubts and difficulties that beset the master. The attitude of the Venetians towards art in the fifteenth century, when Gian Bellini started his work, differed from that of the Florentines by reason of the splendid isolation of Venice.

The State was a law to herself; she instituted her own customs, she ruled her own life. Her wars had less effect than her commercial victories upon those of her citizens who turned their thoughts towards art, the stress and strife beyond her boundaries left her artists comparatively untouched. The wider significance of the Renaissance hardly reached her, her people were not only pleasure-loving, but self-centred. Happily, Jacopo Bellini was by way of being a traveller and his experiences were not lost upon his children. He knew Florence and worked in the city at a time when her great men were beginning to rise in all their lasting glory, he may have seen Brunelleschi himself at work upon the

Duomo. He knew Padua, where the tradition of Giotto was very strong, though that great master himself had long passed away, and so he brought to the art he practised in his own city something of the technique of the new movement, as well as the very definite touch of the pagan sentiment that was to be developed in all its beauty by his son's pupils Titian and Giorgione. The effect of his travels, limited though they were, was very lasting, and though Gian Bellini did not see life as his father had seen it, his work paved the way for the masters whose work was in some aspects greater than his. In his early days Venice had no very distinctive art. What there was seems to have been ecclesiastical in thought and extremely formal in design. It was the appeal of the clericals to a people who could neither write nor read, but although a State may erect boundaries and may devote itself to the enjoyment of prosperity, those who care for the claims of art cannot escape altogether from the forces that are at work in surrounding cities. One of the chief forces at work in Northern Italy was the revival of learning that seems to have marched side by side with the discovery of personal beauty. The Church had kept beauty in the background, the Renaissance brought it to the canvas of every artist. Bellini turned the discovery of personal beauty to the service of the Madonna.

Students of the life of Fra Angelico know that a Dominican preacher exercised a very great effect upon the painter's life, and was responsible for sending him, at a very early age, to the great Convent of the Dominicans at Fiesole. There he was received as a brother, and from the shelter of the cloister he gave his art message to the world, his story being preserved to us at the same time because the progress of the Dominicans was recorded. A few years later Giovanni Bellini, then a boy newly in his teens, would seem to have fallen under a very similar influence. He was not fourteen when St. Bernardino came to Padua and preached the doctrine of godliness and Jew-baiting to a people who were not ill-disposed towards asceticism. In the fifteenth century a boy of fourteen was a man. The Pope made Cardinals of lads who were still younger and many, who have left their names written large in Italian history, were married when they were fifteen. Gian Bellini would have been assisting his father in the decoration of the Gattemelata Chapel of Padua at the time and there is no doubt that St. Bernardino's addresses impressed him very deeply. To be sure he did not go into a religious house after the fashion of Fra Angelico, but he turned his thoughts towards religion, and for the rest of his long life his brush was kept almost exclusively for the service of sacred art. The tendencies towards paganism that his father is known to have shown held no attraction for him. He sought to express the beauty of the New Testament stories, and it is hard to find throughout all Italy an artist whose achievements in that direction can vie with his, for Gian Bellini brought sensuous beauty and rare qualities of emotion to canvas for the first time in the history of painting.

In those early days of the middle century there were two acknowledged leaders of painting in the world that young Bellini knew. The first was his father, who is said to have studied in the studios of Gentile da Fabriano (1370 to 1450), and that of Pisanello who was born somewhere about the same time as da Fabriano, and died a year later. It is worth noting that Jacopo Bellini called one of his sons Gentile after his earliest master, though whether Gentile or Giovanni was the elder son remains uncertain. Mr. Roger Fry, who writes with great authority upon the subject, is of opinion that Gian may have been a natural son of Jacopo, and in those days when Popes had "nephews" in abundance, and the marriage vow was more honoured in the breach than the observance, very little stigma attached to illegitimacy. The other great painter of Gian Bellini's time was the Paduan painter Squarcione, who presided over a large and flourishing school in his native city, and did work that was quite as good as that of his contemporaries. He adopted as his son a lad from Padua or Mantua named Andrea Mantegna, who was destined to take such high rank among the painters of the Venetian School.

Although Padua and Venice were in a sense rivals, there

seems to have been a very friendly understanding for many years between Squarcione and Jacopo Bellini, so that Gian and Gentile were able to watch the progress of the Paduan master and his pupils, and to decide for themselves how much they would accept, and what they would reject of the teaching. In early years these influences must have been of great value to the painter, but happily they were not destined to be lasting, for when Gian's sister married Andrea Mantegna, Squarcione quarrelled with his adopted son, and the intimacy with the Bellini family came to an end. This is as it should have been in the best interests of Gian Bellini's art, for when he returned to Venice and settled down there permanently, he was able to follow his own ideas, and free himself from what was bad in the influence of the stiff, formal, and lifeless school of Padua.

Venice must have been a remarkable city in those years. To-day it stimulates the imagination as few cities in Europe can do, then it must have been one of the wonders of the world. There are some striking accounts of the city written in the latter part of the fifteenth century, and though space does not permit any quotation at length, one brief paragraph will not be out of place. Philippe de Comines, envoy of Charles VIII., came to Venice in 1494, and recalled his impressions of that city in his memoirs. "I was taken along the High Street," he writes, "they call it the Grand Canal, and it is very broad, galleys cross it; and it is the fairest street, I believe, that may be in the whole world, and fitted with the best houses; the ancient ones are painted, and most have a great piece of porphyry and serpentine on the front. It is the most triumphant city I have ever seen, and doth most honour to ambassadors and strangers. It doth most wisely govern itself, and the service of God is most solemnly performed. Though the Venetians have many faults, I believe God has them in remembrance for the reverence they pay in the service of His Church." This brief tribute to the charm of Venice is of special value because it helps us to understand why the Venetians were not strenuous seekers after knowledge, why their painters did no more than paint, and why their response to the humanities was so small. It explains the decorative quality of Bellini's pictures, the splendour of their colours. Pageantry and ceremonial were the great desires of Venetian life, the man who could add to the lustre of a State procession along the splendid water-way of the Grand Canal was more to them than the scholar who had written a treatise that moved the more learned Florentines to admiration. Life was so full of pleasure, so varied in its appeals, that the Venetians could not spare time, or even develop the will to study. They had raised the old cry "panem et circenses" and, in the days of Gian Bellini, there was no lack of either. History is full of records that reveal other nations in a similar light, philosophers have drawn the inevitable conclusions – and the trend of life is no wise altered.

Under Bellini, painting lost the conventions that had been regarded as correct or inevitable in Squarcione's studio, and Gian's pictures bear the same relation to those of the Paduan, and his pupil, as Newman's writing bears to bad eighteenth-century English prose. But despite all developments in the technique of his art, Gian Bellini's painting remained quite constant to the mood that St. Bernardino had induced. Doubtless, had his gifts been of another kind, he would have entered the Church, he would have dreamed dreams and seen visions that would not have found such world-wide expression while, being an artist, inheriting artistic traditions from his father, living in the centre of the small world of Venetian and Paduan painters, he expressed his beautiful emotions in fashion that has not weakened its claim upon us in more than four hundred years. The glamour of Venetian life, the extraordinary beauty of the city that was his home, the splendour and the pageants that were part of a Venetian life, the intensity of the colour that surrounded him on all sides – some of it belonging to Venice by right, and even more, brought to her shores by the ceaseless traffic of the sea – all these things developed and deepened the emotion that was to find so exquisite an expression from his brush. To him, as to Fra Angelico, faith was a real and living thing, and like the great monk who died at ripe age while he was yet a boy, Gian Bellini became a lover of the world in its most picturesque aspect, accepting without hesitation the traditional explanation of its creation.

Naturally enough his appeal to the artist is founded upon a dozen considerations, mostly technical, his appeal to the layman is direct and spontaneous. A countryman who has never seen a studio can respond to the exquisite beauty of Bellini's Virgins and Children, can feel the charm of the sunshine that fills the air and lights sea and land, can recognise the infinite glamour of the roads that wind away into the mysterious distance of the background, can enjoy the rich, almost sensuous, colouring. Perhaps had Bellini taken the vows, a great part of these beauties would have been lost, the infinite variety of lovely women and children could hardly have been secured. As a Venetian, and a pleasure lover, he could not have responded, as Fra Angelico did, to the restricted life and rigid discipline of a religious order.

It was not easy for Gian Bellini to devote himself entirely to sacred subjects if he wished to earn a living by his brush, because his father had stood outside the Church. In those days, too, the best church work was in the hands of one family, the Vivarini, whose monopoly was hardly likely to be disturbed by an artist who could show no better credentials than a connection, legitimate or illegitimate, with a painter whose feeling was distinctly pagan. Jacopo Bellini, for all that he was a most admired artist, had no claims upon the Church, and does not seem to have received many commissions from it. Various wealthy societies in Venice had been accustomed to employ him to decorate their halls with work that, as we have said before, has been lost, and their guilds or *scuole* would doubtless have given Gian all the work he wished to do had he been satisfied to do it.

He could not choose for himself. St. Bernardino had chosen for him in those years when his mind was most impressionable. Gian Bellini's hand was doubtless to be seen in Padua where he assisted his father, and his earliest independent work is to be found in the Casa Correr at Venice, where one finds a "Trans-figuration," a "Crucifixion," and two "Pietas." He painted portraits, one from our own National Gallery is to be seen here. This is a picture of the Doge, Leonardo Loredano, who held office from 1501 to 1521.

The early pictures reveal Bellini at the parting of the ways. His figures have many of the defects of the School of Padua. His knowledge of anatomy is decidedly small, he lacks confidence in himself, and yet it is not difficult to recognise that the painter is moving into a new country, that his presentation of sacred subjects is developing on lines that must add considerably to their artistic value and to the permanence of their appeal.

An amusing story is told of the way in which young Bellini acquired his knowledge of oil painting. He is said to have assumed the dress of a Venetian nobleman, and to have gone to the studio of a popular artist of the time, under pretext of having his portrait painted. While the artist, one Antonello of Messina, was busily engaged upon his portrait, Bellini is said to have watched the process very carefully and to have secured the much needed lesson. It is more than likely that the story is untrue, but it has obtained a large measure of credence.

His first big altar-piece is said to have been done for the altar of St. Catherine of Sienna, and after one or two other church paintings had been accomplished, Giovanni was commissioned to decorate the great Council Hall of Venice with historical paintings. But it is well to remember that altar painting never ceased to interest him, his greatest achievements having been accomplished for churches. There are few things in art more beautiful than Gian Bellini's altar-pieces. Ruskin has paid a special tribute to the "Virgin and Four Saints" in the church dedicated to St. Zaccaria, father of the Baptist. He says that the Zaccaria altar-piece, and the one in the Frari, by the same master, are the two finest pictures in the world. Of the big works, however, nothing remains, Gentile being the only one of the family who is represented to-day by pictures painted on a very large scale. Vasari tells us that Gian

painted four pictures in fulfilment of a commission, one representing the Pope Alexander III. receiving Frederic Barbarossa
after the abjuration of the Schism of 1177, the next showing the
Pope saying Mass in San Marco, another representing his Holiness
in the act of presenting a canopy to the Doge, and the last in
which the Pontiff is presented with eight standards and eight
silver trumpets by clergy assembled outside the gates of Rome.
These subjects or some of them had been painted by one
Gueriento of Verona when Marco Corner was Doge. Petrarch had
written the inscriptions for them, but they had faded, and in later
years Tintoretto painted his "Paradiso" over the damaged
frescoes. There is a story to the effect that Giovanni and Gentile
Bellini had promised the councillors that their pictures should last
two hundred years; as a matter of fact, they would seem to have
been destroyed by fire within half that period.

The style of the picture commissioned makes its own
significant commentary upon the times. It was always considered
advisable to stir in the Venetians appreciation for State
ceremonial, which encouraged so much of the pageantry
associated with Venetian life and, even if Giovanni Bellini had no
keen taste for such work, he could not refuse a commission that
would establish his name among his fellow countrymen. To-day
the Sala del Maggior Consiglio holds pictures by Titian, Paul
Veronese, and other artists who followed closely upon Gian
Bellini's era.

III

THE LATTER DAYS

Shortly after the Council Hall pictures had been undertaken, in 1479, to be exact, the Sultan, Mohammed II., conqueror of Constantinople, wished to have his portrait painted, and applied to the Doge of Venice to send him a competent artist to do the work. It should be remembered that the Sultan had been waging a successful war upon Venice, and that in January 1479 the State had ceded Scutari, Stalimene, and other territory and had agreed to pay an indemnity of 200,000 ducats, with a tribute of 10,000 ducats a year for trading rights and the exercise of consular jurisdiction in Constantinople. Naturally the success of the Turks, who had taken Constantinople in 1454, was making a very great impression throughout Europe, and Venice had striven to the uttermost to rouse the Powers to concerted action, but in those days nobody was anxious to trust the Republic. These are matters, of course, that pertain to history rather than art, but it is curious to remember that throughout the times when the watchers from St. Mark's Tower saw the reflected glare of burning cities, when the security of Christian Europe was threatened seriously, when plagues were devastating Venice, Gian Bellini seems to have gone on his way all undisturbed, painting his pictures in the most leisurely fashion, and the fact that art stood right above politics and strife is clearly shown in the action of the Sultan in sending to Venice for a good artist as soon as peace had been restored. There seems to have been some question of sending Gian because his brother was busily engaged on other work in the Ducal Palace, but after a while it was decided to send Gentile, who painted a portrait of the Sultan that found its way afterwards into the Layard Collection in Venice. Some surprise has been expressed that the Sultan should have allowed any one to paint his portrait, because portrait painting is forbidden by the *Koran* [*1], but Mohammed II. was a man of very advanced ideas and he not only gave sittings to Gentile Bellini, but treated him with the greatest favour, dismissing him with many marks of approval and great gifts. Among the presents brought back to Venice by the painter were the armour and sword of the great Doge Dandolo, who had been buried in the year 1205 in the private chapel in St. Sophia. Mohammed II. had caused the great tomb to be destroyed, but he sent the great patriot's armour back to its native land. Vasari tells us that the meeting between the brothers on Gentile's return to Venice was most affectionate.

Mohammed said: "If ye must make pictures, make them of trees and things without souls. Verily every painter is condemned to hell fire."

This journey to Constantinople would seem to have added to the reputation of the house of Bellini, and to have increased the demand for portraits by both brothers. This, in its way, would doubtless have led to the multiplying of school pieces. History has very little to tell of the progress of the brothers during the years that followed. We know that the Doge Loredano, whose portrait has been painted by Gian Bellini, succeeded to his high office in 1501, that Titian would have been working in Bellini's studio then, and that Bellini himself was in the enjoyment of what was known as a broker's patent, and was official painter to the State. His was the duty of painting the portrait of every Doge who succeeded to the control of Venetian affairs during his term of office, and he also painted any historical picture in which the Doge had to figure. There was a salary attached to the office, and the work was quite light. As far as we can tell Gian Bellini was still averse from painting secular subjects. He was now an old man, but he had made great progress in his work, conquering many of the difficulties of perspective, shadow, and colouring that had baffled his predecessors. The pageants demanded by the great Mutual Aid Societies (*Scuole*) from the artists in their employ, he would seem to have left to his brother Gentile, for these pictures had a big political purpose to serve, and they demanded the travel, the experience, and the mood that Gian lacked. His brush was sufficiently occupied with altar-pieces and portraits of distinguished Venetians, now, alas, lost to the world.

One incident that is not without its instructive side in this connection is recorded in the year 1501, when Isabella, Duchess of Mantua, sent her agent in Venice to Gian Bellini to arrange with him to paint a secular subject. The old painter, now in the neighbourhood of his seventieth year, accepted money on account, and then turned his thoughts to other things. The agent worried him from time to time with little or no effect, and wrote despairing letters to the Duchess to convey Bellini's various excuses. Not until 1504, when the Duchess was proposing to take legal action, was the picture finished, and then it does not seem to have been what was required. At the same time it must have been a work of great merit, because a year later we find the Duchess commissioning another picture, and asking for a secular subject, which the old painter after much hesitation refused to paint.

Happily Isabella d'Este was not only a voluminous letter writer, but her correspondence has been preserved, and some forty letters were written in connection with the Bellini picture, by the lady whom Cardinal Bembo called "the wisest and most fortunate of women," and of whom a poet wrote, "At the sound of her name all the Muses rise and do reverence." She had seen Bellini's work, and had admired it in Venice, before she asked a friend, one Signor Vianello, to secure a picture for her *camerino*. At first the old painter raised objections, says Vianello. "I am busy working for the Signory in the Palace," he said, "and I cannot leave my work from early morning until after dinner." Then he asked for 150 ducats and said he would make time, then he came down to 100 ducats and accepted 25 on account Then as has been explained, he declared that he could not undertake the class of subject that the Duchess wanted, and Isabella wrote to say that she would accept anything antique that had a fine meaning. Vianello writes in reply to say that Bellini has gone to his country villa and cannot be reached, and the correspondence and the years pass, until at last the Duchess gets quite cross and writes, "We can no longer endure the villainy of Giovanni Bellini," and goes on to instruct her agent to make application to the Doge, Leonardo Loredano, the one whose portrait, painted by Giovanni Bellini, is in our National Gallery, to commit the old painter for fraud. To this action Bellini responds by showing Vianello that he has a "Nativity" three parts finished, and after a time he sends it to the Duchess together with a very humble letter of apology, that the lady is good enough to accept. She even writes, "Your 'Nativity' is as dear to us as any picture we possess."

In 1506 Albert Dürer was in Venice where he declares that he found the Venetians very pleasant companions, and adds with sly sarcasm that some of them knew how to paint. At the same time he records his fear lest any of them should put poison in his food, but speaks in high terms and without suspicion of Gian Bellini who had praised his work and offered to buy a picture. All these things are small matters enough, but unhappily the records of Bellini's life are so scanty that it is hard to find anything more until the year 1513 when Gian Bellini, well over eighty, found his position as official painter challenged by his pupil Titian, who presented a petition to the Council of Ten, stating *inter alia* that he was desirous of a little fame rather than of profit, that he had refused to serve the Pope, and that he wanted the first broker's patent that should be vacant in the Fondaco de' Tedeschi on the same conditions as those granted to Messer Zuan Bellin.[1] The work that was being done was the restoration of the Great Hall of the Council, and the painting had been in progress for some forty years, Gian Bellini and two pupils being now engaged upon it. There is no doubt that this application by Titian annoyed Bellini's friends and pupils, and even to us it seems a little unreasonable and in bad form to clamour so eagerly for a place that was already occupied. But it would seem to have been the custom of the time to apply early for any privilege of this kind, for we find in later years that Tintoretto applied for Titian's place long before the older master's capacity for working had come to an end.

This was the Venetian way of spelling Gian Bellini's name. Bellini's friends were successful, although it would appear that the old painter's progress had been too slow completely to satisfy the Council of Ten. In the following year Titian, who had been allowed to start work, was told that he must wait until older claims were satisfied, the expenses of his assistants were disallowed, and his commission came to an end. In the autumn of that year Titian brought another petition to the Council, asking once more for the first vacant broker's patent, and mentioning the fact that Bellini's days could not be long in the land. Just about this time the Venetian authorities seem to have held an inquiry into the progress of the work that was being done in the Hall of the Great Council, only to find that the amount of money they had spent should have secured them a far larger amount of work than had been accomplished. It is hardly surprising that these inquiries should have become necessary, there must have been a great laxity in the State departments in the years following the working out of the plans that had been made by France, Austria, Spain, and the Pope at Cambrai. In the last few years Venice had been fighting for her life, Lombardy had passed out of her hands, Verona, Vicenza, and Padua had followed. The Republic had even been forced to seek aid from the Sultans of Turkey and Egypt, and although Venice was destined to emerge from her troubles and light the civilised world a little longer there is small cause for wonder if, in the times of exceptional excitement, her statesmen had not given their wonted attention to the progress of the arts. Doubtless Gian Bellini's leisurely methods and failing strength were accountable for the slow progress of the pictures in the Council Hall, and Titian took advantage of the fact to send in a third petition, offering to finish some work at his own expense, but he had no occasion to take much more trouble.

On November 29, 1516, Gian Bellini died, well on the road to his ninetieth year, "and there were not wanting in Venice," says Vasari, "those who by sonnets and epigrams sought to do him honour after his death as he had done honour to himself and his country during his life." One cannot help thinking that half-a-dozen pages of biography would have been worth a bushel of sonnets.

With Gian Bellini the last great painter of purely religious subjects passed away. He had stood between art and paganism. Perhaps the younger men found him narrow and pedantic, but it is certain that so long as Gian Bellini was the leading painter of Venice it was not easy for pictures to respond to the ever growing demands that followed the Renaissance. Now the road was clear, painting was to reach its highest point in the work of Giorgione and Titian, and was then to decline almost as rapidly as it had risen.

Gian Bellini for all the wide influence that he exerted, not only upon contemporary painting, but upon sculpture too, sent very little work out of Venice. Examples are to be seen in cities that are comparatively close at hand, Rimini, Pesaro, Vicenza, Bergamo, and Turin, but his genius seems to have been too completely recognised in his own city for his work to travel far afield, and the portrait of himself in the Uffizi Gallery is no more than a pupil's work with a studio signature. One of his last undisputed paintings was for the altar of St. Crisostom in Venice. It is said that he painted it at the age of eighty-five. After death his fame suffered by the rise of those stars of Venetian painting, Titian, Giorgione, and Tintoretto, and throughout three centuries his work was held in comparatively small esteem, perhaps because it was often judged by the studio pictures with the forged signatures. As late as the middle of the nineteenth century nobody seemed quite to know the real pictures from the false ones, but with the rise of critics like Crowe, Morelli, and Berenson a much better state of things has been established. Copies and student works have been separated from the originals, careful study of technique and mannerism has made clear a large number of points that were doubtful and in dispute, and although the process of separating the sheep from the goats has reduced considerably the number of works that can be accepted as genuine, the gain to the artist's reputation atones for the loss.

Illustrations of art by contemporaries of Giovanni Bellini on the following pages.

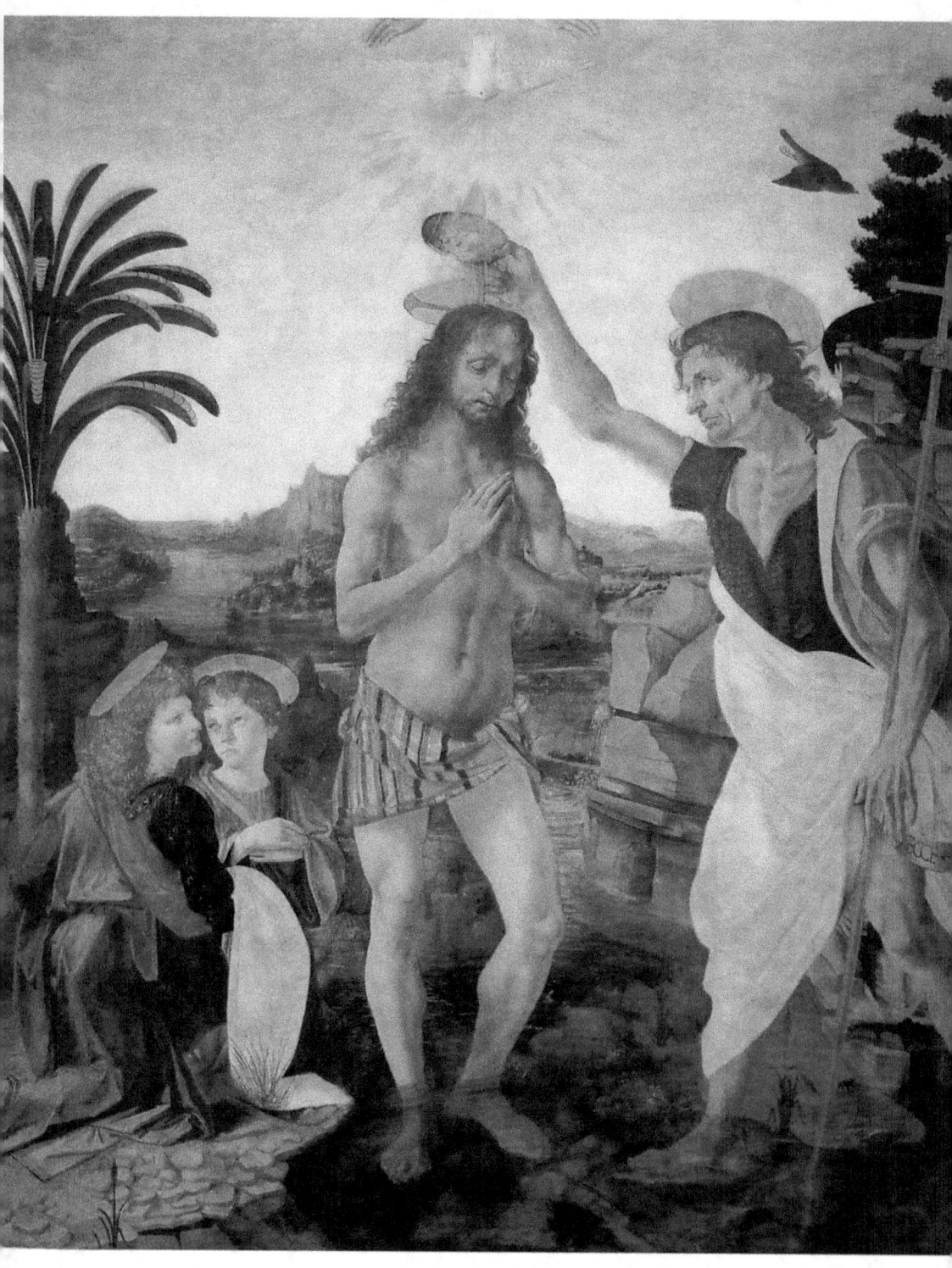

Andrea del Verrocchio, The Baptism of Christ

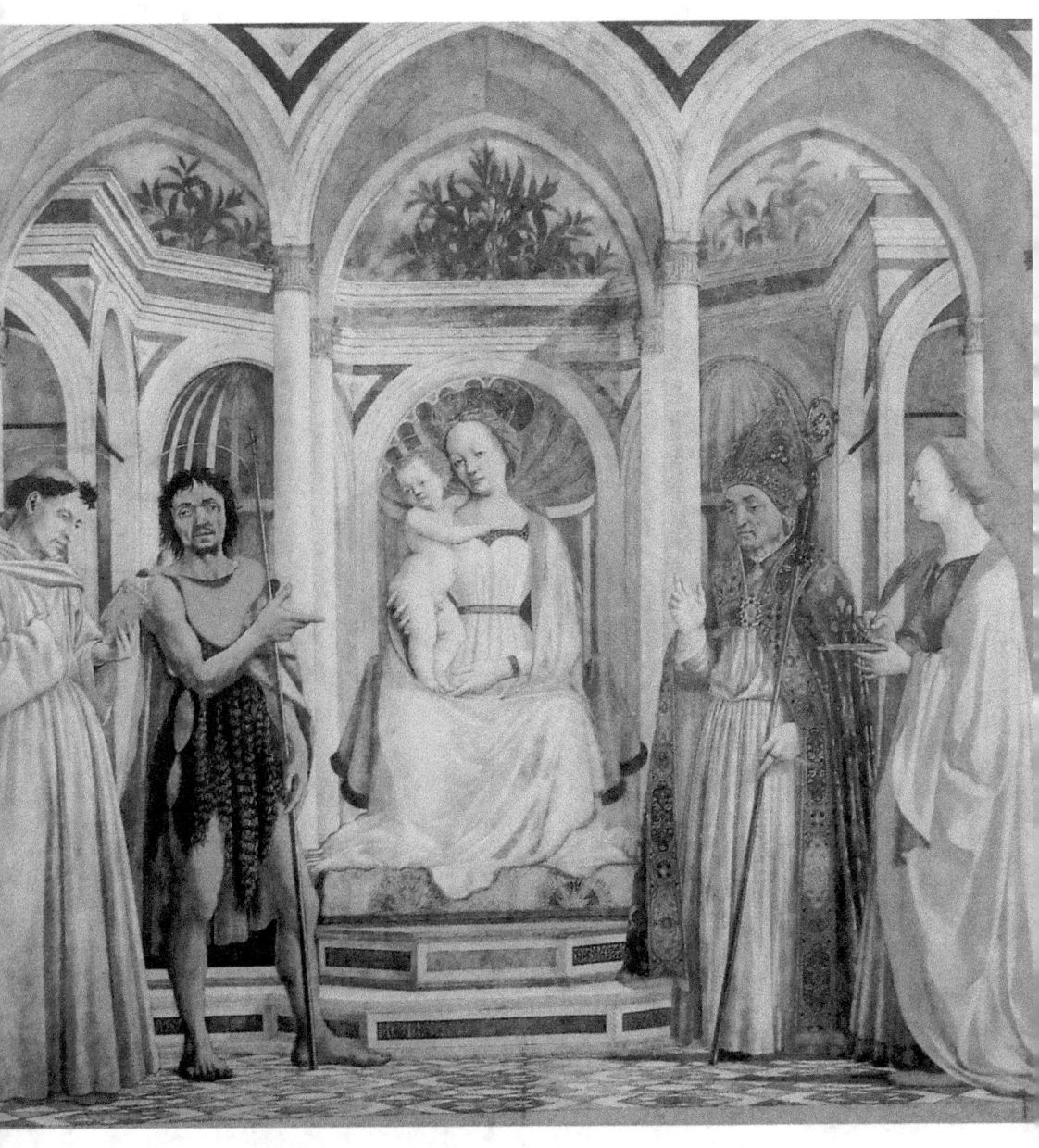

Domenico Veneziano, Madonna and Child With Saints, 1445, Uffizi Gallery

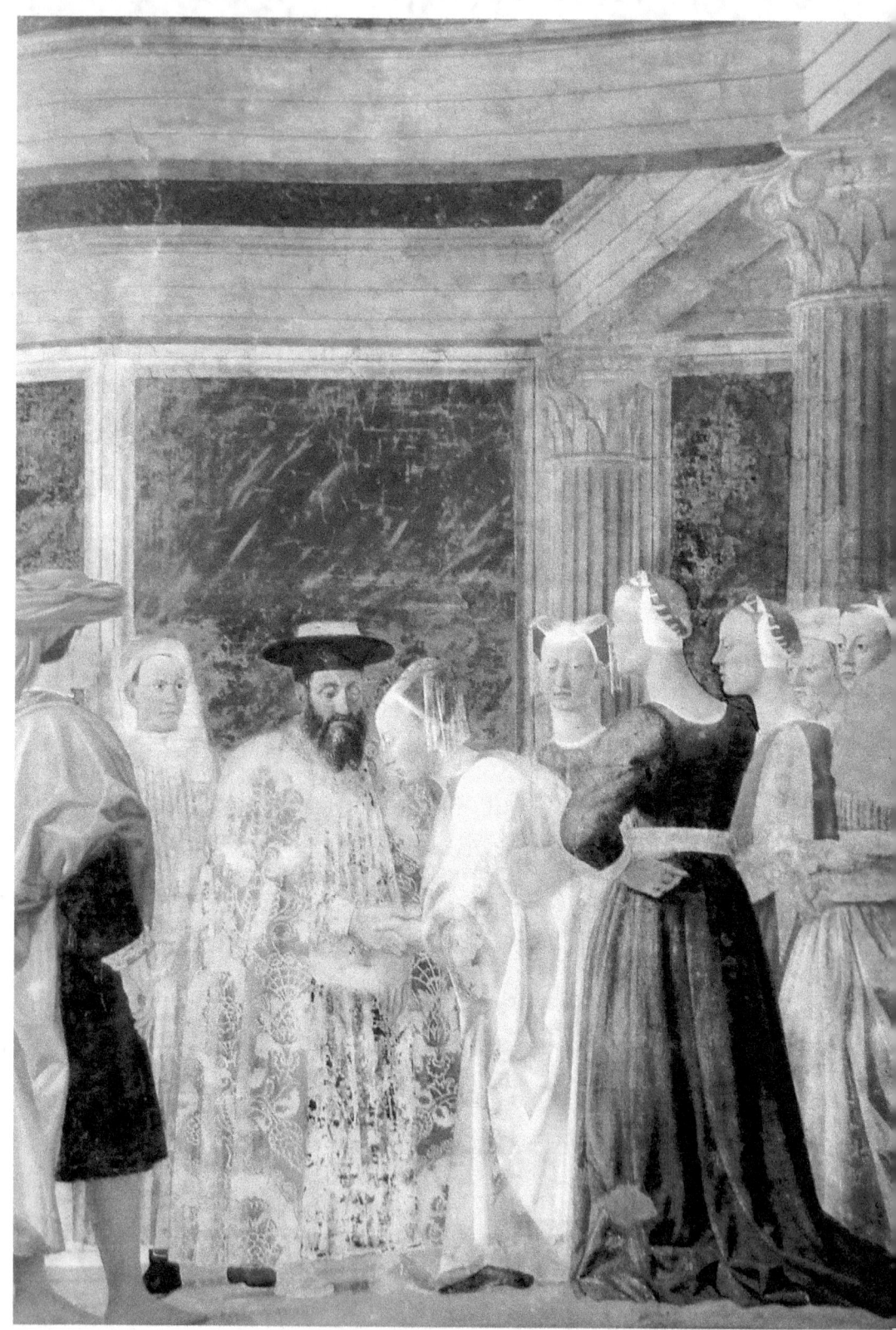

Piero della Francesca, frescoes, Arezzo

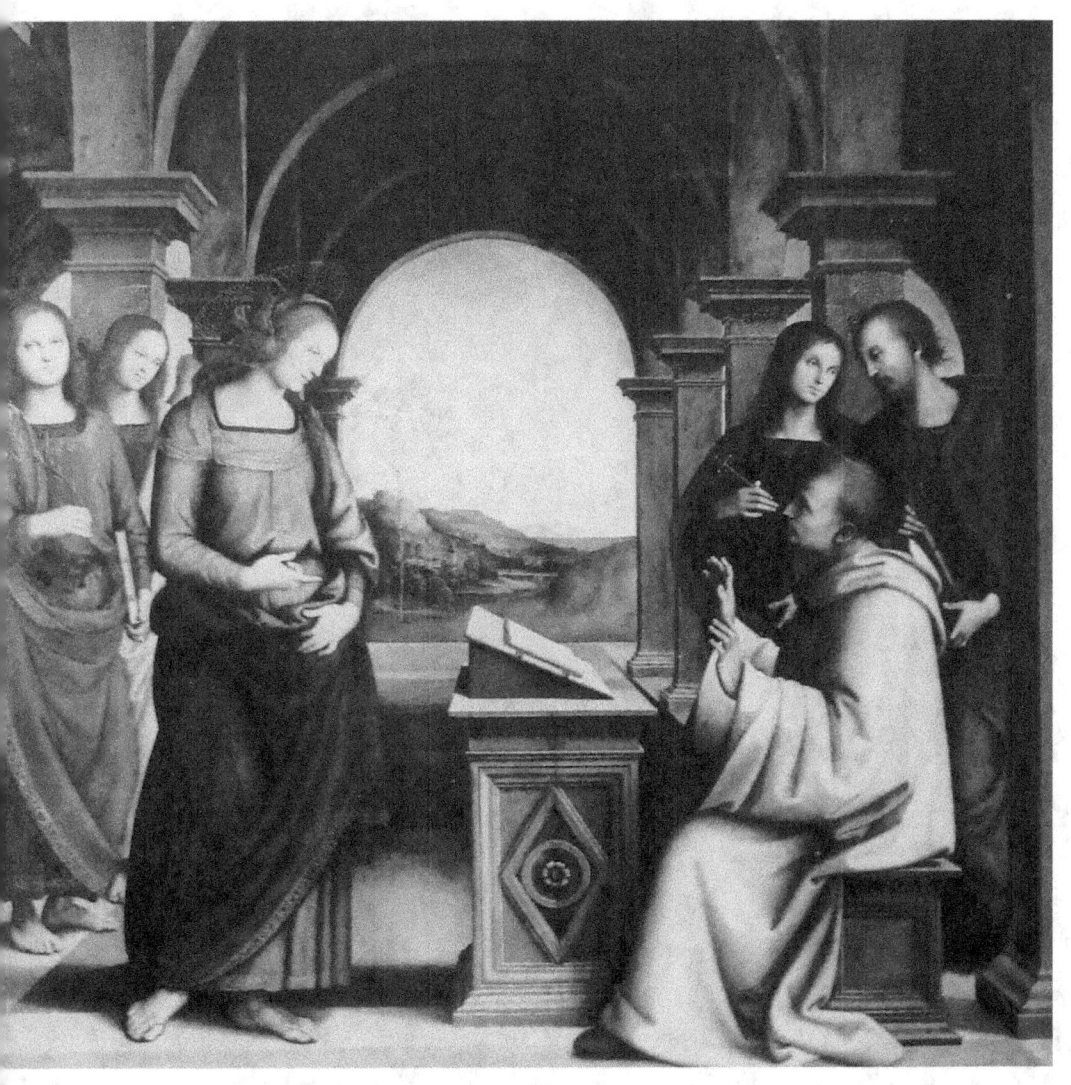

Perugino, Vision of St Bernard, 1488

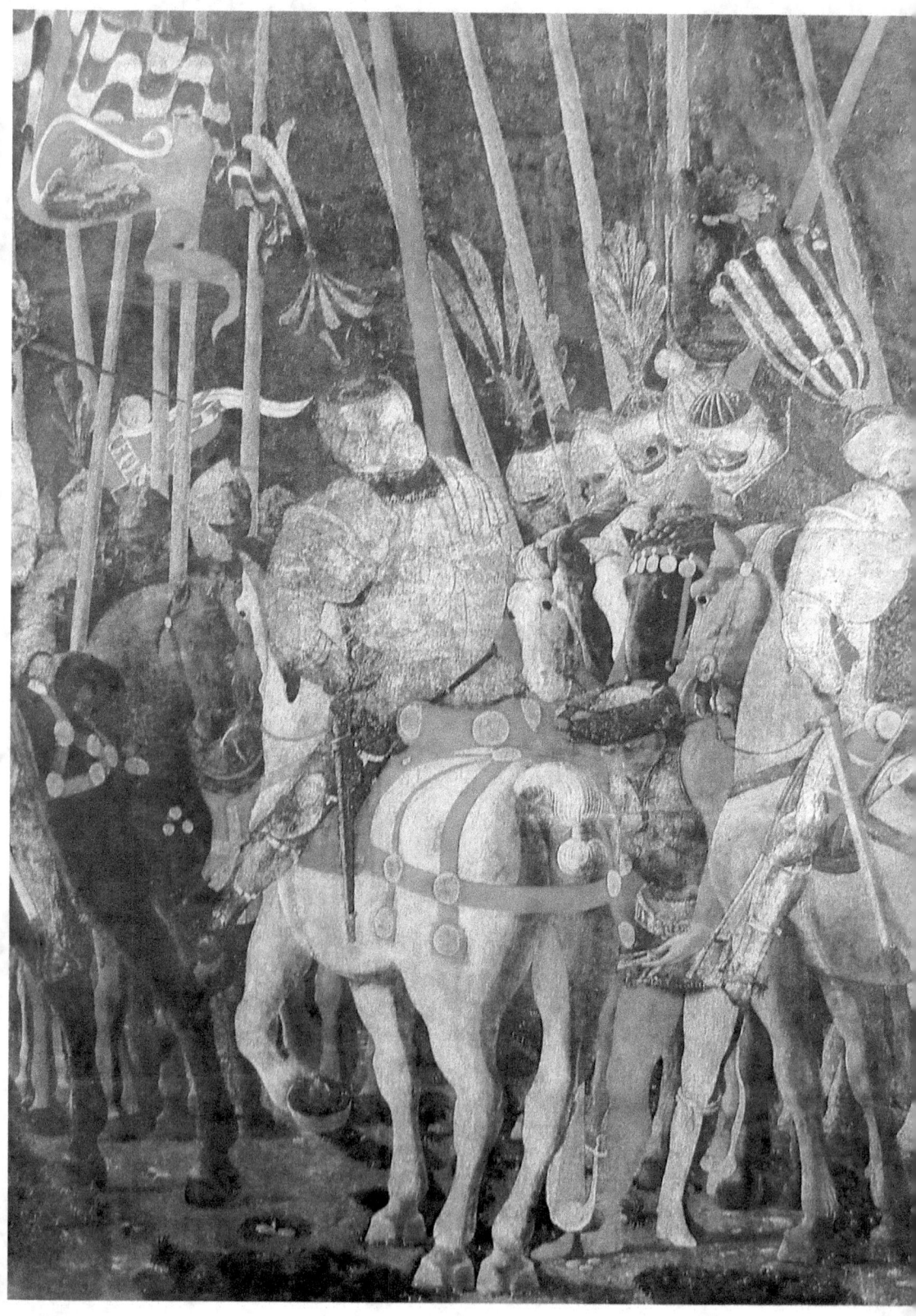

Paolo Uccello, The Battle of San Romano, Paris

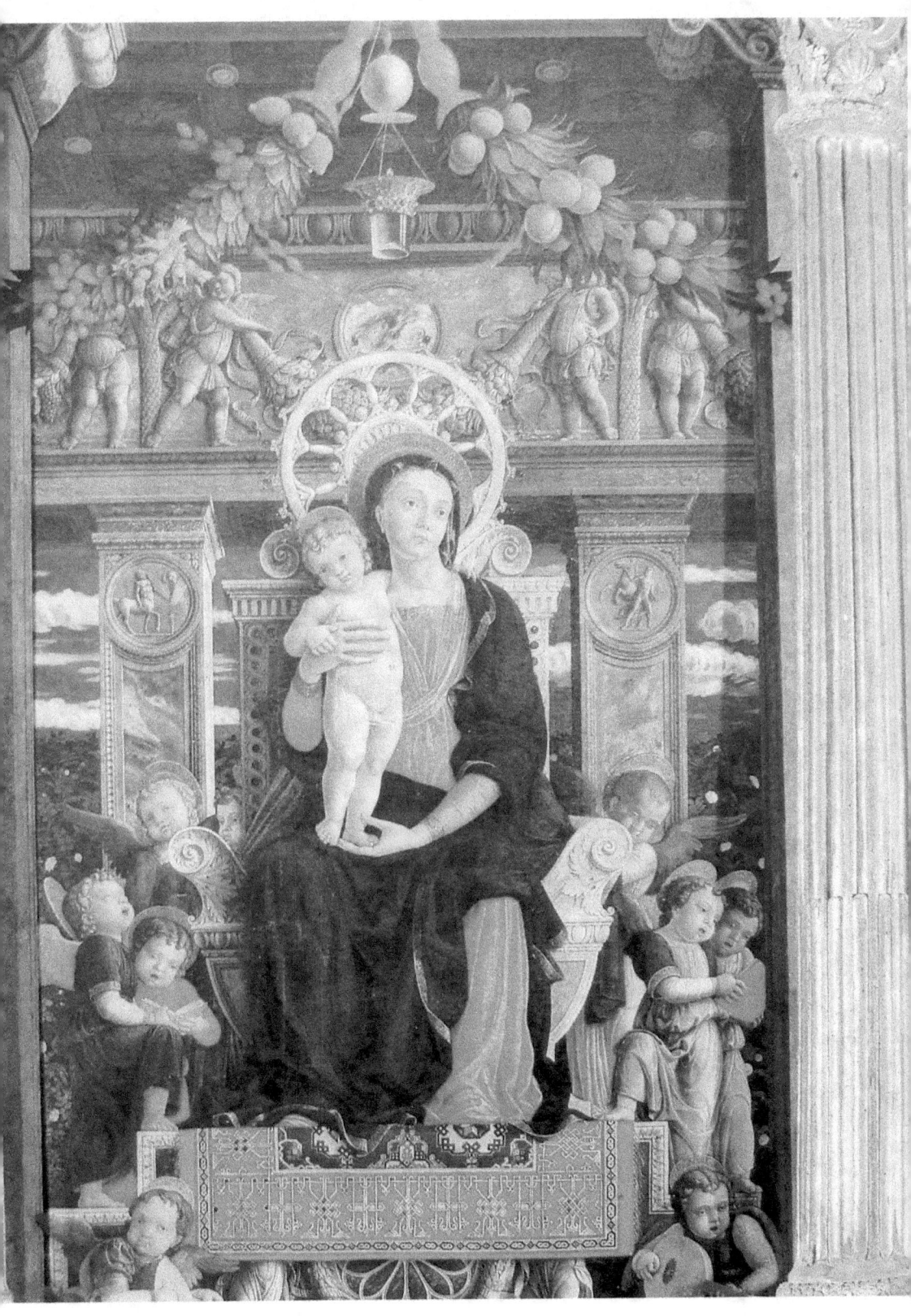

Andreas Mantegna, Madonna and Child Enthroned, 1457-60, Verona

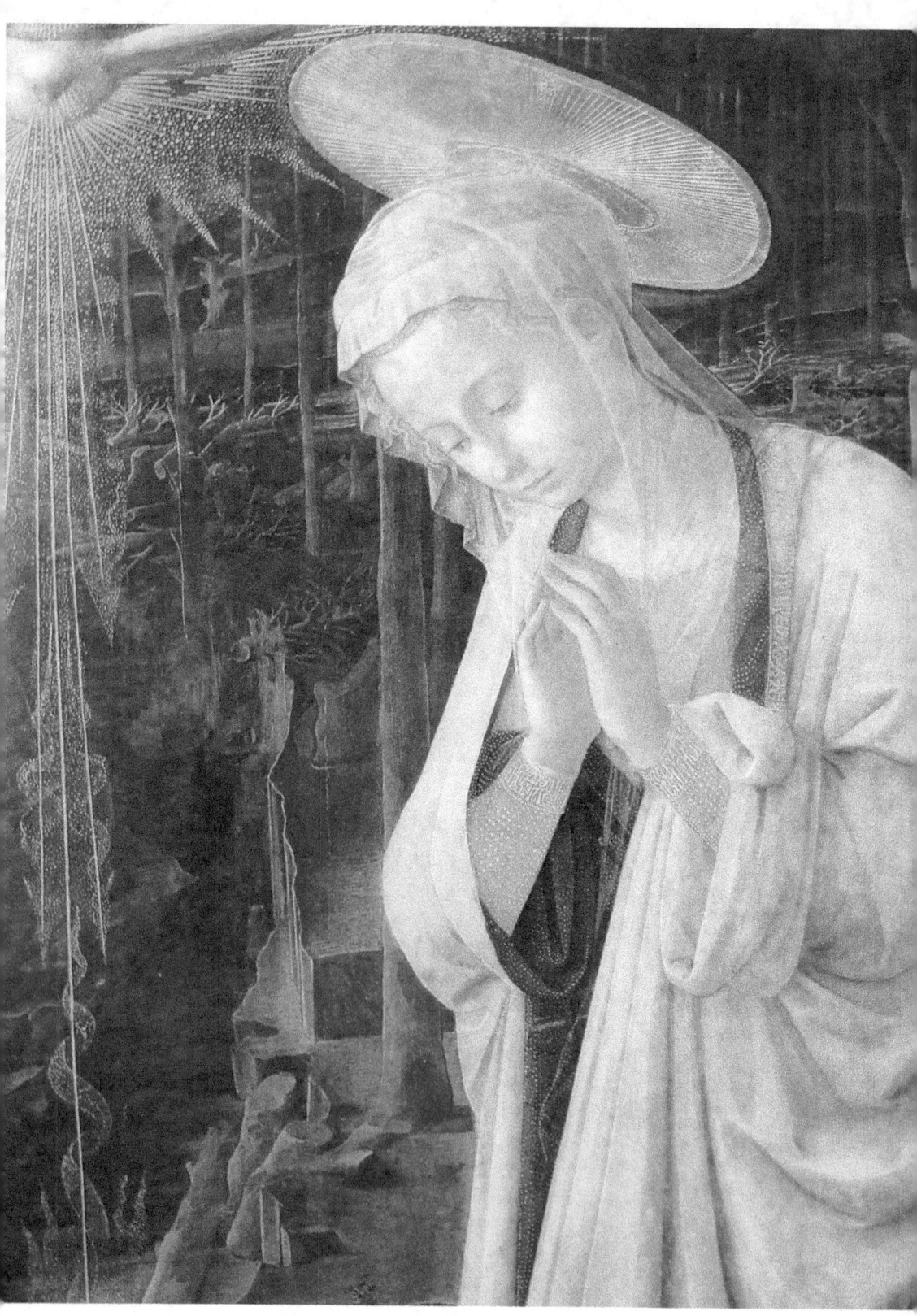

Fra Filippo Lippi, The Adoration of the Virgin, Berlin, detail

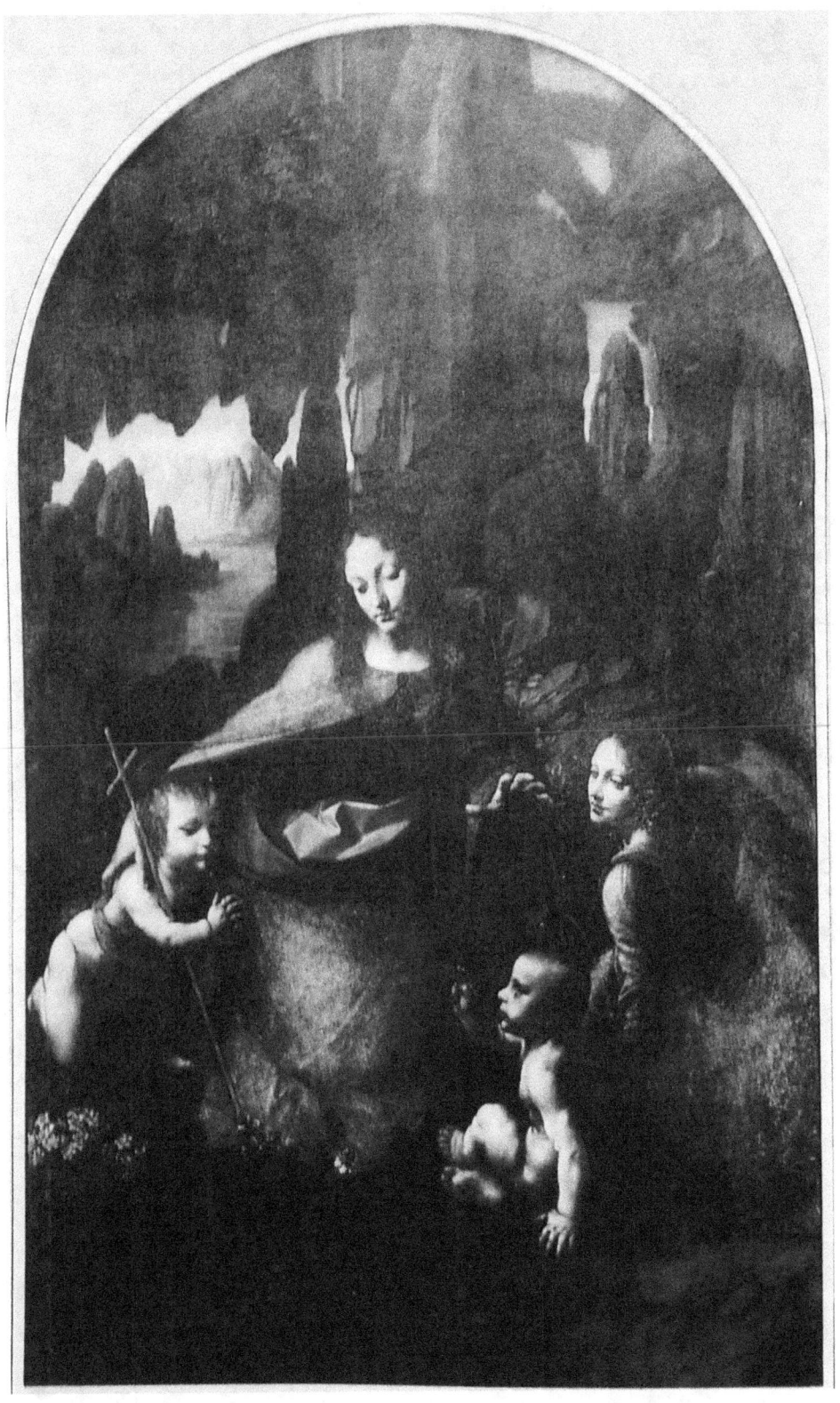

Leonardo da Vinci, The Madonna of the Rocks, London

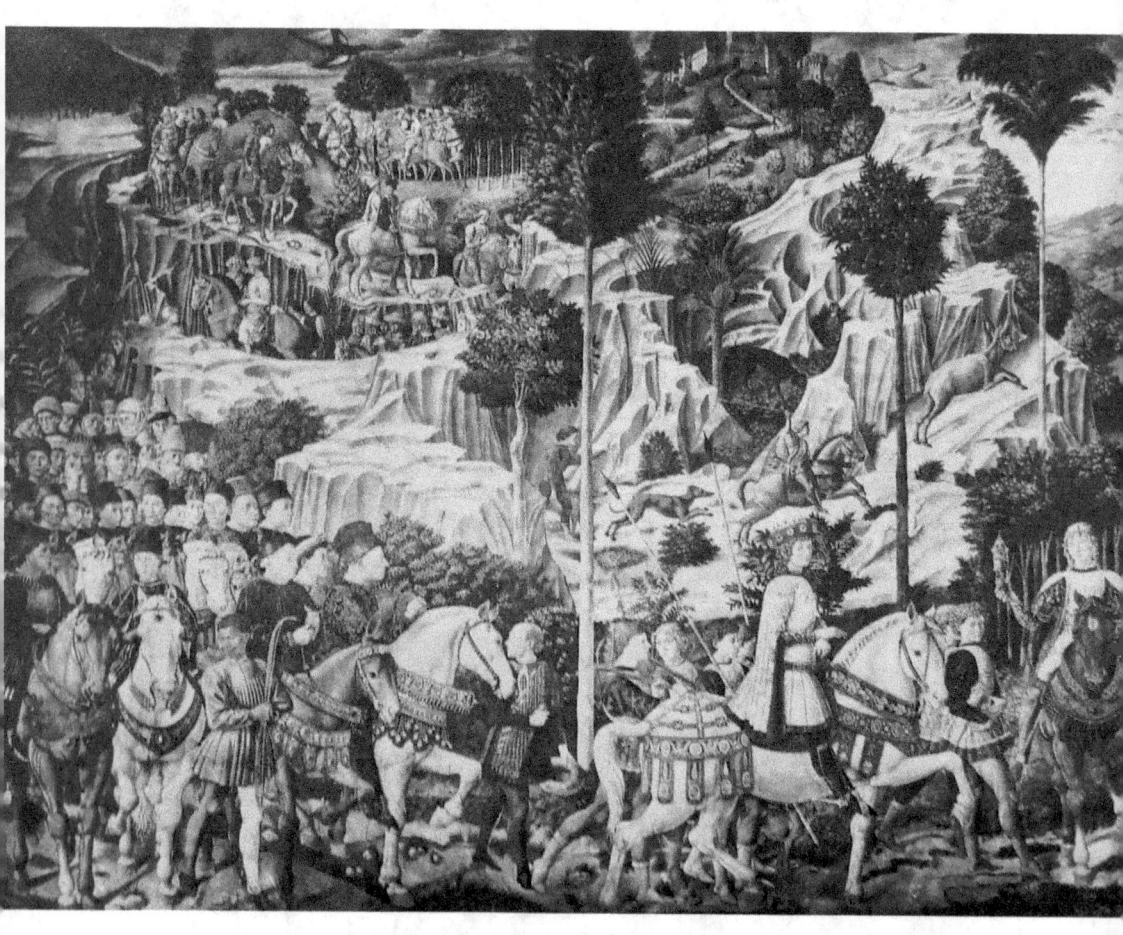

Benozzo Gozzoli, Journey of the Magi

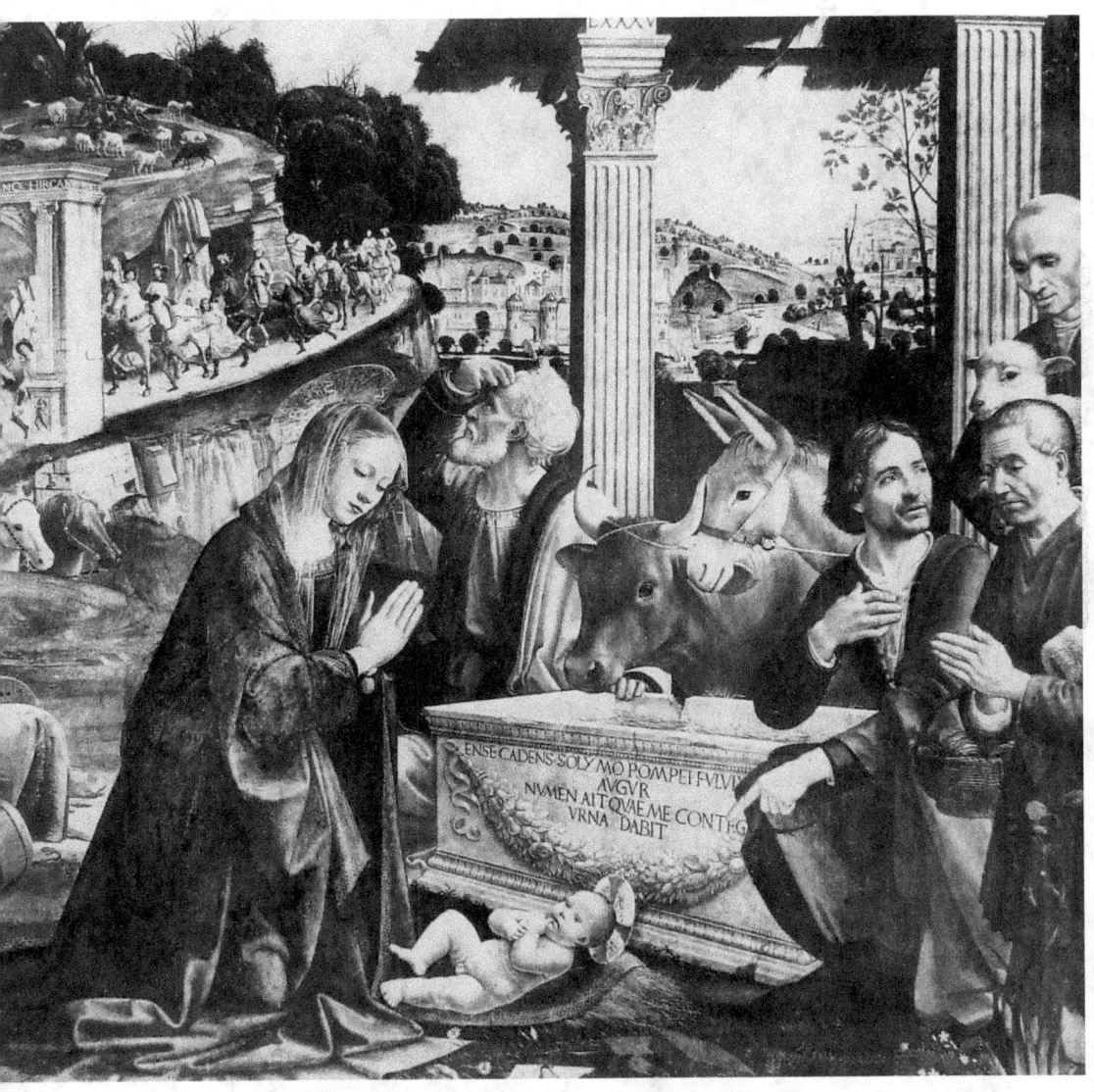

Domenico Ghirlandaio, Adoration of the Shepherds, 1485

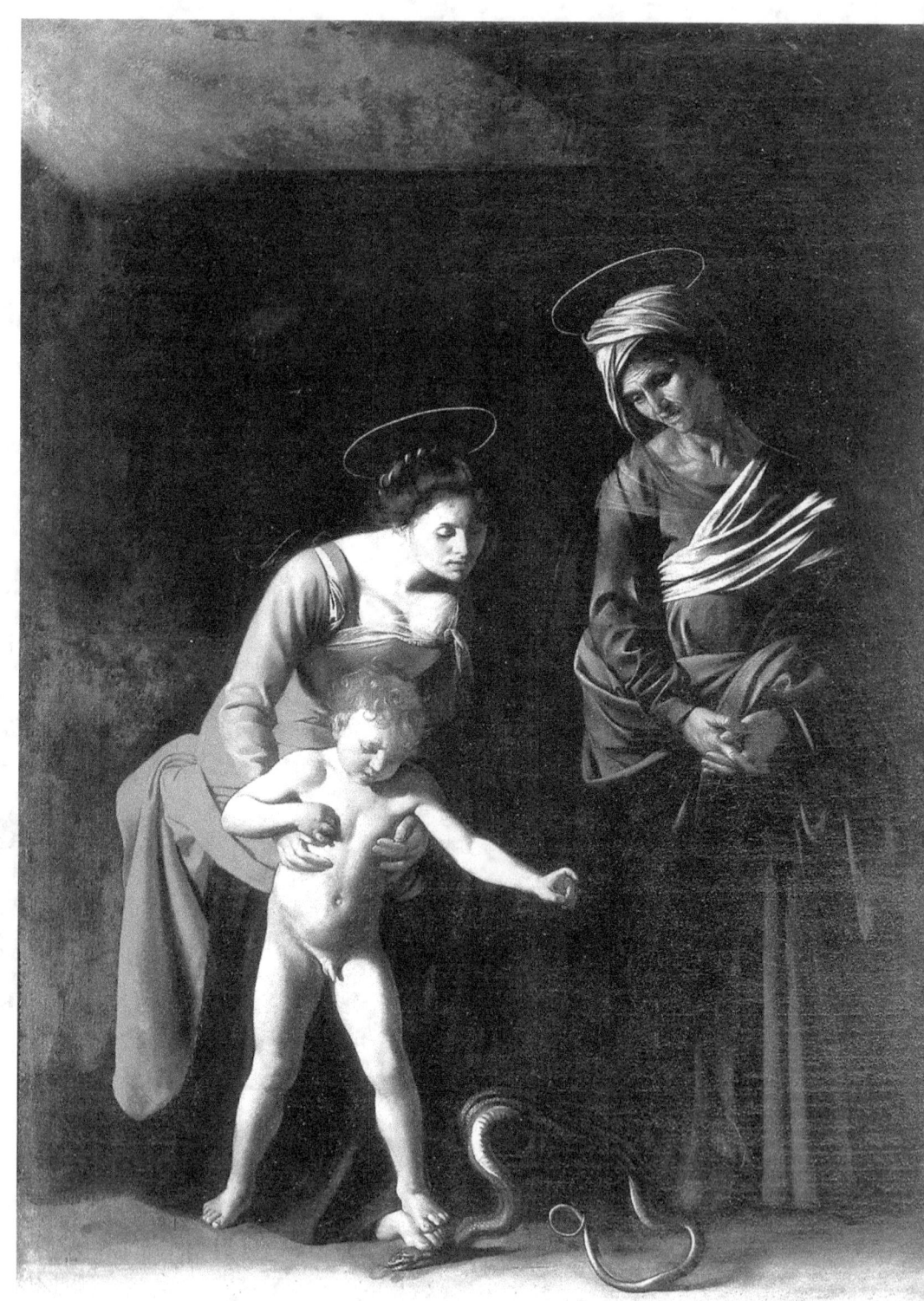

Michelangelo Merisi da Caravaggio, Madonna of the Palafrenieri,
1605-06, Galleria Borghese, Rome

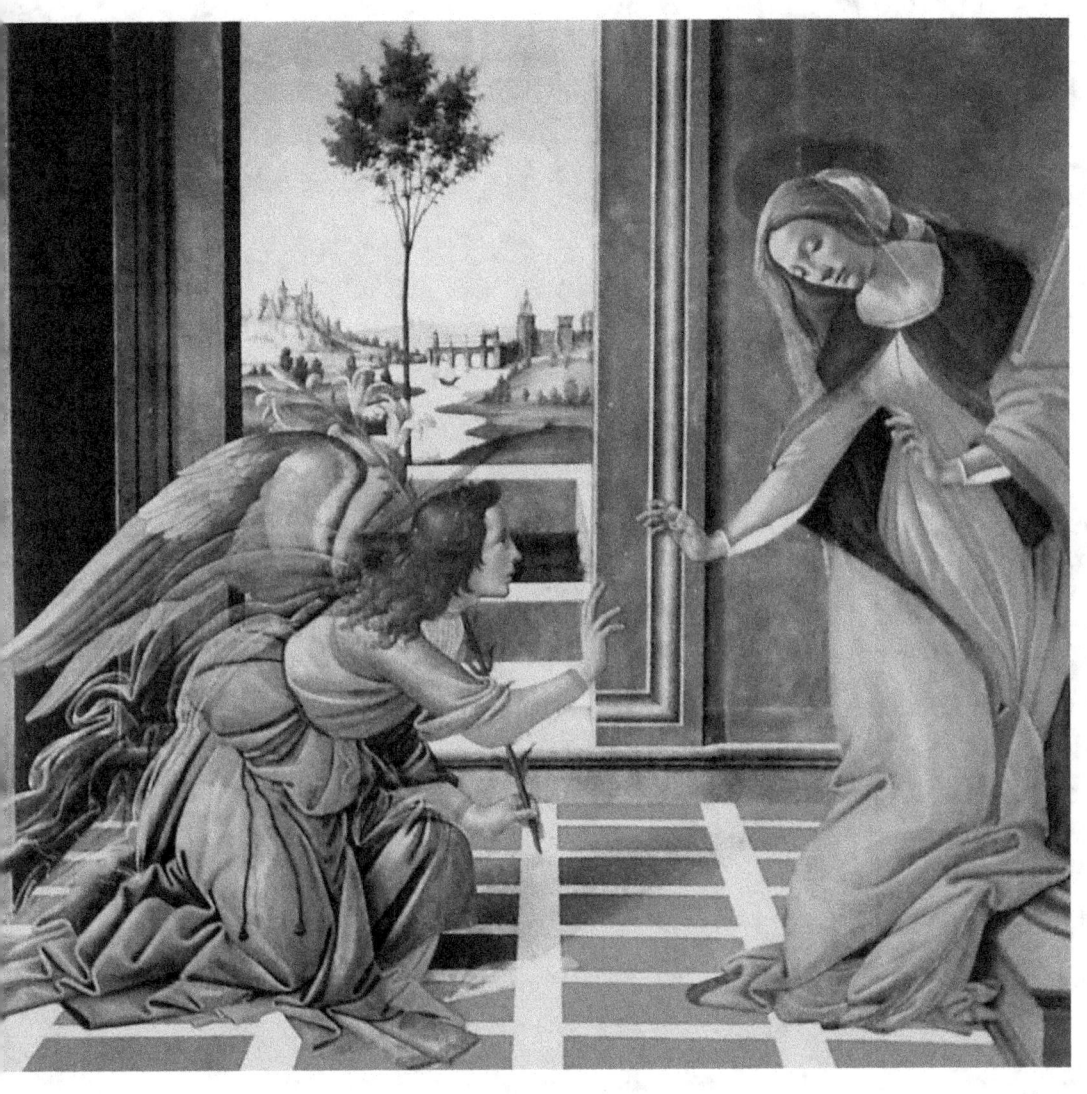

Sandro Botticelli, The Annunciation, Uffizi Gallery, Florence

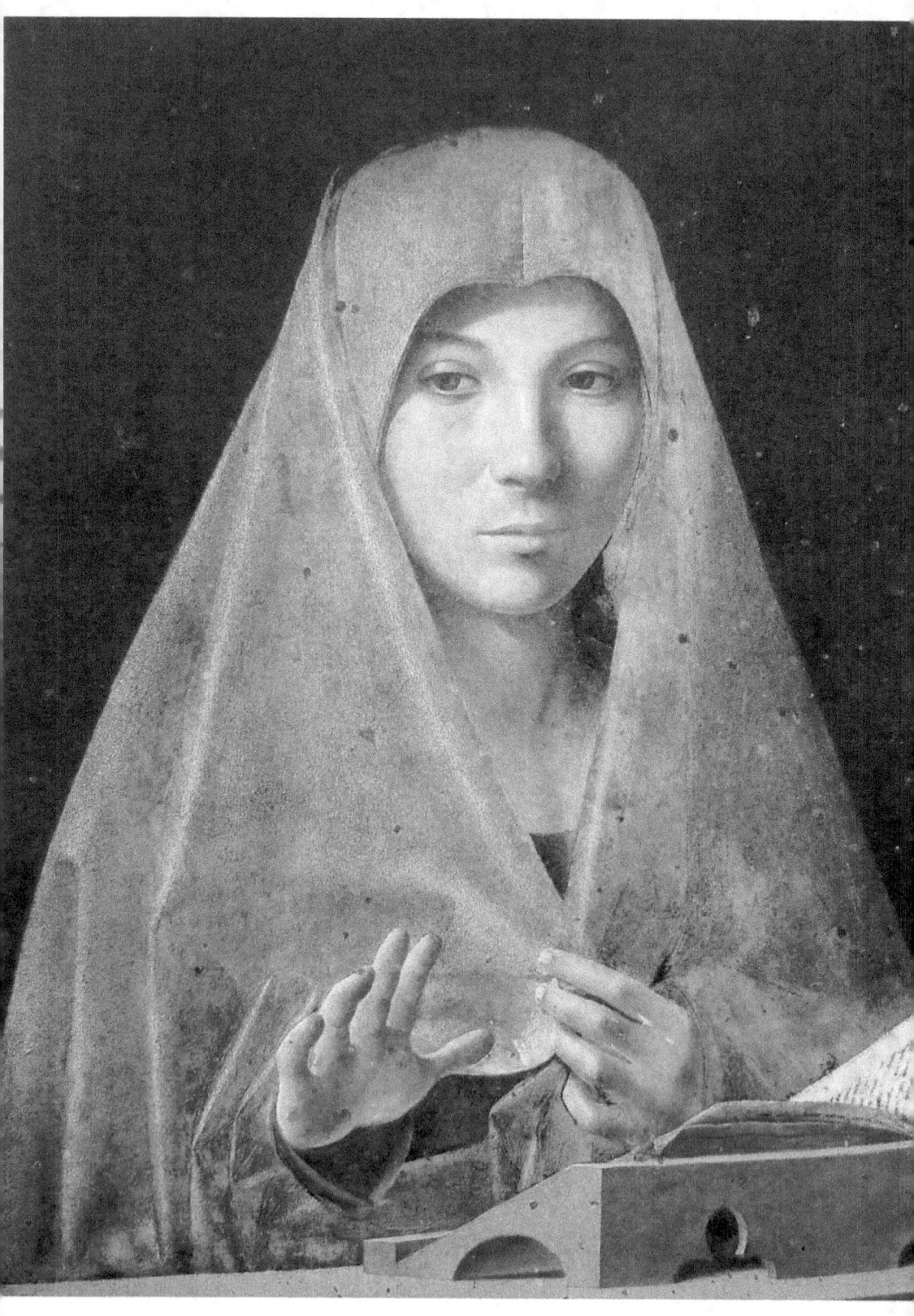

Antonello da Messina, The Virgin of the Annunciation, 1475, Palermo

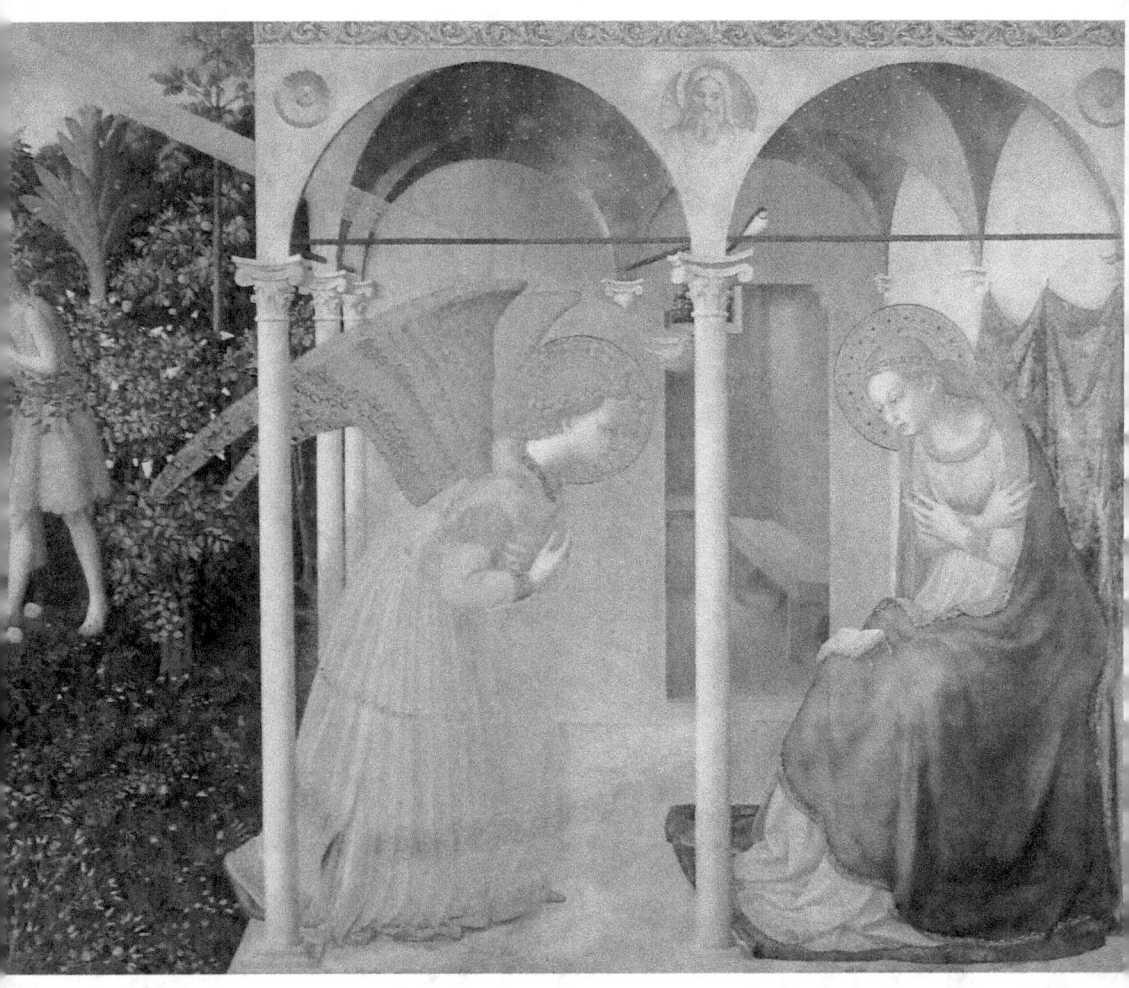

Fra Angelico, Annunciation, Prado, Madrid

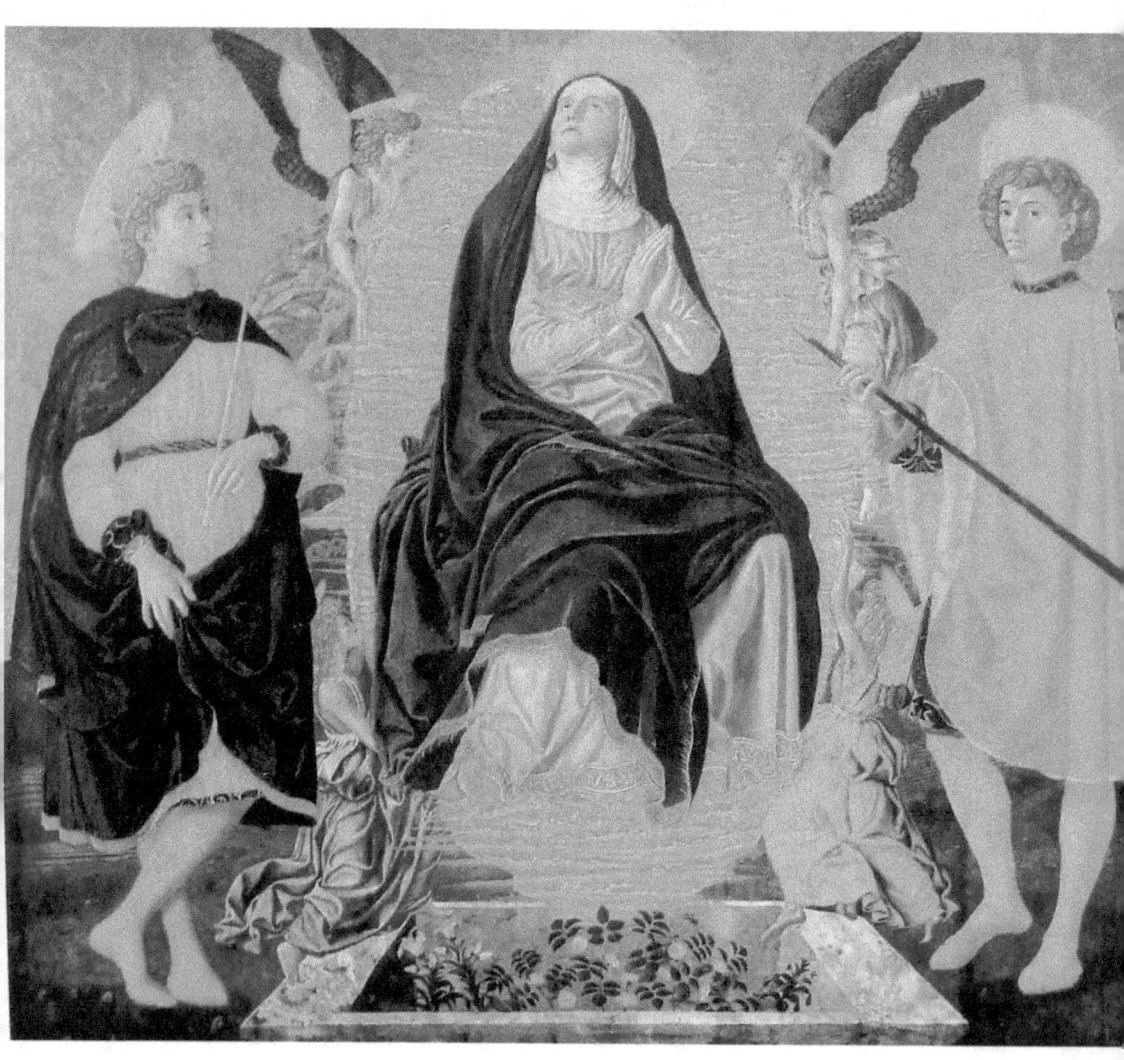

Andrea del Castagno, Assumption, Berlin

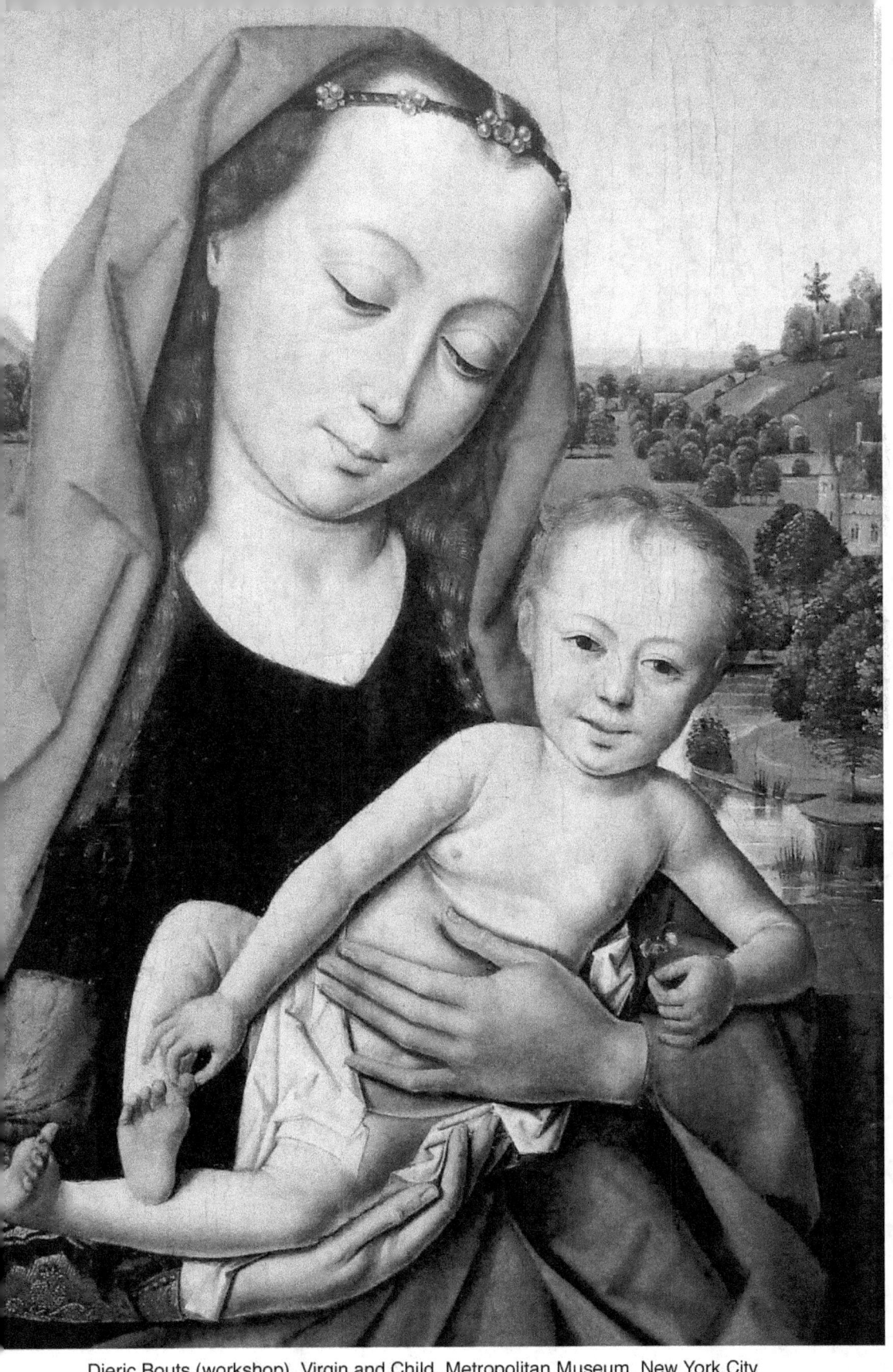

Dieric Bouts (workshop), Virgin and Child, Metropolitan Museum, New York City

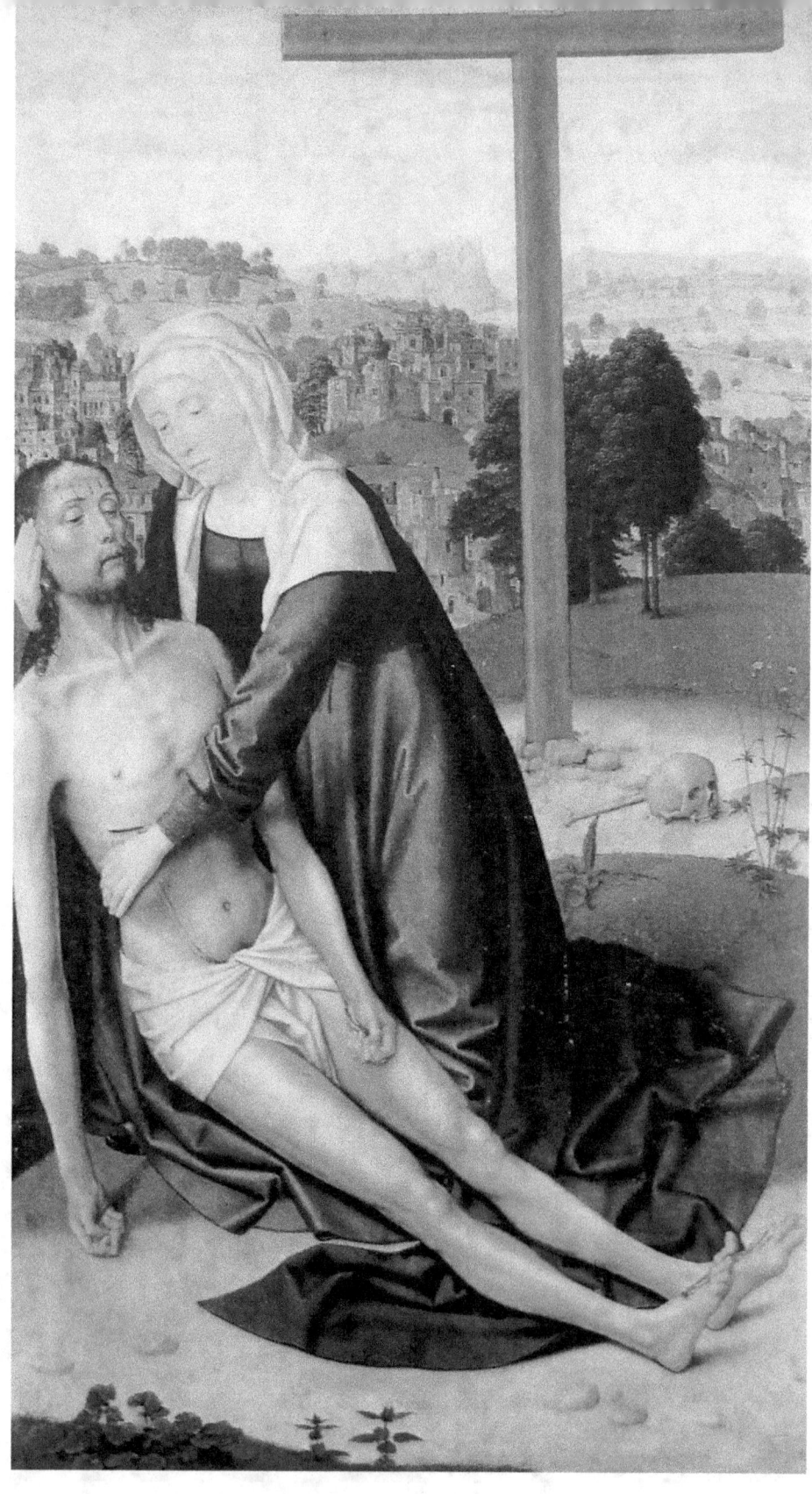

Gerard David, Pietà, Winterhur

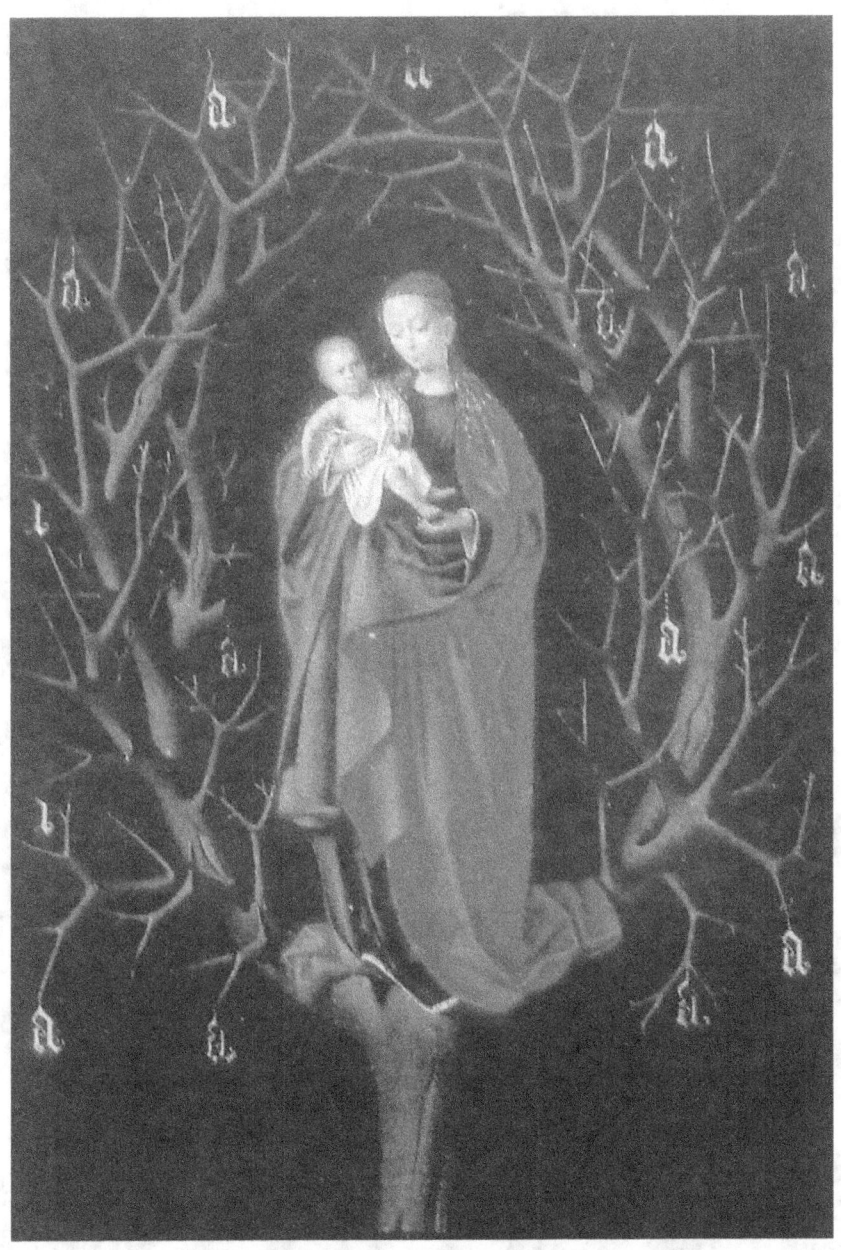

Petrus Christus, Madonna In a Barren Tree, 1450,
Prado, Madrid

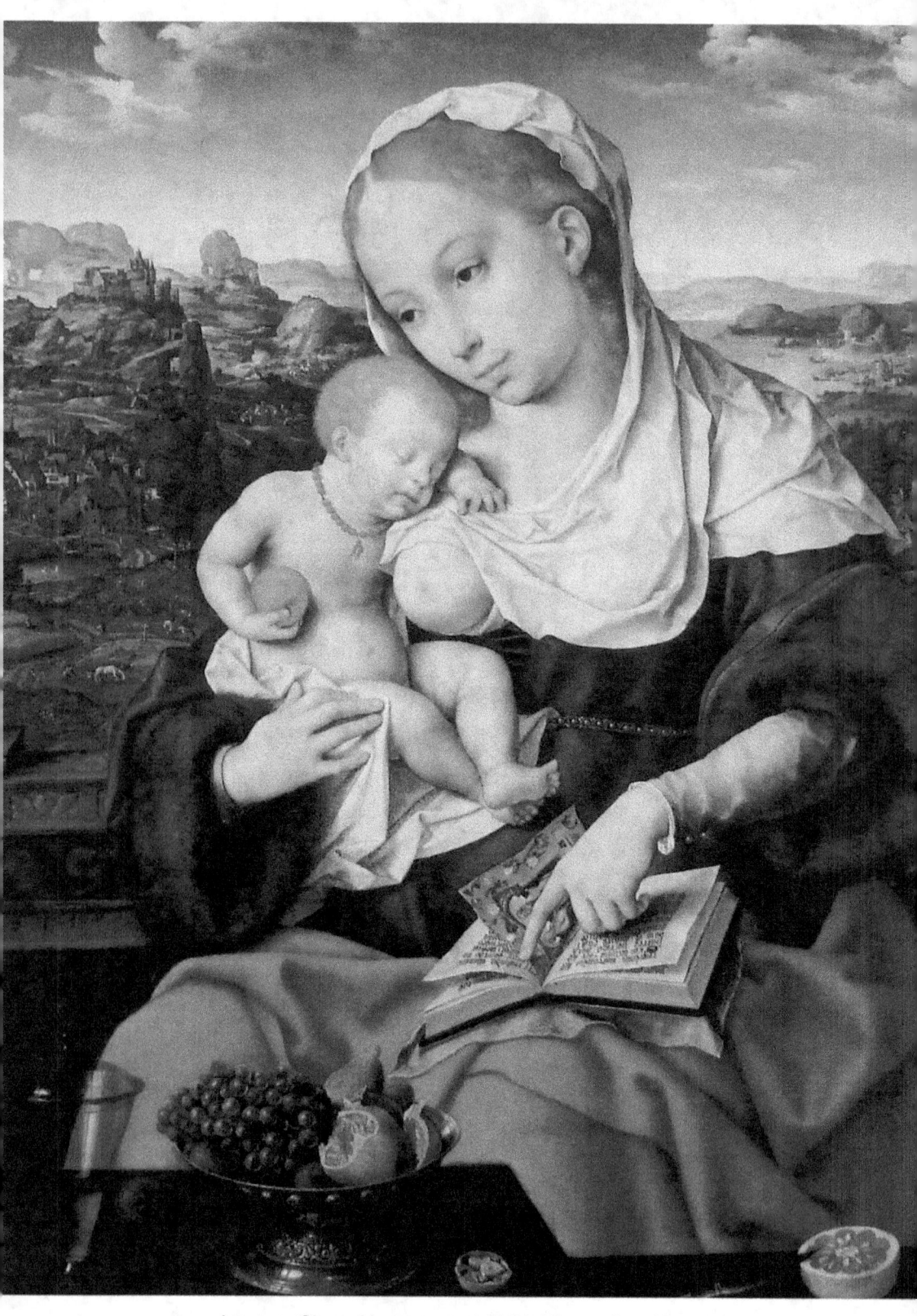

Joos van Cleve, Madonna and Child, Metropolitan Museum,
New York City

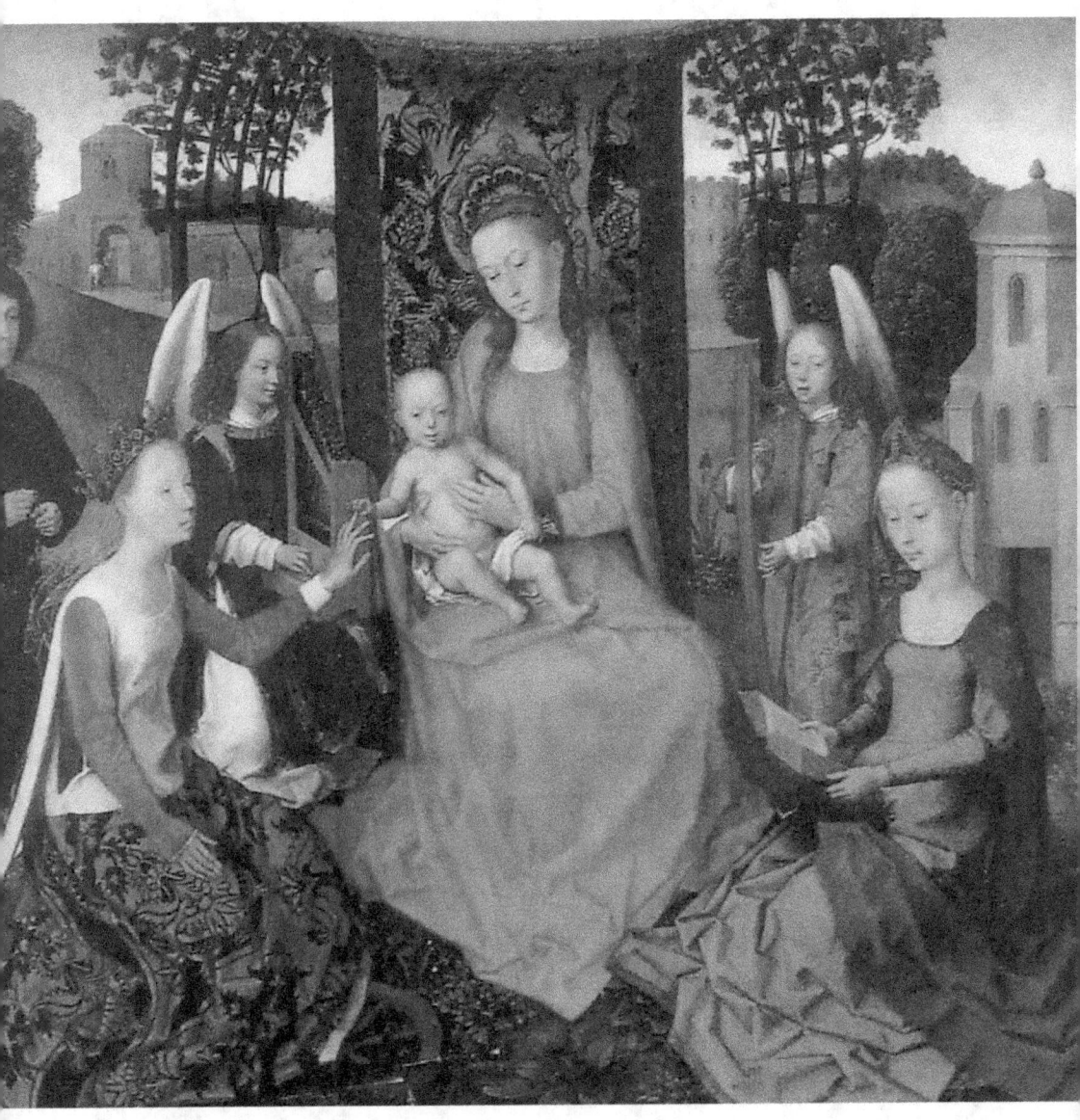

Hans Memling, The Mystic Marriage of St Catherine, Metropolitan
Museum, New York City

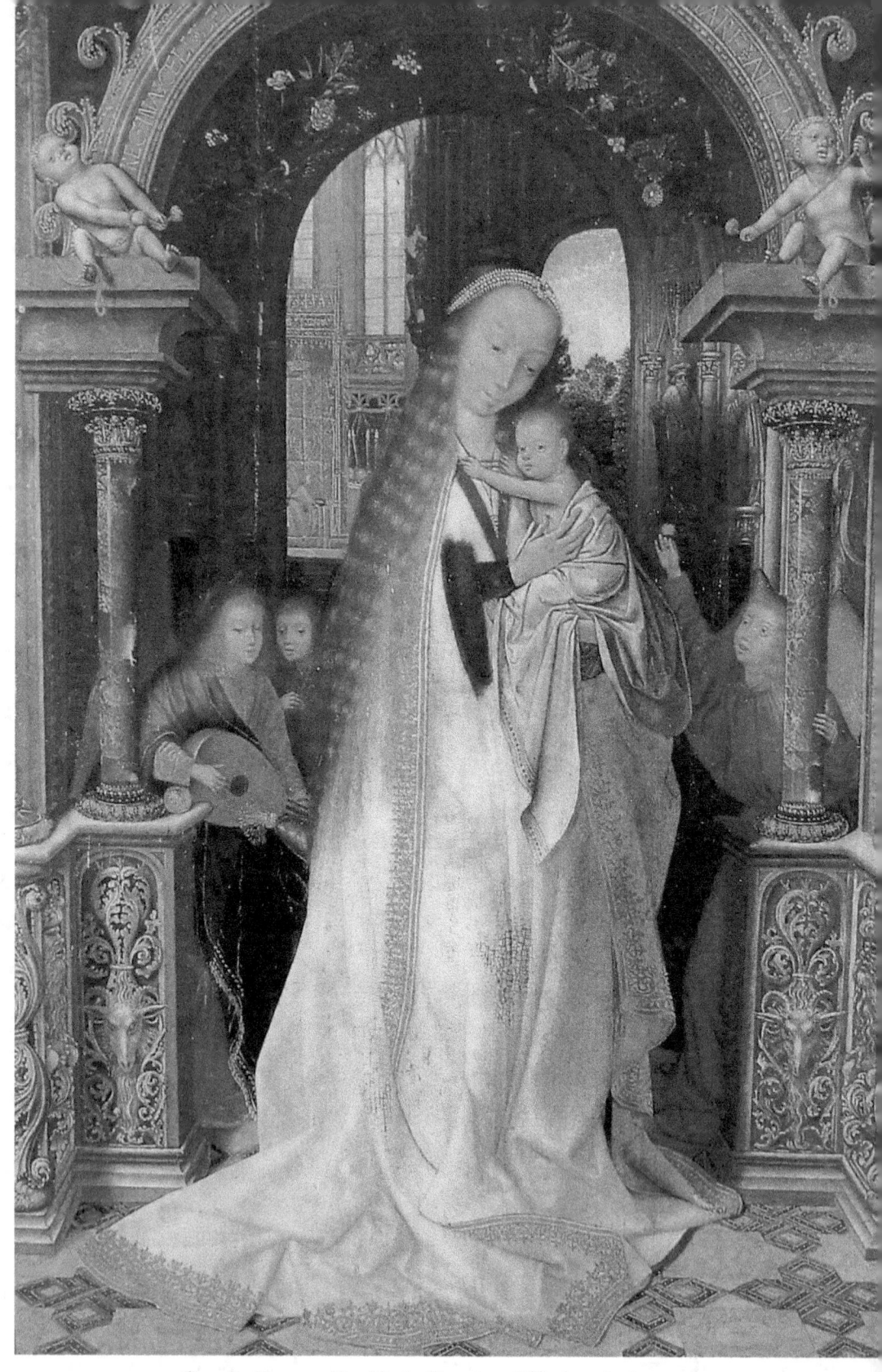

Quentin Massys, The Virgin Standing, With Angels, Lyons

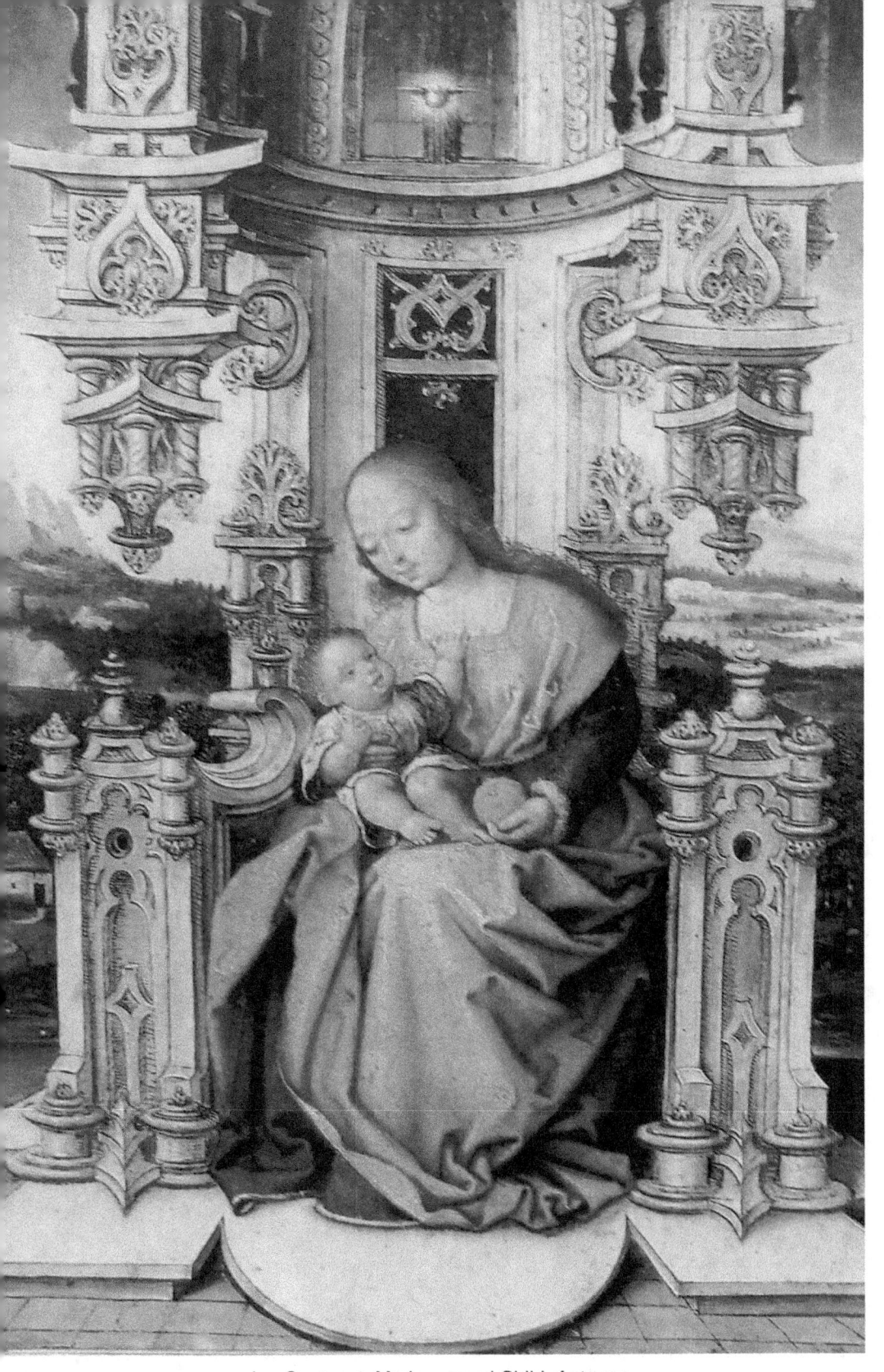

Jan Gossaert, Madonna and Child, Antwerp

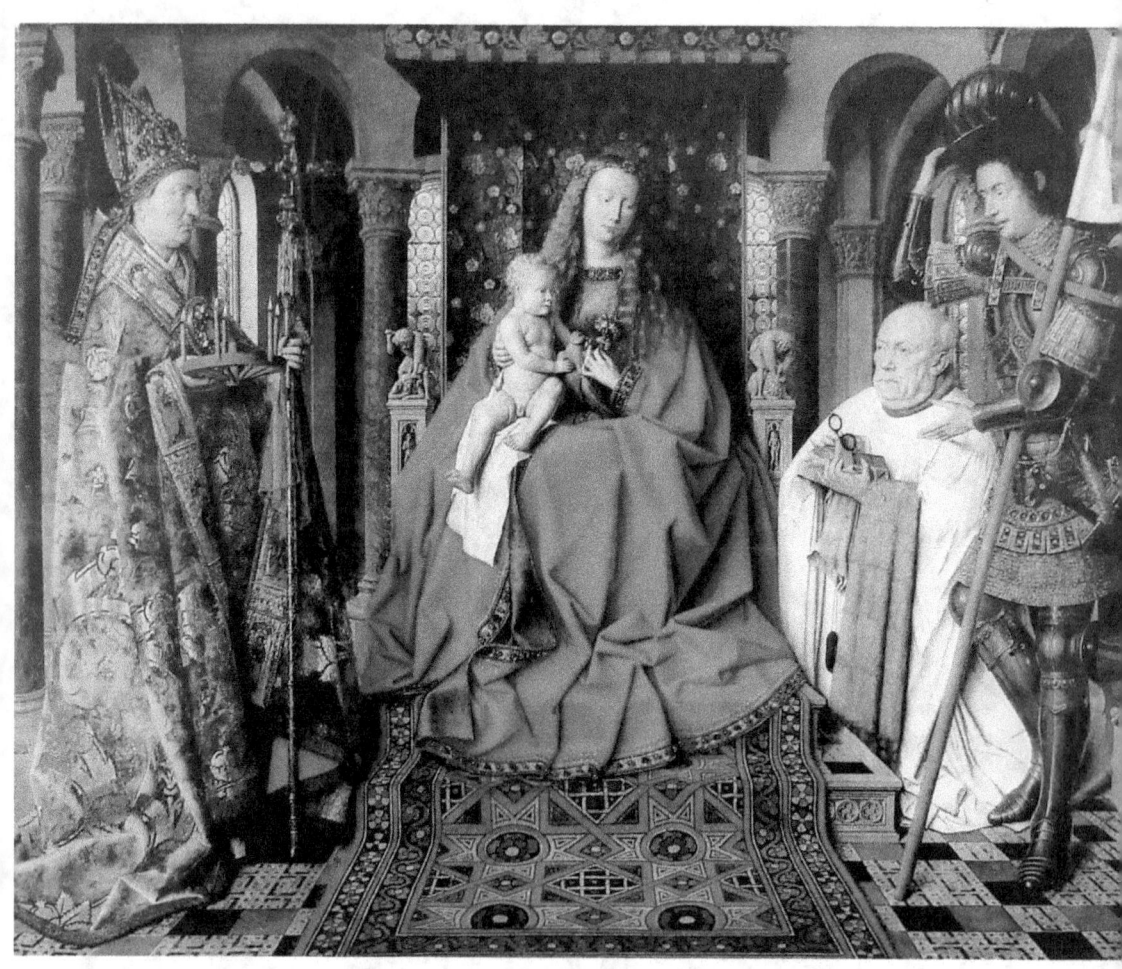

Jan van Eyck, The Paele Madonna, 1436, Bruges

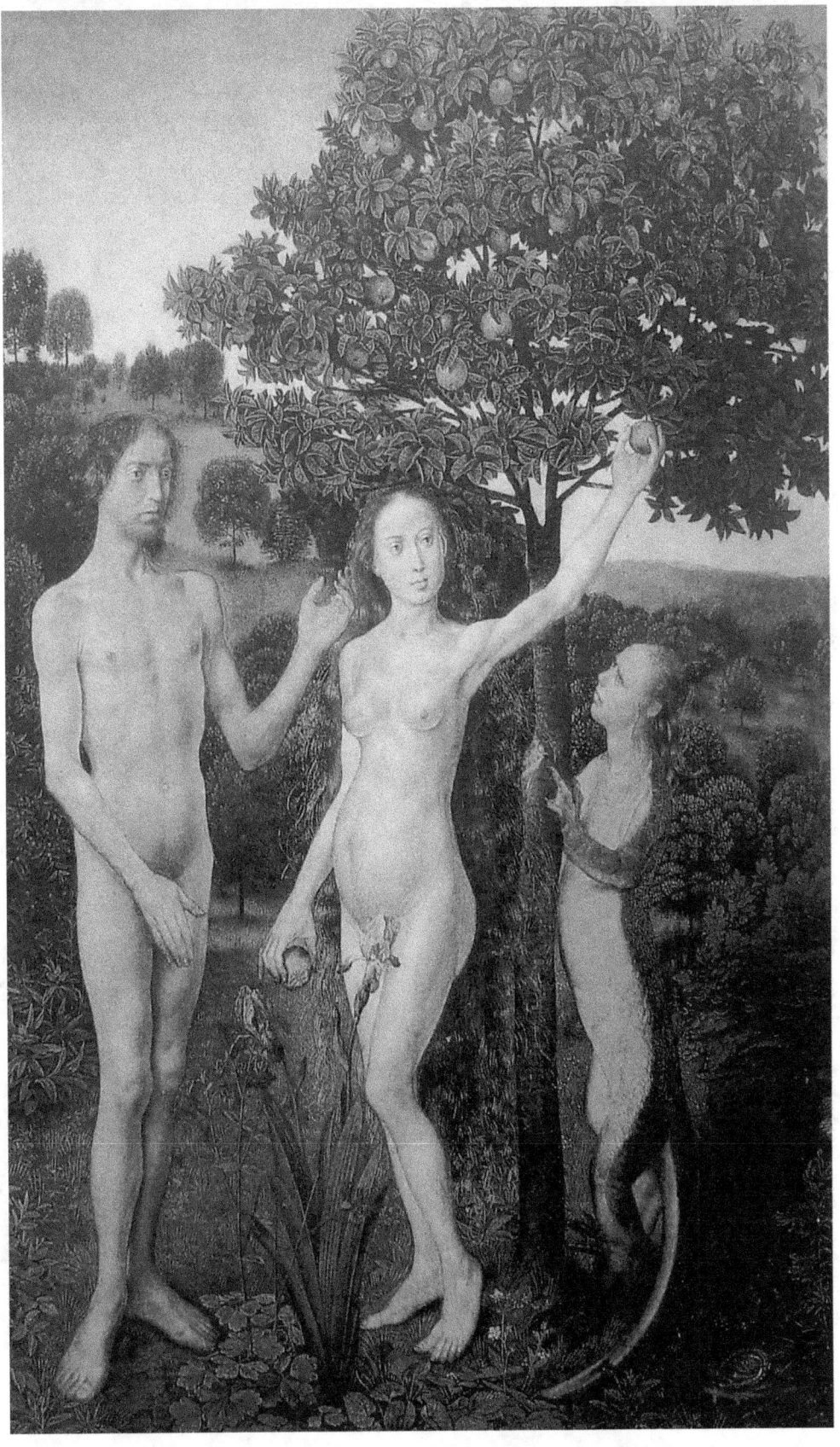

Hugo van der Goes, Fall of Man, 1470, Vienna

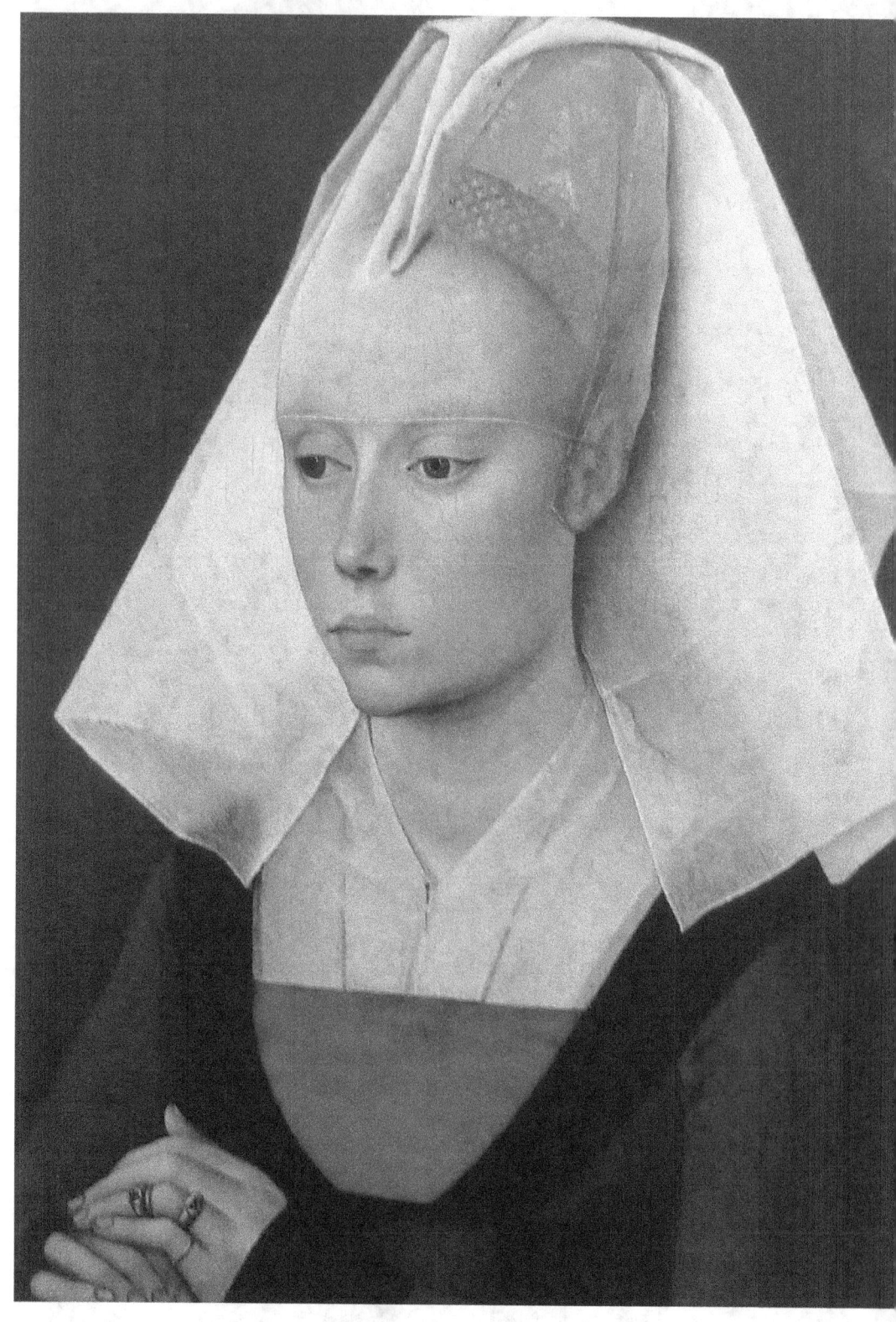

Rogier van der Weyden, Woman Praying, detail, National Gallery, London

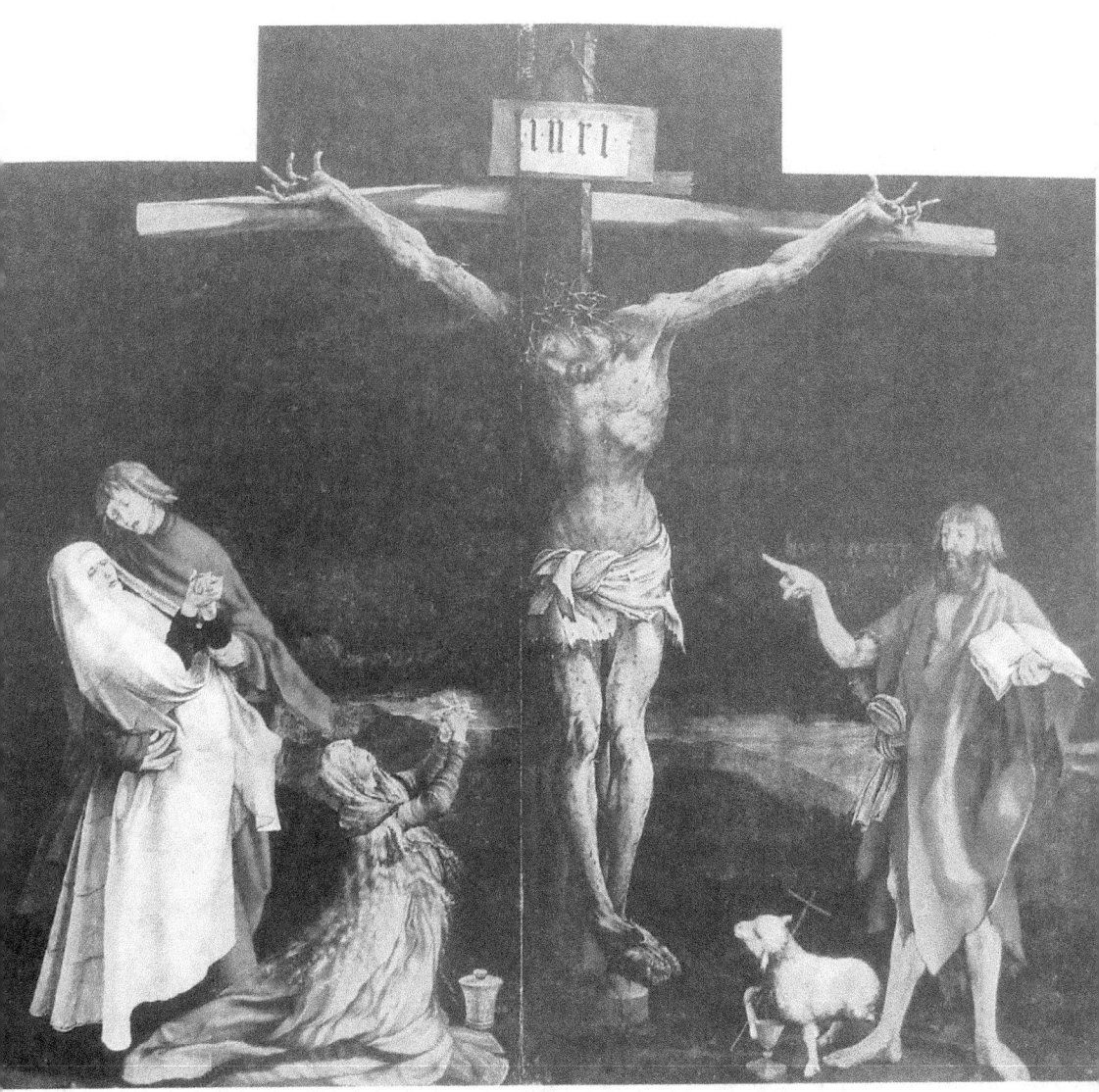

Matthias Grünewald, Crucifixion, Isenheim Altarpiece

Bibliography

On Giovanni Bellini

Hans Belting. *Giovanni Bellini Pietà: Ikone und Bilderzählung in der venezianischen Malerei,* Frankfurt 1985

Stefano Bottari: *Tutta la pittura di Giovanni Bellini,* Milan 1963

Peter Cannon-Brookes: *The Cornbury Park Bellini: A Contribution towards the Study of the Late Painting of Giovanni Bellini,* Birmingham 1977

David Cast: "The Stork and the Serpent: A New Interpretation of the *Madonna of the Meadow* by Bellini", *Art Quarterly,* 32, 1969, 247-258

Susan J. Delaney: "The iconography of Giovanni Bellini's *Sacred Allegory*", *Art Bulletin,* 59, 1977, 331-5

Colin Eisler: "'Saints Anthony Abbot and Bernardino of Siena'" Designed by Jacopo and Painted by Gentile Bellini", *Arte Veneta,* 39, 1985, 32-40

Everett: "'Coronation of the Virgin'", *Art Bulletin,* 46, 1964, 216-8

J. Fletcher: "Isabella d'Este and Giovanni Bellini's 'Presepio'", *Burlington Magazine,* 123, 1981, 453-67, 602-8

Roger Fry: *Giovanni Bellini,* London 1899

Rona Goffen: *Giovanni Bellini,* Yale University Press, New Haven 1989

—. *Renaissance Venice,* Yale University Press, New Haven 1986

— "Icon and Vision: Giovanni Bellini's Half-Length Madonnas", *Art Bulletin,* 57, 1975, 487-518

— "Giovanni Bellini and the Altarpiece of St. Vincent Ferrer", *Renaissance Studies in Honour of Craig Hugh Smyth,* ed. A. Morrogh, Florence, 1985

Christiane Joost-Gaugier: "A Pair of Miniatures by a Panel Painter: The Earliest Works of Giovanni Bellini?", *Paragone,* 30, 1979, 48-71

Julia Helen Keydel: "A Group of Altarpieces by Giovanni Bellini Considered in Relation to the Context for Which They Were Made",

Ph.D thesis, Harvard University 1969

Rodolfa Pallucchini: *Giovanni Bellini*, Milan 1959

Giles Robertson: "The Earlier Works of Giovanni Bellini", *Journal of the Warburg and Courtauld Institutes*, 23, 1960, 45-5

—. *Giovani Bellini*, Oxford, 1968

Martin Robertson: "A Possible Classical Echo in Bellini", *Burlington Magazine*, 121, 1979, 650-3

Carolyn Wilson: "Giovanni Bellini's *Pesaro Altarpiece*, Studies in Its Context and Meaning", Ph.D thesis, Institute of Fine Arts, 1976

Edgar Wind: *Bellini's Feast of the Gods: A Study of Venetian Humanism*, Cambridge, Mass., 1948

Others

Emile de Antonio & Mitch Tuchman: *Painters Painting*, Abbeville Press, New York 1984

C.G. Argan: *The Renaissance*, Thames & Hudson 1969

Karen Armstrong: *The Gospel According to Woman; Christianity's Creation of the Sex War in the West*, Pan 1987

Geoffrey Ashe: *The Virgin: Mary's Cult and the Re-emergence of the Goddess*, Arkana 1987

Patrick Bade: *Femme Fatale: Images of evil and fascinating women*, Ash & Grant 1979

Michael Baxandall: *Painting and Experience in 15th Century Italy*, Oxford University Press 1988

—*Patterns of Intention: On the Historical Explanation of Pictures*, Yale University Press 1985

James Beck: *Italian Renaissance Painting*, Harper & Row, New York 1981

Ean Begg: *The Cult of the Black Virgin*, Routledge 1985

Bernard Berenson: *The Italian Painters of the Renaissance*, Phaidon 1952

—*Looking at Pictures with Bernard Berenson*, selected by Hann Kiel, Abrahams, New York 1974

Pamela Berger: *The Goddess Obscured*, Robert Hale 1988

Bruce Bernard: *The Queen of Heaven: A Selection of Painting the Virgin from the Twelfth to the Eighteenth Centuries*, Macdonald/ Orbis 1987

—*The Bible and Its Painters*, Orbis 1983

Carlo Bertelli: *Piero della Francesca*, Yale University Press, New Haven 1992

Anthony Bertram: *Piero della Francesca*, Studio Publications 1949

Frances Bonner, *et al*, eds: *Imagining Women Cultural Representations and Gender*, Polity Press, Cambridge 1992

Botticelli: *The Complete Paintings of Botticelli*, Granada 1980

Serge Bramly: *Leonardo: The Artist and the Man*, Michael Joseph 1992

Allan Brahama: *Italian Renaissance Painters of the Sixteenth Century*, National Gallery 1985

Robert Briffault: *The Mothers: A Study of the origins of Sentiments and Institutions*, Allen & Unwin, 3 vols 1927

Stephanie Brown: *Religious Painting*, Phaidon 1979

Jacob Burckhardt: *The Altarpiece in Renaissance Italy*, Phaidon 1988

Titus Burckhardt: *Sacred Art in East and West,* Perennial Book, Middlesex 1967

Ritchie Calder: *Leonardo and The Age of the Eye*, Heinemann 1970

Joseph Campbell: *The Power of Myth*, with Bill Moyers, ed. Betty Sue Flowers, Doubleday, New York 1988

Michael P. Carroll: *The Cult of the Virgin Mary*, Princeton University Press, New Jersey 1986

Whitney Chadwick: *Women, Art, and Society*, Thames & Hudson 1990

Andre Chastel: *Art of the Italian Renaissance*, tr Peter & Linda Murray, Alpine Fine Arts Collection 1985

— *The Studios and Styles of the Renaissance, Italy 1460-1500*, tr Griffin, Thames & Hudson 1966

Herschel B. Chipp, ed. *Theories of Modern Art*, University Press of California, Los Angeles 1968

J.E. Cirlot: *A Dictionary of Symbols*, Routledge 1981

Kenneth Clark: *Landscape into Art*, Reader's Union 1965

— *Piero della Francesca*, Phaidon 1969

Bruce Cole: *The Renaissance Artist at Work*, John Murray 1983

— *Piero della Francesca: Tradition and Innovation in Renaissance Art*, Harper ancesca: Tradition and Innovation in Renaissance Art, Harper n S. Roudiez, Columbia University Press 1987

J.C. Cooper: *An Illustrated Dictionary of Traditional Symbols*, Thames & Hudson 1978

Pierre Courthion: *Flemish Painting,* Thames & Hudson 1958

Martin Davies: *Rogier van der Weyden*, Phaidon 1972

Lene Dresen-Coenders, ed: *Saints and She-Devils: Images of Women in the 15th and 16th Centuries*, Rubicon Press 1987

Georges Duby & Michele Perrot: *Power and Beauty: Images of Women in Art*, Tauris Parke Books,

Andrea Dworkin: *Intercourse*, Arrow 1988

— *Pornography: Men Possessing Women*, Women's Press 1984

Colin Eisler: *Early Netherlandish Painting: The Thyssen-Bornemisza Collection*, Sotheby's Publications 1989

Mircea Eliade: *Ordeal by Labyrinth*, University of Chicago Press 1984

—*A History of Religious Ideas, I,* Collins 1979

—*Patterns in Comparative Religion,* Sheed & Ward 1958

—*Symbolism, the Sacred and the Arts,* Crossroad, New York 1985

Joan Evans, ed: *The Flowering of the Middle Ages,* Thames & Hudson 1966

Giorgio T. Faggin: *The Complete Paintings of the Van Eycks,* Weidenfeld & Nicolson 1970

George Ferguson: *Signs and Symbols in Christian Art,* Oxford University Press 1961

John Ferguson: *An Illustrated Encyclopaedia of Mysticism,* Thames & Hudson 1976

Peter Fingesten: *The Eclipse of Symbolism,* University Press of California 1970

S.J. Freedberg: *Painting of the High Renaissance in Rome and Florence,* Harper & Row, New York 1972

Sigmund Freud: *Leonardo da Vinci,* tr Alan Tyson, Penguin 1963

Max J. Friedlander: *From Van Eyck to Bruegel,* Phaidon 1969

Elinor Gadon: *The Once and Future Goddess,* Aquarian Press 1990

Niny Garavaghlia: *The Complete Paintings of Mantegna,* Weidenfeld & Nicholson 1971

Fred Gettings: *The Hidden Art: A Study of the Occult Symbolism in Art,* Studio Vista 1978

Marija Gimbutas: *The Language of the Goddess,* Thames & Hudson 1989

Carlo Ginzburg: *The Enigma of Piero: Piero della Francesca, The Baptism, The Arezzo Cycle, The Flagellation,* Verso 1985

Rona Goffen: *Giovanni Bellini,* Yale University Press, New Haven 1989

Robert Goldwater & Marco Treves, eds. *Artists on Art,* John Murray 1975

E.H. Gombrich. *Symbolic Images,* Phaidon, 1985

—. *Norm and Form,* Phaidon, 1985

Cecil Gould: *Leonardo: The Artist and the Non-Artist,* Weidenfeld & Nicholson 1975

John Hale: *Italian Renaissance Painting,* Phaidon 1977

F.C.Happold, ed. *Mysticism,* Penguin 1970

Frederick Hartt: *History of Italian Renaissance Art: Painting, Sculpture, Architecture,* Thomas & Hudson 1987

—*Sandro Botticelli,* Collins 1954

Michael Jacobs: *A Guide to European Painting,* David & Charles 1980

Diane Kelder: *Pageant of the Renaissance,* Pall Mall Press 1969

Julia Kristeva. *The Kristeva Reader,* ed. Toril Moi, Blackwell, Oxford, 1986

—. *Desire in Language: A Semiotic Approach to Literature and Art,* ed. Leon Roudiez, tr. Thomas Gora, Alice Jardine & Leon Roudiez, Blackwell, Oxford, 1982

—. *Black Sun: Depression and Melancholy,* tr. L.S. Roudiez, Columbia University Press, New York, NY, 1989

—. *Strangers to Ourselves*, tr. L.S. Roudiez, Harvester Wheatsheaf, Hemel Hempstead, 1991

—. *About Chinese Women*, tr. A. Barrows, Boyars, 1977

—. *Tales of Love*, tr. Leon S. Roudiez, Columbia University Press, New York, NY, 1987

—. *Revolution in Poetic Language*, tr. Margaret Walker, Columbia University Press, New York, NY, 1984

—. *Powers of Horror: An Essay on Abjection*, tr. Leon S. Roudiez, Columbia University Press, New York, NY, 1982

Weston La Barre: *The Ghost Dance*, Allen & Unwin 1972

Leonardo da Vinci: *The Drawings of Leonarrillan*, New York 1961

—*The Complete Paintings*, introduction by L.D. Ettinger, Weidenfeld & Nicolson 1969

—*Selections from the Notebooks*, Oxford University Press 1952

Michael Levey: *High Renaissance*, Penguin 1975

—*Early Renaissance*, Penguin 1967

Lucy Lippard: *From the Center: feminist essays on women's art*, Dutton, New York 1976

Christopher Lloyd: *Fra Angelico*, Phaidon 1979

—*A Picture History of Art*, Phaidon 1979

Fiona MacCarthy: *Eric Gill*, Faber 1989

Emile Male: *The Gothic Image*, Collins 1961

K.B. MacFarlane: *Hans Memling*, Clarendon Press 1971

Roy McMullen: *Mona Lisa: The Picture and the Myth*, Macmillan 1975

J.C.J. Metford: *Dictionary of Christian Lore and Legend*, Thames & Hudson 1983

Michelangelo: *The Complete Paintings*, Granada 1980

Toril Moi: *Sexual/ Textual Politics: Feminist Literary Theory*, Routledge 1988

Edward Mullins: *The Painted Witch: Female Body, Male Art*, Secker & Warburg 1985

Peter & Linda Murray: *The Penguin Dictionary of Art and Artists*, Penguin 1976

Linda Murray: *High Renaissance*, Thames & Hudson 1977

Lynda Nead: *Female Nude: Art, Obscenity and Sexuality*, Routledge 1992

Erich Neumann: *The Great Mother*, Princeton University Press, New Jersey 1972

Shirley Nicholson, ed. *The Goddess Re-awakening: The Goddess Principle Today*, Theosophical Publishing House, New York 1989

Rudolf Otto: *The Idea of the Holy*, Oxford University Press 1958

Erwin Panofsky: *Studies in Iconology*, Harper & Row, New York 1972

—*Early Netherlandish Painting*, Harvard University Press, Mass., 1953

Rozsika Parker & Griselda Pollock: *Old Mistresses: Women, Art and ideology*, Routledge & Kegan Paul 1981

Geoffrey Parrinder: *Mysticism in the World's Religions,* Sheldon Press 1976

Walter Pater: *The Renaissance,* Oxford University Press 1980

Michael Payne: *Reading Theory: An Introduction to Lacan, Derrida, and Kristeva,* Blackwell 1993

Robert Payne: *Leonardo da Vinci,* Robert Hale 1979

Karen Petersen & J.J. Wilson: *Women Artists: Recognition and Reappraisal from the Early Middle Ages to the Twentieth Century,* Women's Press, 1978

Piero della Francesca: *The Complete Paintings of Piero della Francesca,* intr. Peter Murray, notes by Pierluigi de Vecchi, Penguin, 1985

Griselda Pollock: *Vision and Difference: femininity, feminism and histories of art,* Routledge 1988

John Pope-Hennessy: *Fra Angelico,* Phaidon 1974

Jeremy Robinson: *Glorification: Religious Abstraction in Renaissance and 20th Century Painting,* Crescent Moon 1994

— *The Madonna Glorified: The Paintings of Karen Arthurs and the Exhibition Hours of the Virgin, Based on Scenes From the Life of the Virgin Mary,* Crescent Moon 1991

Robert Rosenblum: *Modern Painting and the Northern Romantic Tradition,* Thames & Hudson 1978

Mark Roskill: *What is Art History?,* Thames & Hudson 1976

John Ruskin: *Works,* ed. E. T.Cook & A.Wedderburn, 39 vols, Allen 1903-12

Monica Sjöo & Barbara Mor: *The Great Cosmic Mother,* Harper & Row, San Francisco 1987

Alistair Smith: *Early Netherlandish and German Painting,* National Gallery 1985

Frank Stella: *Working Space,* Harvard University Press, Cambridge, Mass., 1986

Victor I. Stoichita: *Leonardo da Vinci,* Abbey Library 1978

Susan Rubin Suleiman, ed: *The Female Body in Western Culture: Contemporary Perspectives,* Harvard University Press, Cambridge, Mass., 1986

Nicholas Usherwood: *The Bible in 20th Century Art,* Pagoda Books 1987

Lionello Venturi: *Renaissance Painting, from Leonardo to Dürer,* Skira/Macmillan 1979

— *Italian Paintings,* Zwemmer 1950

— *Botticelli,* Phaidon 1964

M. Warner. *Alone Of All Her Sex: The Myth and Cult of the Virgin Mary,* Picador 1985

— *Monuments and Maidens,* Weidenfeld & Nicholson 1985

Alan Watts: *The Myth and Ritual of Christianity,* Thames & Hudson 1983

Margaret Whinney: *Early Flemish Painters,* Faber 1966

John White: *The Birth and Rebirth of Pictorial Space*, Faber 1957/87
Edward C.Whitmont: *Return of the Goddess,* Routledge 1987

CRESCENT MOON PUBLISHING

web: www.crmoon.com e-mail: cresmopub@yahoo.co.uk

ARTS, PAINTING, SCULPTURE

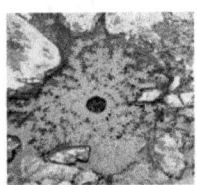

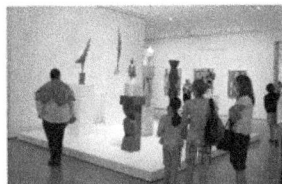

The Art of Andy Goldsworthy
Andy Goldsworthy: Touching Nature
Andy Goldsworthy in Close-Up
Andy Goldsworthy: Pocket Guide
Andy Goldsworthy In America
Land Art: A Complete Guide
The Art of Richard Long
Richard Long: Pocket Guide
Land Art In the UK
Land Art in Close-Up
Land Art In the U.S.A.
Land Art: Pocket Guide
Installation Art in Close-Up
Minimal Art and Artists In the 1960s and After
Colourfield Painting
Land Art DVD, TV documentary
Andy Goldsworthy DVD, TV documentary
The Erotic Object: Sexuality in Sculpture From Prehistory to the Present Day
Sex in Art: Pornography and Pleasure in Painting and Sculpture
Postwar Art
Sacred Gardens: The Garden in Myth, Religion and Art
Glorification: Religious Abstraction in Renaissance and 20th Century Art
Early Netherlandish Painting
Leonardo da Vinci
Piero della Francesca
Giovanni Bellini
Fra Angelico: Art and Religion in the Renaissance
Mark Rothko: The Art of Transcendence
Frank Stella: American Abstract Artist
Jasper Johns
Brice Marden
Alison Wilding: The Embrace of Sculpture
Vincent van Gogh: Visionary Landscapes
Eric Gill: Nuptials of God
Constantin Brancusi: Sculpting the Essence of Things
Max Beckmann
Caravaggio
Gustave Moreau
Egon Schiele: Sex and Death In Purple Stockings
Delizioso Fotografico Fervore: Works In Process 1
Sacro Cuore: Works In Process 2
The Light Eternal: J.M.W. Turner
The Madonna Glorified: Karen Arthurs

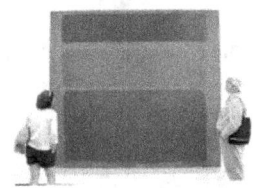

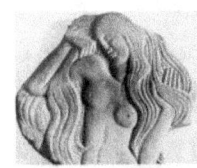

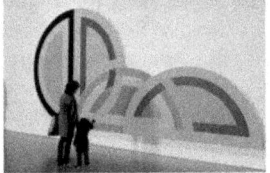

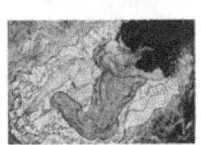

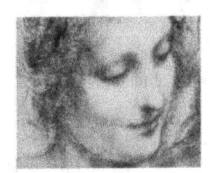

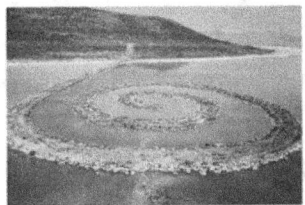

LITERATURE

J.R.R. Tolkien: The Books, The Films, The Whole Cultural Phenomenon
J.R.R. Tolkien: Pocket Guide
Tolkien's Heroic Quest
The *Earthsea* Books of Ursula Le Guin
Beauties, Beasts and Enchantment: Classic French Fairy Tales
German Popular Stories by the Brothers Grimm
Philip Pullman and *His Dark Materials*
Sexing Hardy: Thomas Hardy and Feminism
Thomas Hardy's *Tess of the d'Urbervilles*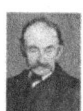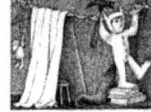
Thomas Hardy's *Jude the Obscure*
Thomas Hardy: The Tragic Novels
Love and Tragedy: Thomas Hardy
The Poetry of Landscape in Hardy
Wessex Revisited: Thomas Hardy and John Cowper Powys
Wolfgang Iser: Essays and Interviews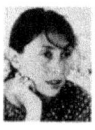
Petrarch, Dante and the Troubadours
Maurice Sendak and the Art of Children's Book Illustration
Andrea Dworkin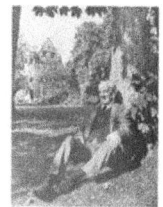
Cixous, Irigaray, Kristeva: The *Jouissance* of French Feminism
Julia Kristeva: Art, Love, Melancholy, Philosophy, Semiotics and Psychoanalysis
Hélène Cixous I Love You: The *Jouissance* of Writing
Luce Irigaray: Lips, Kissing, and the Politics of Sexual Difference
Peter Redgrove: Here Comes the Flood
Peter Redgrove: Sex-Magic-Poetry-Cornwall
Lawrence Durrell: Between Love and Death, East and West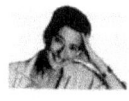
Love, Culture & Poetry: Lawrence Durrell
Cavafy: Anatomy of a Soul
German Romantic Poetry: Goethe, Novalis, Heine, Hölderlin
Feminism and Shakespeare
Shakespeare: Love, Poetry & Magic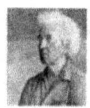
The Passion of D.H. Lawrence
D.H. Lawrence: Symbolic Landscapes
D.H. Lawrence: Infinite Sensual Violence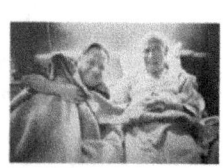
Rimbaud: Arthur Rimbaud and the Magic of Poetry
The Ecstasies of John Cowper Powys
Sensualism and Mythology: The Wessex Novels of John Cowper Powys
Amorous Life: John Cowper Powys and the Manifestation of Affectivity (H.W. Fawkner)
Postmodern Powys: New Essays on John Cowper Powys (Joe Boulter)
Rethinking Powys: Critical Essays on John Cowper Powys
Paul Bowles & Bernardo Bertolucci
Rainer Maria Rilke
Joseph Conrad: *Heart of Darkness*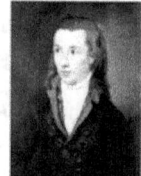
In the Dim Void: Samuel Beckett
Samuel Beckett Goes into the Silence
André Gide: Fiction and Fervour
Jackie Collins and the Blockbuster Novel
Blinded By Her Light: The Love-Poetry of Robert Graves
The Passion of Colours: Travels In Mediterranean Lands
Poetic Forms

POETRY

Ursula Le Guin: Walking In Cornwall
Peter Redgrove: Here Comes The Flood
Peter Redgrove: Sex-Magic-Poetry-Cornwall
Dante: Selections From the Vita Nuova
Petrarch, Dante and the Troubadours
William Shakespeare: Sonnets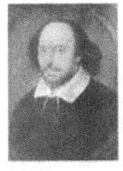
William Shakespeare: Complete Poems
Blinded By Her Light: The Love-Poetry of Robert Graves
Emily Dickinson: Selected Poems
Emily Brontë: Poems
Thomas Hardy: Selected Poems
Percy Bysshe Shelley: Poems
John Keats: Selected Poems
Joh n Keats: Poems of 1820
D.H. Lawrence: Selected Poems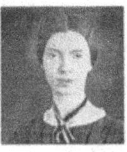
Edmund Spenser: Poems
Edmund Spenser: Amoretti
John Donne: Poems
Henry Vaughan: Poems
Sir Thomas Wyatt: Poems
Robert Herrick: Selected Poems
Rilke: Space, Essence and Angels in the Poetry of Rainer Maria Rilke
Rainer Maria Rilke: Selected Poems
Friedrich Hölderlin: Selected Poems
Arseny Tarkovsky: Selected Poems
Arthur Rimbaud: Selected Poems
Arthur Rimbaud: A Season in Hell
Arthur Rimbaud and the Magic of Poetry
Novalis: Hymns To the Night
German Romantic Poetry
Paul Verlaine: Selected Poems
Elizaethan Sonnet Cycles
D.J. Enright: By-Blows
Jeremy Reed: Brigitte's Blue Heart
Jeremy Reed: Claudia Schiffer's Red Shoes
Gorgeous Little Orpheus
Radiance: New Poems
Crescent Moon Book of Nature Poetry
Crescent Moon Book of Love Poetry
Crescent Moon Book of Mystical Poetry
Crescent Moon Book of Elizabethan Love Poetry
Crescent Moon Book of Metaphysical Poetry
Crescent Moon Book of Romantic Poetry
Pagan America: New American Poetry

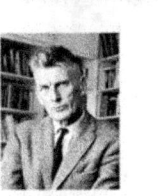
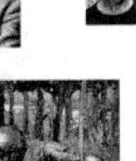
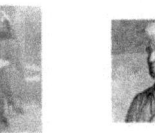
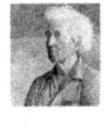
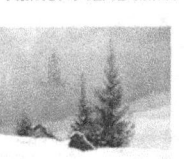
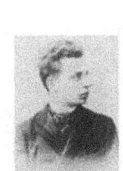
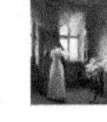
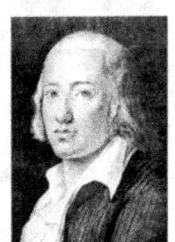
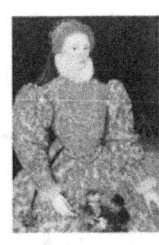

MEDIA, CINEMA, FEMINISM and CULTURAL STUDIES

J.R.R. Tolkien: The Books, The Films, The Whole Cultural Phenomenon
J.R.R. Tolkien: Pocket Guide
The *Lord of the Rings* Movies: Pocket Guide
The Cinema of Hayao Miyazaki
Hayao Miyazaki: *Princess Mononoke*: Pocket Movie Guide
Hayao Miyazaki: *Spirited Away*: Pocket Movie Guide
Tim Burton : Hallowe'en For Hollywood
Ken Russell
Ken Russell: *Tommy*: Pocket Movie Guide
The Ghost Dance: The Origins of Religion
The Peyote Cult

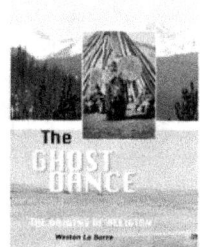
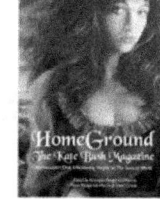

Cixous, Irigaray, Kristeva: The *Jouissance* of French Feminism
Julia Kristeva: Art, Love, Melancholy, Philosophy, Semiotics and Psychoanalysis
Luce Irigaray: Lips, Kissing, and the Politics of Sexual Difference
Hélene Cixous I Love You: The *Jouissance* of Writing
Andrea Dworkin
'Cosmo Woman': The World of Women's Magazines
Women in Pop Music
HomeGround: The Kate Bush Anthology
Discovering the Goddess (Geoffrey Ashe)
The Poetry of Cinema
The Sacred Cinema of Andrei Tarkovsky
Andrei Tarkovsky: Pocket Guide
Andrei Tarkovsky: *Mirror*: Pocket Movie Guide
Andrei Tarkovsky: *The Sacrifice*: Pocket Movie Guide
Walerian Borowczyk: Cinema of Erotic Dreams
Jean-Luc Godard: The Passion of Cinema
Jean-Luc Godard: *Hail Mary*: Pocket Movie Guide
Jean-Luc Godard: *Contempt*: Pocket Movie Guide
Jean-Luc Godard: *Pierrot le Fou*: Pocket Movie Guide
John Hughes and Eighties Cinema
Ferris Bueller's Day Off: Pocket Movie Guide
Jean-Luc Godard: Pocket Guide
The Cinema of Richard Linklater
Liv Tyler: Star In Ascendance
Blade Runner and the Films of Philip K. Dick
Paul Bowles and Bernardo Bertolucci
Media Hell: Radio, TV and the Press
An Open Letter to the BBC
Detonation Britain: Nuclear War in the UK
Feminism and Shakespeare
Wild Zones: Pornography, Art and Feminism
Sex in Art: Pornography and Pleasure in Painting and Sculpture
Sexing Hardy: Thomas Hardy and Feminism

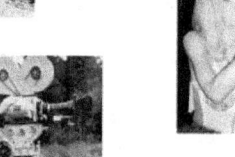
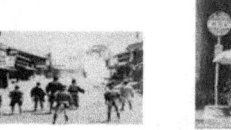
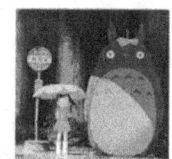
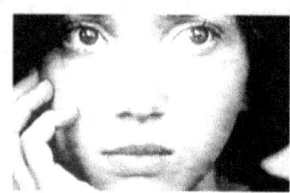

The Light Eternal is a model monograph, an exemplary job. The subject matter of the book is beautifully
organised and dead on beam. (Lawrence Durrell)
It is amazing for me to see my work treated with such passion and respect. (Andrea Dworkin)

CRESCENT MOON PUBLISHING
P.O. Box 1312, Maidstone, Kent, ME14 5XU, Great Britain. www.crmoon.com

cresmopub@yahoo.co.uk   www.crescentmoon.org.uk

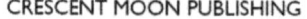

www.ingramcontent.com/pod-product-compliance
Lightning Source LLC
Chambersburg PA
CBHW051316220526
45468CB00004B/1370